Changing Japanese Capitalism

Economic crisis tends to spur change in the "rules of the game" – the "institutions" – that govern the economic activity of firms and employees. But after more than a decade of economic pain following the burst of the Japanese Bubble Economy of the 1980s, the core institutions of Japanese capitalism have changed remarkably little. In this systematic and holistic assessment of continuity and change in the central components of Japanese capitalism, Michael A. Witt links this relatively slow rate of institutional change to a confluence of two factors: high levels of societal coordination in the Japanese political economy, and low levels of deviant behavior at the level of individuals, firms, and organizations. He identifies social networks permeating Japanese business as a key enabler of societal coordination and an obstacle to deviancy, and he sheds light on a pervasive but previously underexplored type of business networks, intra-industry loops.

MICHAEL WITT is Assistant Professor of Asian Business and Comparative Management in the Economics and Political Science Area of INSEAD.

Changing Japanese Capitalism

Societal Coordination and Institutional Adjustment

MICHAEL A. WITT

CAMBRIDGE
UNIVERSITY PRESS

CAMBRIDGE UNIVERSITY PRESS
Cambridge, New York, Melbourne, Madrid, Cape Town, Singapore, São Paulo

Cambridge University Press
The Edinburgh Building, Cambridge CB2 2RU, UK

Published in the United States of America by Cambridge University Press, New York

www.cambridge.org
Information on this title: www.cambridge.org/9780521868600

First published 2006

Printed in the United Kingdom at the University Press, Cambridge

A catalogue record for this publication is available from the British Library

Library of Congress Cataloguing in Publication data

ISBN-13 978-0-521-86860-0 hardback
ISBN-10 0-521-86860-2 hardback

Contents

Figures

Tables

Foreword to Michael Witt, Changing Japanese Capitalism

In the years after the Second World War, we have witnessed a succession of waves of societal development, in different parts of the world, some of which have been labelled "miracles". There was the German miracle in the 1960s and 1970s, the East Asian miracle of the 1980s – the age of the little dragons, and more recently the miracle of China's emergence as the 'workshop of the world'. But none of these took the world of business by storm as did the great Japanese miracle of the 1970s and 1980s. This was due to the growth of the Japanese economy to immense size, second in the world after the US, still a very long way ahead of any other rivals, and still four times greater than that of China. A related feature was that its starting point was one of almost complete devastation.

Adding to the sense of intrigued respect that gradually accumulated among the observers and competitors of the Japanese as they rose to control massive industrial power, was a sense that there was a mystique in how they did things. Not only were their firms managed in ways foreign to Western managers, but the relations among the major components of the society – government, owners, banks, workforces – were quite distinct. The political system itself seemed not to follow that of other democracies, and the complex web at the top of the structure became an object of fascination to outsiders.

Such was their success in penetrating markets, that Japanese management systems led a widespread revolution in global production efficiency. The current global concerns with quality, with customer needs, with the re-engineering of processes, with worker engagement, with constant product improvement – even though not always initiated in Japan – seemed to reach their earliest full flowering there. Japanese management came to be seen as the standard in many industries, especially where production was involved. Here was a beautiful machine running smoothly in top gear.

Then suddenly it went off the rails. Japan entered a crisis in the 1990s, suffering severely from an assets inflation of such proportions that its effects carry forward still. But more particularly it entered a crisis of purpose and of will, as the elaborate system of balanced power bases appeared to absorb pressure without yielding when reforms were proposed. These pressures came from inside its own structure, as well as outside. The most common themes were transparency, efficiency, the ending of collusion, flexibility. To many Japanese it seemed as if the West wanted them to behave against their own traditions, to adopt "international best practice". Whether they would is closely bound up with whether they could, and in the event they have chosen in the main to do it their own way, and slowly.

The story of how Japanese capitalism has been changing is significant in two senses. In the first place, this is a major phenomenon in global terms, and the shaping and evolving of its future has big ramifications in many economies and markets. But secondly, it illustrates how societies vary in the trajectories they follow for their progress. If societies behave so differently, then nostrums thought to be universal may not be as widely relevant as much current policy and practice suggests.

This book contains a fine-grained analysis of a complex social system, and it illustrates especially the highly coordinated nature of the Japanese economy. Vested interests, and elaborate connections across a range of exchanges, obligations, and flows of information, need to be understood if Japan's progress is to be mapped fully. In this account, we find a more complete picture than average, as the author has deliberately taken on board the need to depict society holistically. He has also delved into the detailed workings of the social networks that hold the system in balance, revealing that they are also capable of holding the system in check. Social capital can be an obstacle to adaptation, a downside not often acknowledged in accounts of its workings.

Japan is far more significant than its coverage in the press these days suggests. It is also likely to be capable of that permanent challenge to all societies as they grow – to adapt while remaining true to themselves. If its slowly returning confidence rises to earlier levels across more of its industries than its continually spectacular automotive sector, then the lessons of this book will be needed by those again facing the mystique.

Acknowledgements

I owe thanks to a great number of individuals for their roles in the genesis of this book. First and foremost, I have incurred a great debt of gratitude to Gordon Redding, Arie Y. Lewin, and Peter A. Hall. At INSEAD, I have been blessed with having Gordon Redding as colleague and mentor. I have benefited much from his work on comparative business systems as well as from joint research undertaken on the question of executive rationale, both of which inform especially Chapter 2 of this book. A great boon has also been the opportunity to explore the question of institutional change in national institutional configurations in cooperation with Arie Y. Lewin, who has opened my eyes to research on co-evolution and organizational theory. Chapter 3 of this book is partially based on joint research with Arie, and his kind permission for me to draw on this work for this book is greatly appreciated. Peter Hall piqued my interest in varieties of capitalism and firm-level research during my time at Harvard, and he has provided much important input and feedback.

I am further deeply indebted to my advisors at Harvard – Susan J. Pharr, James E. Alt, and Steven K. Vogel – for their patient guidance. Their advice and insights were invaluable assets for me in producing my dissertation, out of which the present work has grown. Susan has since offered constant encouragement for me to take the project forward to its present shape, and continued input from Steven has proved extremely helpful.

Great thanks go also to all my contacts and contributors in Japan – some of them listed in the Appendix but most of them interviewed under the condition of anonymity – who have made this work possible by taking the time and trouble to meet me and provide data and advice. I am especially indebted to Yuko Unoki for her introductions of senior executives. Several officials of the Ministry of Economy, Trade and Industry (METI) were also particularly helpful, not least by providing key introductions.

Thanks are due further to Peter Marsden for offering untiring and prompt advice about social network analysis on numerous occasions; to Nobuhiro Hiwatari and Jonathan Lewis for their support of my field work in Japan and their hosting me at the Institute of Social Science at the University of Tokyo; to Richard Dyck for patiently helping me explore and understand the intricacies of the Japanese semiconductor equipment industry; and to E. Keith Henry for drawing my attention to intra-industry loops in 1996. Christina L. Davis, Lorraine Eden, Martin Gargiulo, Witold J. Henisz, Patricia A. Nelson, Gabriel Szulanski, Douglas Webber, and Peter Williamson read part or all of the manuscript at various stages or other work leading up to it and provided helpful feedback and encouragement for which I am thankful. I have also received much valuable feedback from discussants and participants at various seminars and conferences, especially at Harvard, INSEAD, AIB, AOM, and EGOS.

Financial support for this project was at various stages provided by the Lee Foundation of Singapore, the Studienstiftung des deutschen Volkes (German National Merit Foundation), the US–Japan Relations Program at Harvard University, the Department of Government at Harvard University, and INSEAD. The contribution of these sponsors is noted with much gratitude, as is the institutional support for my research provided by the Department of Government as well as the US–Japan Relations Program at Harvard University, the Institute of Social Science at the University of Tokyo, the Euro-Asia and Comparative Research Center at INSEAD, and INSEAD.

Last, but not least, I would like to thank my family for their patience and support. This book would not have been possible without them.

1 | Introduction

I T HAS BEEN SAID, not least by the Japanese themselves, that Japan has changed only twice over the past 150 years: once in the Meiji Restoration of 1868, which marked the downfall of the Tokugawa shogunate after some 265 years of continuous rule, and again in 1945, when Japan had lost the Pacific War.

This is, of course, a vast overstatement. Nothing, and certainly no social system, ever stands still, and Japan is no exception. However, in the context of developments in the Japanese business system[1] over the past fifteen years, it contains a kernel of truth. A comprehensive review of the available empirical evidence, presented later in this book, suggests that the core structure of the Japanese business system today is not much different from that in 1990. Viewed from the perspective of the business system as a whole, institutional[2] change in Japan seems to be proceeding at a relatively slow rate.

This would not be remarkable had this slow rate of change not occurred in the face of extended economic crisis, which should have been conducive to institutional change (Katznelson 2003; Krasner 1976; North 1990; Oliver 1992). With the burst of the bubble economy of the 1980s, real economic growth in Japan slowed from an average 4.1 percent in the 1980s to 1.5 percent in the 1990s (OECD 2004). Asset prices collapsed: at their nadir in 2003, stock prices were more than 80 percent off their 1989 highs, and 2005 prices of residential land in Japan's six major cities stood some 65 percent lower than at the peak in 1991 (Kurosu 2003; Miyawaki 2005). The

---

[1] The institutional structure governing economic activity of firms and employees (cf. Redding 2005; Whitley 1999), where the term "institutions" is defined as "humanly devised constraints that structure human interaction. They are made up of formal constraints (e.g., rules, laws, constitutions), informal constraints (e.g., norms of behavior, conventions, self-imposed codes of conduct), and their enforcement characteristics" (North 1994:360).

[2] See the previous note for a definition of the term "institution."

consequences were severe for individuals, firms, and especially the financial sector, which was heavily exposed through direct ownership and lending. Bankruptcies, once rare, tripled between 1989 and 2001 (Kurosu 2003) and came to include firms previously thought too large or prestigious to fail, such as Hokkaido Shokutaku Bank, Yamaichi Securities, and (almost) Nissan. Unemployment more than doubled, from around 2.5 percent in the 1980s, to a peak of 5.4 percent in 2002 (Kurosu 2003), a level unknown since the immediate postwar era. The Japanese banking crisis is possibly the costliest ever worldwide, with bad debts in 1999 amounting to about one-third of Japanese GDP (Amyx 2004).

Scholars and observers have proffered a wide range of possible explanations that shed light on the relatively low level of change from different angles and bear witness to the multicausality of the phenomenon. Among the mechanisms blamed for slow change are the weakening of the coordinating role of the Liberal Democratic Party (LDP) in the policy-making process following its electoral defeat and subsequent 11-month stint in opposition in 1993–4 (Amyx 2004); the relative absence of pressure on the private sector to initiate institutional adjustment given a corporate governance system that isolates firms from profitability pressures (Lincoln 2001); and the possibility that the Japanese people may, despite the crisis, not want fundamental institutional change (e.g., Curtis 1999; Lincoln 2001).

Of special relevance to this work are two other mechanisms laid out in the literature: the delaying role of vested interests (e.g., Amyx 2004; Katz 2002; Lincoln 2001; Sakakibara 2003; Yamamura 2003) and lock-in of the present institutional structure because of institutional complementarities (e.g., Amyx 2004; Lincoln 2001). Vested interests may delay the change process by offering resistance in the policy-making process. They exist in many quarters, including labor unions bent on maintaining their influence and employment for their members, firms keen on preserving barriers to competition and privileges such as subsidies, bureaucrats fearing loss of influence and shrinking empires, and indeed large portions of the population, who seem to equate structural reform with convergence on Anglo-Saxon-style capitalism (Yamamura 2003).

Institutional complementarity may reduce the rate of institutional change by increasing the complexity of change. Complementarity exists where the effective functioning of one set of institutions is contingent on the presence of another set of "fitting" institutions (Aoki 1988; Hall and Soskice 2001). Adjustment in one set of institutions may break the functionality of the complementary set, which then also requires adjustment, which in turn may necessitate changes in other parts of the system.

Vested interests and complementarities have no doubt played their part in limiting the rate of institutional adaptation in Japan. But their ability to do so gives rise to a new puzzle. Vested interests and institutional complementarities exist in any institutional structure (North 1990; Pierson 2004), including in other advanced industrialized nations that have handled institutional adjustment processes with greater swiftness. Why is it that their delaying influence seems to be relatively more elaborated in the Japanese case? One may conjecture that the Japanese system shows relatively higher levels of vested interests and lock-in, or that vested interests are relatively more able to delay institutional change. Both are very likely the case. At the same time, this leaves unanswered the question of where this variation in the salience of vested interests and complementarities comes from.

Societal coordination and institutional adjustment

In this book, I argue that *societal coordination* in the political economy is a key source of this variation. Recent research on cross-national differences in the make-up and functioning of capitalist political economies has established societal coordination as a central dimension of variation across different varieties of capitalism (Hall and Gingerich 2004; Hall and Soskice 2001). Hall and Soskice (2001) differentiate between two broad types of coordination, strategic coordination and market coordination. Since the term "strategic" implies careful goal-oriented design that is not necessarily present in these processes, I will deviate from Hall and Soskice's nomenclature and refer to it as "societal coordination" or, for the sake of simplicity and readability, just "coordination." As the name implies, market coordination draws on market forces, especially the price mechanism (cf. Hayek 1945), to achieve order in the political economy. By contrast, in societal coordination, the organization of economic activity and the building of economic institutions occurs through formal and informal nonmarket interaction and cooperation of actors (cf. Hall and Soskice 2001; Streeck and Yamamura 2003). Social

networks and the social capital underlying them play a key role
in societal coordination processes (Hall and Soskice 2001) as they
facilitate cooperation (Fukuyama 1995; Putnam 1993a, 1993b) and
the sharing and diffusion of information, values, and norms (DiMaggio
and Powell 1983; Meyer and Rowan 1977; Oliver 1991; Pfeffer and
Salancik 1978; Podolny and Page 1998).

A key notion advanced by Hall and Soskice (2001) is that different
varieties of capitalism draw on market and societal coordination to
different extents. In their work, this is expressed in a dichotomy
between liberal market economies (LMEs) and coordinated market
economies (CMEs), with the former relying more on market
coordination and the latter on societal coordination. The result is a
distinction, consistent with other works in the varieties of capitalism
literature (e.g., Albert 1993; Dore 2000), between the Anglo-Saxon
camp, representing the LMEs, and the continental European
and Japanese camps, representing the CMEs. While societal coordination is not the only dimension along which different types of
capitalism vary (e.g., Amable 2003; Boyer 1997; Orrù, Biggart, and
Hamilton 1997; Redding 2005; Schmidt 2002; Whitley 1999),
recent empirical evidence (Hall and Gingerich 2004) suggests that it
is a key one.

In terms of economic outcomes, CMEs seem to have done at least as
well as LMEs through the early 1990s (Hall and Soskice 2001), but
lately a performance gap seems to have opened. When assessing the
same groups of countries classified as LMEs and CMEs in Hall and
Soskice (2001), OECD data indicate that, from 1993 through 2003,
average growth rates of GDP reached 4.0 percent in the LMEs, but
only 2.5 percent in the CMEs. OECD data on per capita GDP at
purchasing power parity show the LMEs in the lead at an average of
US$30,350, as opposed to a CME average of US$29,355. This is a
reversal from the period 1985–1997, when CMEs were still ahead by
US$17,902 to US$16,890 (Hall and Soskice 2001). The OECD also
indicates that unemployment rates, which used to be lower in the
CMEs than in the LMEs, over the 1993–2003 period declined by 5.2
percentage points in the LMEs, but by only 1.1 percentage points in the
CMEs. Given widespread agreement in the literature that the quality
of institutional structures and economic performance as expressed in
long-term growth and unemployment rates are linked (e.g., Blanchard
and Wolfers 2000; Nickell et al. 2003; North 1990, 1994; OECD

2005), this suggests that the institutional structures of CMEs may in recent years have lost some economic efficacy relative to those in LMEs.

Underlying this loss in relative efficacy is intense pressure on all economies to adapt their institutional structures to new and still evolving conditions in at least three areas: the ongoing transition to the information technology age, increased uncertainty and competition in the world economy, and societal ageing. Perhaps most important among these is the entry of the world economy into the information technology age (Lewin, Long, and Carroll 1999; Lewin and Stephens 1993; Perez 2002; Yamamura 2003). Transitional periods tend to be marked by massive reallocation of resources to new technologies, encompassing "radical changes in the patterns of production, organization, management, communication, transportation and consumption, leading ultimately to a different 'way of life', . . [T]he whole process takes around half a century to unfold, involving more than one generation" (Perez 2002:153). Assuming this transitional age started with the announcement of the Intel 4004 microprocessor in 1971, as Perez (2002) suggests, it is likely to last another fifteen years, with an attendant need for institutional adjustment.

The pains of the transition to the information technology age have been exacerbated by increased uncertainty and competition in the international economy (Yamamura 2003). The 1970s saw the end of the Bretton Woods regime, resulting in floating exchange rates and subsequent long-term depreciation of the US dollar, as well as two oil shocks. Financial deregulation from the late 1970s onward as well as continuing trade liberalization under successive GATT/WTO agreements fueled globalization of markets. The result has been an increase in economic interdependence, which not only allows for more efficient financial flows and more trade, but has been accompanied by higher volatility in financial markets as well as increased competition, and thus pressure on margins, in tradables. These latter trends have been reinforced by the arrival in international markets of emerging economies with feeble financial systems and highly competitive labor forces. Estimates suggest that the entry of China, India and the former Soviet Union into the world economy has effectively doubled the global labor force (*Economist* 2005). This has led to downward pressure on wages in the advanced industrialized nations and has forced firms to seek new ways, such as web-based organizational structures (Fulk and DeSanctis 1995) and offshoring, to exploit these new developments in order to remain competitive.

Societal ageing poses a further challenge to extant institutional structures in many advanced industrial nations, and especially CMEs such as Japan and Germany. Ageing implies structural shifts in the economy toward providing goods and services for the elderly. It also threatens to undermine pension and medical insurance schemes, with concomitant implications for other spheres of the economy. For instance, a transition from today's increasingly unaffordable pay-as-you-go pension schemes to funded systems would have profound implications for the economy. Massive funds would seek investment opportunities in stock markets, with possible knock-on effects on areas such as corporate governance and the availability of long-term capital.

Institutional adjustment processes in LMEs seem to be able to respond to these challenges in a more timely fashion than those in CMEs. CMEs have exhibited a relatively slower rate of adaptation in response to these adjustment pressures because their societally coordinated adjustment processes tend to involve extensive bargaining and consensus-finding before any changes can be put into place. These coordinated and often political processes are relatively time intensive. By contrast, the rate of response tends to be quicker in the market-coordinated adjustment processes typical of LMEs, in which relatively more institutional adjustment occurs through autonomous action at the micro level of individuals, organizations, and firms with subsequent diffusion of institutional innovation through evolutionary and isomorphic processes (cf. DiMaggio and Powell 1983; Meyer and Rowan 1977; Williamson 1985). I will develop this argument in detail in Chapter 3.

Variation in the relative prevalence of coordinated versus autonomous adjustment processes helps shed light on the question posed at the beginning of this chapter of why vested interests and institutional complementarities seem to have a relatively greater impact on institutional adjustment processes of countries such as Japan. Vested and other conservative interests can delay institutional adaptation only if they get a say in the change process. This is often the case in societally coordinated adjustment processes, especially where there are norms of extensive consultation and consensus-building, as is the case in Japan.

In autonomous adjustment processes, by contrast, micro-level actors by definition initiate change without active consultation with other actors, which denies conservative forces the opportunity to exert influence. At the same time, societally coordinated processes are more likely to build complementary institutional structures. For one, it tends to be easier to do so when the major actors governed by these institutional structures cooperate in designing them. In addition, CMEs by definition tend to feature higher levels of formal institutionalization – as evident, for example, in higher levels of formal regulation – around which actors' expectations can converge to form complementarities.

An additional adjustment dynamic tends to develop at the micro level of individuals, organizations, and firms. As environmental change moves the extant institutional structure out of alignment with actors' needs (cf. Seo and Creed 2002) and coordinated adjustment processes fail to provide for speedy adjustment, micro-level actors may seek to isolate themselves from the cost of this misalignment through the adoption of a range of micro-level responses (cf. Oliver 1991). While these responses can be political in nature – for example, political bargaining, grassroots movements, or demonstrations (cf. Aoki 2003; Buchanan and Tullock 1962; Henisz and Zelner 2005; Knight 1992; North 1990; Seo and Creed 2002; Streeck and Thelen 2005; Thelen 2004; Tullock, Seldon, and Brady 2002; Van de Ven and Hargrave 2004) – many responses are likely to be at least initially autonomous, apolitical, and undertaken without intention to induce systemic institutional change. For instance, tax evasion or capital flight are rarely undertaken as political acts, but rather to reduce the economic costs of an institutional structure perceived to be out of alignment with actors' needs. As these responses and their costs accumulate and spread through the system, they can contribute to deinstitutionalization (cf. Oliver 1992) and serve to increase the felt pressure for adjustment by threatening the legitimacy of the societally coordinated adjustment processes and those involved in them. This feedback mechanism linking apolitical autonomous action at the micro level with coordinated adjustment processes represents an underexplored dynamic in the literature on institutional change.

The picture that emerges for Japan is that institutional adjustment there has been slowed by a combination of highly coordinated and thus time-intensive adjustment processes paired with relatively limited adjustment pressure from the micro level. The causes of the latter phenomenon are at least three-fold. First, the insular geography of Japan dampens at least one part of common micro-level actions seen elsewhere, namely those that depend on legal or illegal exit of actors or their resources. Second, the present institutional structure seems to continue to enjoy legitimacy, which dampens the perceived need to take action. Third, micro-level action that deviates from established norms is seen as socially illegitimate. Enforcement of compliance with the extant institutional structure is facilitated by the extensive social networks that pervade the Japanese political economy. As mentioned earlier, these networks are conducive to coordination. At the same time, however, their role as conduits of information, norms, and values (cf. Oliver 1991) also makes them effective means of stabilizing established institutions by fostering compliance (DiMaggio and Powell 1983; Galaskiewicz and Wasserman 1989; Meyer and Rowan 1977; Oliver 1991, 1992) even when these institutions have moved out of alignment with the needs of those they govern. The overall effect of these three factors is to reduce the relative prevalence of micro-level action and the concomitant pressure for change, with the result of a relatively slower pace of institutional adaptation.

Social networks, social capital, and societal coordination

Social networks are formally defined as "any collection of actors (N ≥ 2) that pursue repeated, enduring exchange relations with one another and, at the same time, lack a legitimate organizational authority to arbitrate and resolve disputes that may arise during the exchange" (Podolny and Page 1998:59). Their effects are closely linked to the concept of social capital, which is "the sum of the actual and potential resources embedded within, available through, and derived from the network of relationships possessed by an individual or social unit. Social capital thus comprises both the network and the assets that may be mobilized through that network" (Nahapiet and Ghoshal 1998:243). Social capital may have private good character; that is, the effects of social networking accrue at the level of the individual holders of social relations (cf. Adler and Kwon 2002; Inkpen and Tsang 2005). However, it may also have public good character, in which case any effects of social networking are felt at the level of the community as a whole (cf. Adler and Kwon 2002; Inkpen and Tsang 2005).

The bulk of the literature has focused on illustrating the presence of benefits at the private goods level. For example, networks have been found to foster learning "because they preserve greater diversity of search routines than hierarchies and they convey richer, more complex information than markets" (Podolny and Page 1998:62). Networks may play this role either by acting as conduits for pieces of information (Burt 1992; Contractor and Lorange 1988; Hamel 1991; Kogut 1988; Liebeskind et al. 1995; Root 1988) or by creating learning synergies (Fountain 1998; Powell and Brantley 1992; Powell, Koput, and Smith-Doerr 1996). Networks may also allow actors to share the legitimacy or status of affiliated networking actors, which can affect such aspects as chances of organizational survival (Baum and Oliver 1992; Uzzi 1996), market value (Stuart, Hoang, and Hybels 1999), or access to scarce resources (Stark 1996). Further, networks can improve economic performance, for example by reducing transaction costs through trust (Dore 1983; Sako 1992), providing better information than markets and thus allowing higher quality in production (Sako 1992; Uzzi 1997a), and allowing actors to adjust more quickly to environmental changes (Powell 1990).

A separate stream of literature has taken a more macro approach and explored the public goods nature of social capital. The core argument of these works has been to link the degree of social capital, expressed in terms such as propensity of citizens to engage in voluntary associations, to the well-being and functioning of political entities and their economic performance characteristics (e.g., Fukuyama 1995; Harrison 1992, 1997; Jackman and Miller 1998; Putnam 1993a, 1993b, 2000; Yamagishi 2003). For instance, in his classic study contrasting northern and southern Italy, Putnam (1993a) argues that the dismal economic performance of southern Italy can be linked to the relative absence of civil society, and thus by implication to reduced levels of social capital.

Much less well explored[3] is the dark side of social networks (cf. Gargiulo and Ertug 2006). Networks may represent a private bad.

---

[3] Leaving aside the blanket dismissal of social networks by neo-classical economists as statutory market distortions.

For instance, the transmission of conformity pressures through network ties, as discussed earlier, may represent a private bad if the institution in question has negative utility for the individual actor. In addition, the trust implied in many social networks may lead to a decrease in vigilance and monitoring of information that is received (Szulanski, Cappetta, and Jensen 2004). This effect is especially detrimental when information is ambiguous and thus requires higher levels of verifying and monitoring. Third, network ties may entail needlessly burdensome obligations for the involved parties, a phenomenon known as "over-embedding" (Uzzi 1997a) of economic transactions. These obligations may negate the positive effects of the network ties in question. Failure to sever detrimental ties may be the result of enforcement of compliance through community pressure (e.g., Portes 1998; Portes and Sensenbrenner 1993) or by an external third party such as the state. In addition, actors may not recognize the private bad character of the tie because of cognitive lock-in, which occurs when strong bonds serve as filters of external information that prevent realization of the negative impact of these ties (Gargiulo and Benassi 2000).

Social capital may also represent a public bad. Putnam (2000) notes that social capital may facilitate not only socially desirable activities, but also undesirable ones. For instance, criminal organizations, such as the mafia, typically exhibit dense social networks and attendant high social capital. This social capital may work to the benefit of the individual member (or it may not, if s/he would prefer to quit), but is typically undesirable from the perspective of society at large.

In the concrete context of societal coordination and institutional adjustment in the present fast-changing environment, social capital can further constitute a public bad in two ways. First, as discussed, it acts as a conduit for conformity pressures, thus forestalling micro-level action that could contribute to the building of pressure for coordinated adjustment. Second, social capital facilitates coordination by fostering cooperation (Fukuyama 1995; Putnam 1993a, 1993b) and the sharing and diffusion of information, values, and norms (DiMaggio and Powell 1983; Meyer and Rowan 1977; Oliver 1991; Pfeffer and Salancik 1978; Podolny and Page 1998). Networks thus make it easier for actors to coordinate with one another directly, for instance, in the context of societally coordinated adjustment processes mentioned earlier. In addition, networks enable tacit coordination through information exchange. Shared information will tend to be socially constructed (cf. Weick 1979); that is, it will tend to contain implicitly an interpretation of reality by the actor offering the information. Information can thus betray the propensity of the actor offering it to adopt one kind of action over another and allow the recipient of the information to adjust its actions accordingly. Overall, this suggests that societal coordination is more likely to occur in the presence of high degrees of social capital, with the known consequences for the rate of institutional adaptation.

Social networks in the Japanese political economy and intra-industry loops

The Japanese business system is so rich in networks that it has been dubbed a "network economy" (Kumon 1992; Lincoln 1990b). It was not least the prevalence and perceived efficacy of these networks in the booming Japanese economy of the 1980s that helped spur the current scholarly interest in social networks (Podolny and Page 1998). Prominent among the kinds of Japanese social networks explored in the literature are business groups, vertical *keiretsu*, R&D consortia, and the state–associations–firms nexus. All of these structures have been criticized for constituting sources of rigidity through the social obligations they entail. In addition, as I will discuss in Chapter 4, prior research suggests that all of these mechanisms contribute to the coordinated character of the Japanese political economy and, to the extent that comparable structures exist elsewhere, the evidence suggests that they tend to be relatively highly elaborated in Japan.

However, probably the most pervasive kind of social networks in the Japanese political economy, and thus a potential source of coordination, has so far largely escaped systematic exploration in the literature. Business groups can foster coordination among large firms in different industries. Vertical *keiretsu* can support coordination between suppliers and buyers. R&D consortia aim to create temporary coordination among competing firms in the same industry. And the state–associations–firms nexus can represent an important source of coordination between industry and state and, within the confines of associations, among firms.

What is missing from this picture is the continuous informal social networking that occurs among the actors active within the same industry. Japanese firms have numerous incentives for coordinating their actions with their peers in their industries, including risk aversion (Hofstede 1997; Lincoln 2001) and a strong incentive to ensure the survival of the firm for the benefit of its employees. Coordination helps firms reduce risk by providing access to more information and shared interpretations of data, and by making it easier to mobilize help from banks or government should any decision prove flawed. The effect of coordination at the level of the industry is visible in the tendency of firms to mimic each other and to exhibit undifferentiated corporate behavior, which has led strategy scholars to suggest that most Japanese firms in effect possess no strategy (Porter and Takeuchi 1999).

Industry-level networking goes beyond the state–associations–firms nexus in two important ways. First, a considerable degree of informal networking occurs among firms outside the confines of the industry associations. Second, information exchange within industries involves not only firms, associations, and the state, but also a variety of other actors with significant interest in the industry, such as universities, banks, and the press. Despite their prevalence in the Japanese economy and despite hints at their existence in works on the state–associations–firms nexus (e.g., Okimoto 1989; Schaede 2000; Tilton 1996), these networks have gone largely unexplored in the literature (known exceptions are Henry 1992; Watanabe, Irawan, and Tjahya 1991). Henry (1992) described these networks as the "Tokyo Loop." Recognizing his contribution, but also acknowledging the geographic dispersion of these networks beyond Tokyo, I will refer to them as "intra-industry loops."

Given the importance of intra-industry loops to coordination in the Japanese political economy, Chapters 4 through 6 will explore this phenomenon in detail. I describe the make-up and functioning of intra-industry loops, and I produce evidence that is consistent with the notion that loop networking represents a response by Japanese firms to coordination requirements. I further show evidence suggesting that the Japanese state may facilitate the creation of intra-industry loops through public R&D consortia.

So what? Or, Is this book for you?

The arguments and facts provided in this book should prove a rewarding reading experience for a number of audiences, including scholars of various fields in the social sciences, policy-makers and political commentators, and anyone doing business in Japan.

Scholars of Japan may find new insights in at least three areas. One is, of course, the argument that societal coordination, and by implication the extensive social networks permeating Japan, represent an important component in the slow rate of institutional adjustment we have witnessed in Japan. I intentionally cast the argument, where possible, in comparative perspective. Prior works on present-day institutional change in Japan focus either exclusively on Japan (e.g., Katz 2002; Lincoln 2001; Sakakibara 2003) or on a small sample of countries, such as Germany, Japan, and the United States (Yamamura and Streeck 2003). This approach runs the risk of identifying causal relationships that are spurious or miss an important part of the picture, as illustrated in the debate about vested interests and institutional complementarities already mentioned.

A second probable point of interest for Japan scholars lies in the identification and discussion of intra-industry loops. Despite their pervasiveness in the Japanese political economy, this form of social networking has so far largely eluded systematic exploration. This study helps fill this empirical gap. I describe the makeup and functioning of intra-industry loops, present evidence that networking intensity varies by the demand for coordination by firms, and show that the Japanese state plays an important role in the nurturing of these networks in infant industries through the formation of public R&D consortia.

Likely to be of value for Japan scholars is also the holistic, data-driven business systems analysis I undertake to shed light on the question of institutional change, or lack thereof, in the Japanese political economy over the past fifteen years. Prior works (e.g., Inagami and Whittaker 2005; Jackson 2003b; Lincoln 2001) have tended to focus on individual elements of the business system. By contrast, one chapter of this book evaluates all key components of the business system (cf. Redding 2005). The data presented in the context of this analysis may also provide a useful point of departure for further exploration of the Japanese business system and institutional change within it.

The key point of interest for scholars of varieties of capitalism is likely to be the argument linking societal coordination to the rate of institutional adjustment in rapidly changing environments. The adjustment difficulties of CMEs have not escaped scholarly attention (e.g., Yamamura and Streeck 2003), though empirical research in this vein has again tended to focus on a small sample of countries. In this work, I push our understanding of the phenomenon further by laying out a set of mechanisms underlying the observed variations in rates of institutional adaptation and supporting its contentions with data from a broad sample of advanced industrialized nations.

Scholars of institutional change may find two points of particular value. First, the extent of societal coordination emerges as an important contingency that co-determines the characteristics of institutional adjustment processes. This includes the level of society at which adjustment occurs, mechanisms of diffusion of institutional innovation, uniformity of output, riskiness of institutional adjustment, and of course the rate of institutional adjustment.

Second, I point to an additional dynamic of institutional adjustment. Most research on institutional change at the level of the nation state has been on change through political processes that involve power and bargaining (e.g., Aoki 2003; Buchanan and Tullock 1962; Henisz and Zelner 2005; Knight 1992; Niskanen 1990; North 1990; Seo and Creed 2002; Streeck and Thelen 2005; Thelen 2004; Tullock, Seldon, and Brady 2002; Van de Ven and Hargrave 2004). I argue that an *additional* source of pressure for formal institutional change can emerge from actions at the micro level that are at least initially autonomous, apolitical, and undertaken without intention to induce systemic formal institutional change. This dynamic has been under-explored in the literature.

Scholars of social networks and social capital may find two large points of interest. First, this study provides additional evidence that social networks and social capital may represent a obstacle to institutional adjustment. One mechanism previously described in the literature is that social networks stabilize extant institutions by transmitting isomorphic pressures that discourage institutional innovation (Oliver 1992). This effect is clearly visible in the relatively low levels of autonomous micro-level action in the Japanese context.

A second effect of social networks that emerges from the discussion is that they facilitate coordination and thus constitute an important contributing factor in the relatively slower rate of institutional adjustment in CMEs. To the extent that institutional adaptability is a desirable feature of an institutional structure, there may be such as a thing as too much social capital.

Second, social network and social capital scholars may be interested in the empirical evaluations of intra-industry loops. From a theoretical perspective, the linkage between public R&D consortia and the emergence of intra-industry loops may be of interest. Prior studies have elucidated the volitional formation of social capital (e.g., Bouty 2000; Browning, Beyer, and Shetler 1995; Rosenkopf, Metiu, and George 2001). By contrast, networking in public R&D consortia tends to be governed by "enforceable trust" (Portes 1998); that is, it is in principle compulsory. Using data from the Japanese micromachine industry, I show evidence that networking under conditions of enforceable trust may create conditions for other sources of social trust to develop, which in turn can help maintain social networking after the formal termination of the R&D consortium.

For practitioners in business, this book could prove valuable in at least three ways. First, by shedding light on one of the major mechanisms underlying the slow rate of institutional change in Japan, this book illustrates a source of political risk for business in Japan. The political risk literature has tended to focus on institutional change as a source of host country risk for foreign investment (Berg and Guisinger 2001; Henisz 2002; Kobrin 1982). Underlying this approach is the notion that investment that looked favorable under the conditions under which it was undertaken may turn unprofitable if political processes *ex post* result in changes in policies and institutions. But there is also an inadaptability risk. This is relevant for both foreign and domestic investors, as both need to consider at least implicitly the possibility that institutional adjustment will fall behind environmental changes, with concomitant implications for economic performance and political dynamics. To the extent that firm capabilities co-evolve with the institutional environment (e.g., Anderson 1999; Arthur 1994b; Dooley and Van de Ven 1999; Gell-Mann 1994; Kauffman 1995; Lewin and Kim 2004; Lewin, Long, and Carroll 1999; Lewin and Volberda 1999;

Volberda and Lewin 2003), domestic firms further face the risk that adjustment failure in their home market will erode their competitiveness on international markets and reduce their options for developing requisite capabilities for the emerging information technology age.

Second, foreigners conducting business in Japan may be especially interested in the exposition of intra-industry loops. Foreign businesses have tended to find Japan a relatively opaque business environment. A closer understanding of intra-industry loops may help these firms devise ways of keeping abreast of developments in their industries.

Third, foreign businesses may find the analysis of change in the Japanese business system useful for understanding the system itself. Experience in numerous executive education programs suggests that even old Asia hands tend to have a limited sense of its key features and their interdependencies. While the analysis in Chapter 2 is intended as an exposition of change in the Japanese business system rather than of the business system as such, it does afford insights into the functioning of the system that may prove useful for operating within it.

Last but not least, it is my hope that this book may be of use for policy-makers involved in institutional change and political commentators, both in Japan and elsewhere. This monograph is not intended as a policy book, and it intentionally abstains from giving policy recommendations. What the book does is to provide theoretical argument and empirical evidence suggesting that societal coordination is inimical to quick institutional adjustment, with concomitant costs in terms of economic performance. This implies neither a need nor a recommendation for convergence on the LME model, as these costs must be weighed against societal values as well as benefits attendant on the present structures, such as institutional competitive advantages (Hall and Soskice 2001). But it does suggest that societal coordination and its costs ought to be subject to debate in the political arena. At a minimum, there ought to be a critical evaluation of whether the key benefits of the present system can be maintained at lower levels of societal coordination that afford the business system faster rates of adaptability and thus increase the likelihood that the benefits of societal coordination can be sustained into the future.

Outline of the book

As befits a book arguing that Japan exhibits a slow rate of institutional adjustment, in Chapter 2, I commence with an empirical analysis of continuity and change in the Japanese business system since 1990. Drawing on Redding's (2005) comprehensive framework for analyzing business systems, I find limited change in the rules of the game of Japanese business despite one-and-a-half decades of economic pain. The major exception is an increase in foreign ownership that is putting pressure on firms to improve profitability and corporate governance, with possible knock-on effects on other parts of the system. However, the analysis shows that there are also at least three sources of institutional rigidity situated within the business system: widespread support of the extant structure, institutional competitive advantage, and coordination.

In Chapter 3, I argue that societal coordination of adjustment processes mediates the rate of institutional adjustment in business systems. In coordinated processes, adjustment typically occurs through bargaining within and among organizational actors such as employer associations, labor unions, interest groups, and government. This contrasts with autonomous processes, in which actors initiate and implement institutional change without the need for formal coordination or bargaining with one or several external actors. I produce cross-sectional evidence from the advanced industrialized nations that suggest that degree of coordination is inversely related to economic indicators of institutional fit, and lay out the underlying mechanisms for a relatively slower rate of adjustment in coordinated systems. I further argue that the rate of progress in societal coordinated adjustment processes is at least partially contingent on pressure for adjustment emanating from actions of micro-level actors such as individuals and firms. These actions can be political in nature and aimed at coordinated adjustment process, but many of them may contribute to building pressure even though they are autonomous, apolitical, and undertaken without intention to induce systemic institutional change. Applied to Japan, this discussion suggests that the relatively slow rate of institutional adjustment is a likely consequence of high levels of societal coordination paired with relatively low levels of pressure for adjustment from micro-level action.

Given the importance of social networks in enabling societal coordination, I dedicate Chapter 4 to exploring the coordinating role of social networks in the Japanese business system. Key forms of networks known from the literature include business groups and vertical *keiretsu*, but also R&D consortia and the state–associations–firms nexus. The chapter introduces and defines a hitherto under-explored but highly prevalent form of networking, intra-industry loops. Intra-industry loops link firms in a given industry with one another as well as with other actors and organizations involved in the industry such as associations, government, and academics. These networks constitute a key mechanism for information exchange and thus coordinating within industries.

Since there is limited literature on intra-industry loops in Japan, I focus on evaluating this phenomenon empirically in the following two chapters. In Chapter 5, I use survey data from three case industries – micromachines, semiconductor equipment, and apparel – to illustrate the shape, contents, importance, and frequency of networking and how these characteristics vary across industry. Network character-istics appear to change with life cycle stage, which is consistent with the idea that industries of different ages tend to coordinate on different dimensions and use coordination as a buffer against uncertainty. For example, perceived network importance and frequency of use of network ties tend to be higher in sunrise and sunset industries than in mature industries, as the former two face greater uncertainty about the future course of the industry. Similarly, networking contents – the kinds of information exchanged – seem to evolve over time in patterns that are consistent with the needs of firms at the respective life cycle stage.

In Chapter 6, I use evidence from the micromachine industry to suggest that the Japanese government may help build intra-industry networks – and thus reinforce coordination in the Japanese business system – by sponsoring R&D consortia in the early stages of an industry. Questionnaire and interview data from the micromachine industry show that firms that participated in a ten-year-long consortium in the industry seem to continue to network more extensively with one another after termination of the consortium than firms that did not participate in the consortium. This suggests that by inducing competing firms to cooperate toward a common goal, the consortium may have laid the foundations for increased intra-industry networking and thus higher potential for coordination among the participant firms.

Chapter 7 concludes the book with a summary and a prediction for the future evolution of the Japanese business system.

2 | Continuity and change in the Japanese business system

T HE MAIN argument of this book is that the coordinated nature of the Japanese business system renders it relatively slow to adjust when faced with high-velocity changes impinging on economic activity. Making this argument requires, first of all, demonstration that institutional adjustment in the Japanese business system has indeed been relatively slow.

I tackle this challenge by exploring the extent to which the Japanese business system has undergone structural changes over the past fifteen years. This period is particularly suitable for this kind of evaluation because all else equal, one would expect the incidence of institutional change to be inversely related with system performance: the lower the performance of the system, the greater the probability of change. The extant institutional structure may not be the result of conscious institutional design (Thelen 2004), but its preservation is contingent on the consent or at least acquiescence of those governed by it. For business systems, the perhaps central variable mediating consent and acquiescence is economic performance. Low performance undermines the legitimacy of the system, increases the incentives for institutional change if higher output is attainable under a different institutional configuration, and weakens the relative economic power of those with a vested interest in the status quo (cf. North 1990; Oliver 1992). As institutions and the interests of those they govern diverge, actors become increasingly likely to spring into action and seek institutional change (North 1990; Seo and Creed 2002). The dismal economic performance of Japan since 1990 should consequently have been conducive to institutional adjustment processes in the Japanese business system.

In my analysis, I find that despite these favorable conditions, institutional change at the core of the Japanese business system over the past fifteen to twenty years has been limited. A holistic analysis of the institutional structure underlying Japanese business using the business system model by Redding (2005) suggests marked divergence from pre-recession conditions in only one area: ownership. There, I find evidence of a rapid increase of foreign ownership and concomitant unwinding of shareholdings by Japanese financial institutions, paired with a decline in long-term shareholdings and cross-shareholdings as well as moves toward corporate governance reform.

I further identify three sources of institutional rigidity in the system: widespread support of the extant system, the significance of existing institutions as a source of competitive advantage, and the coordinated nature of the business system, which is facilitated by extensive social networks.

Analytic framework

Sartre is reputed to have remarked that one could say anything about Americans, all would be true. The same can be said of institutional change, especially in the Japanese context. Some scholars, perhaps the majority, argue that the Japanese business system is highly rigid, little has changed, and that what change has occurred constitutes adaptive tinkering with the extant structure (e.g., Curtis 1999; Lincoln 2001; Sakakibara 2003; Streeck and Yamamura 2003). Others contend that while change is proceeding in an incremental manner, the overall effects may indeed be fundamentally transformational (e.g., Streeck and Thelen 2005; Vogel 2005). The two sides are vulnerable to erring in opposite directions: The former may underestimate the amount of change in the business system if the sum of incremental changes indeed builds up to a fundamental reorientation. Conversely, the latter is prone to overestimate the degree of transformative change. Incremental change occurs in any business system at any given time, but which is transformational and which is not? There are no clear criteria for telling incremental adaptation from incremental transformation.

I propose to define change as transformational if its impact is *systemic* (cf. also Lincoln 2001). The debate about change in Japan shows a tendency to conflate change in parts of business systems with change in the business system itself. Business systems are "systems" by dint of linkages and complementarities among the core features of their component elements (Hall and Soskice 2001; Redding 2005). Absent such linkages, they would merely be loose agglomerations of unrelated institutions. With the need to adapt a constant in life, alterations in the institutional details of component elements and subsystems, such as corporate governance structures (Jackson 2003a) or the redeployment of labor within firms (Vogel 2005), are to be expected. A key question for determining whether these changes are adaptive or transformational is thus whether they alter core components on which the linkages and complementarities of the business system rest. Transformational change in the definition proposed here involves core components, with concomitant knock-on effects through linkages and complementarities that necessitate further change in other parts of the system. A test for the transformational nature of change, then, is to look for the presence of knock-on effects. Where they are absent, one can conclude that change in a component element was probably not transformational.

Evaluating continuity and change in the Japanese business system thus requires a holistic system analysis that takes into account linkages and complementarities among component elements of the system. This raises the question of what these component elements are. To answer this question, I draw on the literature on comparative business systems (also known as "varieties of capitalism" or "co-evolution"). This stream of research in political science, socioeconomics, and business argues that different societies have evolved structurally distinct forms of capitalism (Albert 1993; Amable 2003; Dore 2000; Hall and Soskice 2001; Lewin and Kim 2004; Lewin, Long, and Carroll 1999; Lewin and Volberda 1999; Redding 2005; Streeck and Yamamura 2001; Thelen 2004; Whitley 1999). A central tenet is that economic activity is embedded in society and thus shaped and constrained by societal values and practices. Variation in these values and practices across societies has, through historical and political processes (cf. Thelen 2004), given birth to different ways of organizing economic activity. The resultant institutional configurations, or "business systems," can deviate considerably from the neo-classical ideal many economists espouse (cf. Hall and Soskice 2001; Whitley 1999).

Making the argument that capitalism has evolved in different varieties throws up the same challenge as the analysis in this chapter: devising methods for identifying and comparing the essences of business systems. Several schemes have emerged, all with considerable empirical substantiation. For Hall and Soskice (2001), the central discriminatory variables are the extent and mechanisms of societal coordination of economic activity. Amable (2003) points to five dimensions along which systems differ: product–market competition, labor markets, finance and corporate governance, social protection and welfare, and education. Whitley's model (1999) comprises seven components: at the level of the firm, ownership, management, and networks across firms, and at the level of society, the nature of the state, of the financial system, of the skill development and control system, and of trust and authority relations.

In this chapter, I draw on the business systems model by Redding (2005). The model represents a refinement of Whitley's approach and goes beyond the other models by considering not only the means of coordination in society, economy, and business, but also the socially accepted ends and means of business. The model thus incorporates a general analysis of societal preferences for the institutional structure of business. In addition, it explicitly opens up the possibility that different business systems may not merely represent distinct means toward the same ends, but distinct means toward varying ends. The question of the ends represents an important element in understanding institutional adjustment in the Japanese business system; I will return to this point later in this chapter.

The essence of the Redding model is an analysis of business systems in terms of three layers and their linkages (Figure 2.1): (1) the cultural underpinnings of society, which co-determine the desirable and attainable in society; embedded in culture, (2) the business environ- ment,[1] which provides the institutional infrastructure of financial, human, and social capital; and embedded in the business environ- ment, (3) the business system itself, which constitutes the institutional fabric of business. Key influences on the shaping of these institutional layers are the state and civil society as well as material and ideational logics. As shown in Figure 2.2, each layer consists of three component parts, each of which in turn tends to feature several sub-components. The output of the model is a holistic view of a given business system that takes into account virtually all institutional elements the literature has identified as constitutive of a business system.

---

[1] Redding refers to this layer as "institutions." I adhere to the common usage of "institutions" to denote any formal and informal constraints on human behavior (cf. North 1990). In this sense, all three layers of the Redding model are made up of institutions. To prevent confusion, I refer to Redding's "institutional" layer as the "business environment."

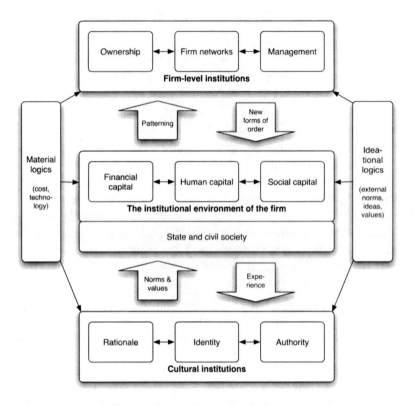

Figure 2.1. The nature of the business system (following Redding 2005)

In the remainder of this chapter, I first use the Redding model to
gain an overview of developments in the component parts of the
Japanese business system over the past fifteen years. Where appropriate and possible, I will also provide external reference points by
including data from two other leadings economies: the United States
as a representative of the liberal market kind of capitalism, and
Germany as a representative of a similar, societally coordinated
market type of capitalism. The main rationale for doing so is that
many measures are, at least implicitly, relative to external reference
points. For example, to say that Japan's society is group-based is in
essence to say that it is relatively more collectivist than other societies,
such as that of the United States and of Germany. The comparative
approach will also make it easier to identify where developments in
Japan are following trends elsewhere and where they are not.

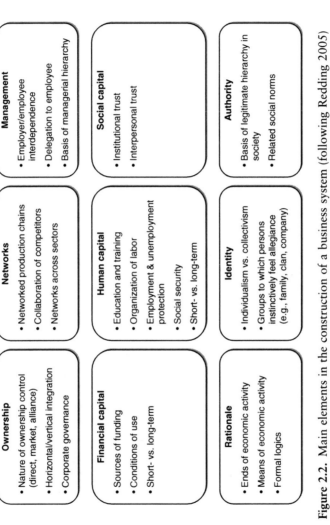

Ownership
- Nature of ownership control (direct, market, alliance)
- Horizontal/vertical integration
- Corporate governance

Networks
- Networked production chains
- Collaboration of competitors
- Networks across sectors

Management
- Employer/employee interdependence
- Delegation to employee
- Basis of managerial hierarchy

Financial capital
- Sources of funding
- Conditions of use
- Short- vs. long-term

Human capital
- Education and training
- Organization of labor
- Employment & unemployment protection
- Social security
- Short- vs. long-term

Social capital
- Institutional trust
- Interpersonal trust

Rationale
- Ends of economic activity
- Means of economic activity
- Formal logics

Identity
- Individualism vs. collectivism
- Groups to which persons instinctively feel allegiance (e.g., family, clan, company)

Authority
- Basis of legitimate hierarchy in society
- Related social norms

Figure 2.2. Main elements in the construction of a business system (following Redding 2005)

Two caveats are in order. First, since the focus in this chapter is on institutions, I concentrate on the three institutional layers in the model – culture, business environment, and business system. I bracket the role of the other, noninstitutional components such as the state in the model.

Second, my analysis is deliberately indicative rather than exhaustive and detailed. Several books could be written about each of the nine boxes. Within the constraints of this book, my analysis is limited to one chapter, so it must remain relatively high-level and cannot do full justice to the richness of and diversity in the institutional fabric.

Following our empirical analysis, I evaluate the impact of changes in the nine boxes on the linkages within the system. I identify change in ownership patterns of companies toward international investors as a key institutional tension with potential for inducing transformational change. At the same time, I find powerful institutional sources of rigidity.

Culture

At the cultural level, the Redding model asks for an analysis of rationale, identity, and authority.

Rationale

Rationale refers to the way in which people in a given national context think about business and the economy. It comprises three elements in their relation to business activity: commonly accepted ends, commonly accepted means, and the use of formal logics. Put in another way, the model asks to explore what people consider the ultimate purpose for the existence of the firm, what they consider the appropriate ways of pursuing this purpose, and how they apply formal logics such as mathematical optimization to business processes. The analysis thus calls for a full reconstruction of the mental landscape of a people, or at least of those occupying leading positions in business and economic life. While complete analyses of rationale are yet to be produced[2] and longitudinal statistics of formal logics do not appear to exist, the available data allow for some exploration of change in the accepted ends and means in the Japanese business system.

---

[2] Gordon Redding and myself are presently working on this issue.

In terms of accepted ends of the firm, the evidence suggests that the idea of stakeholder value is alive and well, both in the minds of the general public and of the corporate elite. An indicator of the acceptance of the stakeholder value view and competing models by the general public may be derived from question 87 of Inglehart's World Value Survey, which asks respondents to choose among four options of ownership and management control. Option 1 is consistent with the shareholder value view: "The owners should run their business or appoint the managers." Option 2, on the other hand, is consistent with a stakeholder view emphasizing both owners and employees: "The owners and the employees should participate in the selection of managers." Option 3 suggests the state should be in charge, and option 4 refers to employee-owned and -run business.

The data for Japan reveal consistent support of stakeholder value (option 2) over shareholder value (option 1). After relative stability in shareholder and stakeholder value views through 1995 at around 40 percent and 50 percent, respectively, both dropped in 2000 to values of 32 percent and 44 percent, with a concomitant increase in "don't know" replies. The reason is unclear, but the proportion of respondents preferring option 2 to option 1 remained almost unchanged between 1995 and 2000 at about 1.35. The United States tends to favor the shareholder over the stakeholder view, with support for the former consistently in the upper 50 percent range since 1981 and reaching 59 percent in 2000. Support for the stakeholder view remained in the lower to mid 30 percent range, with a value of 33 percent in 2000. (West) Germany occupies an intermediate position with 47 percent favoring shareholders and 43 percent, stakeholders both in 1981 and 1990. However, in 1997, it shows a marked shift toward the stakeholder view, with stakeholder support reaching 63 percent and shareholder support plummeting to 29 percent. This is likely a sign of a popular backlash to highly publicized attempts by German business to place greater emphasis on shareholder value in the mid-1990s. No German data are available for 2000.

Further evidence of the persistence of stakeholder value in Japanese management comes from several surveys. Jackson points to survey results that show that "the commitment to employees remains strong among Japanese managers" (Jackson 2003a:294), and notes similar findings for Germany. Inagami and Whittaker determine that only 9 percent of the managers they surveyed agreed with the statement that "the company is the property of the shareholders, and employees are simply a factor of production" (Inagami and Whittaker 2005:77). By contrast, 86 percent agreed that "stakeholders are not limited to shareholders, and management must reflect appropriately multiple interests" (Inagami and Whittaker 2005:77).

These results are consistent with findings from field research on executive rationale I undertook in 2002 and 2003. As part of a large-scale comparative project (cf. Redding and Witt 2004), I queried seventeen high-profile Japanese business leaders about their rationale for the existence of the firm. Most interviews paired two business leaders over dinner. They were conducted in Japanese and lasted an average of two hours. The conversations were recorded, but are not for attribution. A list of the respondents with their respective positions at the time of the interviews is included in the Appendix.

All Japanese executives I interviewed expressed support of a stakeholder value view of the firm. To most executives, their company's ultimate purpose seems to be to contribute to the well-being of society at large and their employees, as expressed in representative statements such as these:

- "Not like that American-style 'shareholder only,' not that way of doing things, but managers have after all a responsibility toward all stakeholders."
- "If I were to say for what the company exists, it is to make the employees it is embracing happy, and to maintain that happiness, we have to give a return to the shareholders from whom we have received the money."
- "As an individual manager, I think the most important thing is, it has to be a company that can continue to contribute to society in its own way in the respective country, including overseas."

The interviews revealed widespread recognition of the increased importance of shareholders and the institutional infrastructure accompanying it, though this tended to be considered an unavoidable consequence of globalization rather than a desirable feature:

- "It's like Las Vegas, today's shareholders. ... I am saying, let's return to the cross-shareholding among friends. That feels more at home to the Japanese manager. It does not fit Japan that people

who don't even speak Japanese sell and buy my company's stocks and profit from that."
- "The rating companies, [their people] are still really young, that bunch levels barrages of fairly rude questions at today's managers, everyone is fairly unhappy."

In clarifying relations with shareholders, one executive compared his company to a child, and his shareholders, to the child's parents, in the sense that the shareholders were the ones to put up the capital to make the foundation of the firm possible. Just as a child owed gratitude to its parents that is to be expressed as filial piety, he explained, the firm owed gratitude to shareholders, expressed in form of dividends. But just as a child at some point began to lead a life of its own free from parental control, so the firm's existence was to be free of interference from shareholders.

On the question of the accepted means of business and economic activity, there is very limited time-series evidence available. The World Values Survey includes five items that can very broadly be construed to be related to four basic parameters of the desirable shape of the business system: the role of technology, incentivization through income differentials, the role of government in the economy, and the role of competition as a general principle. Table 2.1 shows the development of these values from 1990 to 2000 in Japan, 1990 to 1997 in West Germany,[3] and 1990 to 1999 in the United States. Biggest changes in the Japanese time series are a somewhat increased fondness of private business ownership and slightly reduced enthusiasm about technological development. Appreciation of competition has gained very slightly, and views on the role of income equality and government responsibility have remained virtually the same. Taken at face value, it might seem as if Japanese held similar views about incentivization through income differentiation as Germans and Americans while placing relatively more emphasis on technological development and government and relatively less stress on competition. In effect, however, all of the questions except the one on competition ask for respondents' views relative to the perceived status quo. Since perceptions of the status quo on these issues are not

---

[3] For some of these variables, there are data for all of Germany from a 1999 survey. Since West and East German mindsets have not converged, use of these data would prevent comparability over time. I consequently use the latest data point available for West Germany (1997).

Table 2.1. Views related to accepted means

Issue	Country	1990	1997/1999/2000
Technology development	Japan	57.1%	52.9%
	Germany	30.5%	24.3%
	USA	49.3%	47.3%
Income equality	Japan	5.7	5.7
	Germany	6.2	5.4
	USA	6.7	5.7
Private ownership of business	Japan	5.1	4.5
	Germany	3.7	4.0
	USA	3.2	3.5
Government reponsibility	Japan	6.8	6.7
	Germany	4.2	5.4
	USA	3.4	4.3
Competition is good	Japan	4.5	4.2
	Germany	3.3	3.6
	USA	3.2	3.4

Note: Data of second data point is 2000 for Japan, 1997 for Germany, and 1999 for the USA. German data points are for West Germany. Value given for "Technology Development" is the balance of the percentage of positive and negative ratings. Values given for the other variables are means of the answers given on a scale from 1 to 10. Scales used are: income equality: "1: Incomes should be made more equal 10: We need larger income differences as incentives;" private ownership of business: "1: Private ownership of business should be increased 10: Government ownership of business should be increased;" government responsibility: "1: People should take more responsibility to provide for themselves 10: The government should take more responsibility to ensure that everyone is provided for;" competition: "1: Competition is good. It stimulates people to work hard and develop new ideas 10: Competition is harmful. It brings the worst in people."
Source: World Value Surveys.

measured, direct comparison across countries is meaningful only for views on competition.

In sum, there is considerable evidence that the stakeholder view of Japanese business is alive and well. Shareholders are recognized as a constituency that may have gained in importance, but the needs of other stakeholders and especially of employees still appear to loom large in the rationale of Japanese business. The limited available evidence on accepted means shows very limited change.

Identity

In this category, I find that Japanese society seems to have remained relatively collectivist, and that in the economic realm, identification with the company as a reference group seems still strong.

Numerous comparative studies have confirmed that Japan's society is relatively collectivist. Hofstede (1997) concludes that on an individualism scale from 0 (most collectivist) to 100 (most individualistic), Japan scores 46, as compared with 67 for Germany and 91 for the United States. Trompenaars and Hampden-Turner (1997) find similar results in their study, with Japan ranking lowest among the three countries in terms of measures of individual freedom, desirability of individual credit, and desirability of individual responsibility. Inglehart's World Values Survey draws a similar picture for 1995, the only year for which the relevant data are available: When asked which was more important for human relations, understanding the other's preferences (collectivist) or stating one's own preferences clearly (individualistic), 80.3 percent in Japan opted for the former, as compared with 78 percent in Germany and 74.3 percent in the United States. The most recent comparative study, the GLOBE project under Robert House (House et al. 2004), yields similar results for Japan, with Japan receiving the highest collectivism score of 5.19 out of 7, compared with 4.2 for the United States and 3.79 for Germany. The same study also finds evidence that Japanese distinguish more strongly between ingroup and outgroup than Americans and Germans.

Time-series evidence about change in the trade-off between individualism and collectivism comes from the biannual – formerly annual – Survey on Social Consciousness conducted by the Prime Minister's Office. The survey contains two questions that aim at this issue, one asking whether people should turn their attention to country and society or focus on the fulfillment of personal lives, the other probing whether from now on, the Japanese should emphasize personal benefit over that of the entire people or vice versa.

Both series indicate that the interests of the collective tend to continue to supersede those of the individual. In 2004, 44 percent of respondents indicated that people should turn their attention to country and society, as opposed to 34.6 percent pointing toward fulfillment of personal lives. This compares with 1990 values of 41.3 percent and 33.6 percent, respectively. Similarly, in 2004,

38.5 percent of respondents indicated that the Japanese should emphasize national over personal benefit, while 32.0 percent argued the opposite. In 1990, the values were 30.5 percent and 30.3 percent, respectively. Both time series are highly correlated, with correlation coefficients of +0.85 for the collectivist answers and +0.87 for the individualistic answers. For unknown reasons, both series show a marked upswing in the percentage of collectivist answers in 1991 and 1992 before stabilizing around today's values from 1993 onward.

The leading source of group identity in Japan, at least in the economic sphere, is the company (cf. Lebra 1976). The evidence suggests that the community aspect of the Japanese firm is still strong, though somewhat weakening. Given a choice between working with pleasant but incapable vs. unpleasant but capable colleagues, two surveys suggest that a large majority still prefers the former. One 2003 survey finds 66.9 percent of respondents preferring a pleasant but incapable co-worker; the opposite was preferred by 29 percent (NHK Broadcasting Culture Research Institute 2004). A second 2003 survey puts the numbers at 67 and 13 percent, respectively (Institute of Statistical Mathematics 2004). The time series was fairly stable from the 1970s until 1998 with numbers around 70 and 77 percent supporting option 1 and 25 and 11 percent, option 2.

Most people also still prefer a section chief who sometimes pushes too hard but also cares for his people on matters unrelated to work to a section chief who is reasonable but uncaring, though with a somewhat declining trend (Institute of Statistical Mathematics 2004). In 2003, 77 percent preferred a tough but caring boss, down from 87 percent in 1988 but little changed from 81 percent in 1973. 18 percent prefer the opposite, up from 10 percent in 1988 and 13 percent in 1973.

In addition, the majority of employees still socialize with co-workers outside of work, though the preparedness to do so started to weaken as early as the 1970s (NHK Broadcasting Culture Research Institute 2004). In 2003, 37.8 percent of respondents indicated a preference for consulting and helping colleagues with anything, down from 59.4 percent in 1973 and 44.6 percent in 1988. 37.5 percent prefer to limit contact unrelated to work to talk and fun after work, about the same as in 1988 (37.6 percent), but up from 26.4 percent in 1973. Respondents preferring to focus only on work-related issues stand at 21.7 percent, up from 15.1 percent in 1988 and 11.3 percent in 1973.

Table 2.2. Indicators of identification and satisfaction with the firm

Measure	mid-1980s(%)	late 1990s(%)
Self-perception as "living like a company man"	31	31
"Natural to sacrifice one's private life for the sake of the company to some extent"	47	43
Separation from family for job reasons acceptable	47	48
Doing work at home	19	19
"Pursue hobbies, study or social activities away from work and company people"	54	58
Satisfied with company	56	61
Satisfied with work	61	71
Satisfied with status in workplace	57	70
Satisfied with interpersonal relations at workplace	60	70
Satisfied with wages	34	44

Source: Inagami and Whittaker 2005

Inagami and Whittaker (2005) present further evidence for persistent identification with the firm. Comparing various surveys from the mid-1980s and late 1990s (various years), they find that there was no or little change on dimensions such as self-perception as "company man," acceptability of some personal sacrifice for the company and separation from one's family for job reasons, the proportion of employees working at home, or spare time activities away from the company (Table 2.2). Satisfaction with company, work, status, workplace relations all registered increases; even satisfaction with wages rose, despite falling wage levels (Table 2.2).

In sum, the evidence suggests limited change in the identity box. Survey results show that group interests fairly consistently tend to be placed over individual interests, and identification with the company as a major source of identity seems to have remained strong.

Authority

Comparisons of the strength of authority, or power distance, at an international level suggest a considerable degree of power distance in Japan, but draw an otherwise highly inconsistent picture. Hofstede finds power distance to be strongest in Japanese society, followed by the United States and then Germany. GLOBE, on the other hand, suggests that all three cultures feature almost identical power distance, with Germany in first, Japan in second, and the United States in third place. Inglehart's World Value Surveys show the Japanese to be more reluctant to follow orders of which they are not convinced than Americans, but less so than Germans. It is not clear what conclusions to draw from these data about the extent of power distance in Japan, or indeed any of the three countries.

The traditional sources of hierarchy in Japanese society are structured along Confucian lines and include education, age, and sex. None of the major longitudinal studies of the Japanese value system explores to what extent educational attainment commands respect. First-hand observation in Japan suggests that education is still valued, and the top echelons in bureaucracy and business continue to be recruited on the basis of attainment. It is not clear, though, to what extent the degree of obeisance to education has changed since 1990.

The evidence is much clearer for respect of age. Survey data suggest there is virtually no change in the proportion of Japanese considering it appropriate to use honorific (*keigo*) or polite (*teinei*) language toward people that are senior in age as well as the proportion believing that the same language level should be used regardless of age (NHK Broadcasting Culture Research Institute 2004). In 2003, 87.2 percent of respondents indicated the use of polite language, while 10.0 percent said the opposite. The respective percentages are 87.9 and 9.8 percent in 1988 and 84.2 and 13.7 percent in 1973. Since politeness of language in Japanese is indicative of status, the data suggest great resilience in the respect for age.

The traditional male dominance in Japanese society has come under attack over the past decades, and while elements of male domination are still clearly evident, a large amount of evidence consistently points to sex losing importance as a basis of status. The number of people believing that a difference exists in women's ability to consider and handle matters has fallen from 54 percent in 1988 to 45 percent in 2003 (Institute of Statistical Mathematics 2004). Perhaps in part as a consequence, the willingness to invest in women's education has increased. In 2003, 47.7 percent of Japanese indicated they would educate their daughters through college, up from 31.0 percent in 1988 and 21.7 percent in 1971. However, even the latest numbers are still considerably lower than the 67.7 percent for sons (NHK Broadcasting Culture Research Institute 2004). Perhaps again as a partial consequence, more women advance into positions of power, though overall penetration is still low. The proportion of female Diet members has risen from 3.4 percent in 1980 over 5.9 percent in 1990 to 9.2 percent in the early 2005 Diet (Miyawaki 2005). Similarly, the proportion of women in management positions has more than doubled over the past fifteen years, albeit from a miniscule base. In 1990, the proportions of women among the positions of chief clerk (*kakarichou*), section chief (*kachou*), and department chief (*buchou*) were 5.0, 2.0, and 1.1 percent, respectively (Miyawaki 2005). In 2004, these numbers were 11.0, 5.0, and 2.7 percent, respectively (Miyawaki 2005).

In sum, the jury seems out on the strength of authority in Japanese society compared with other nations. What is clear, though, is that age continues to be a source of authority. The same holds true for sex, though the male-dominated nature of Japanese society is eroding. No data are available that allow insights in changes of the link between education and status.

Business environment

The second layer of the Redding business systems model comprises financial capital, human capital, and social capital.

Financial capital

For an analysis of the institutional structure of financial capital, the Redding model proposes to explore sources of funding, terms under which funding is provided, and the degree to which capital is patient. No time-series statistics indicative of the latter two seem to exist, but there is clear evidence on the main sources of funding used by firms.

The key structural characteristic of Japan's postwar financial system was its dependence on indirect finance, with firms obtaining the bulk of their funding from banks rather than from capital markets. The role of banks as intermediaries was crucial for the execution of industrial policy (Johnson 1982; Okimoto 1989). However, with the heyday of industrial policy over (Callon 1995), the financial sector liberalized (Vogel 1996), and with banks still weakened from the bad loans problem of the 1990s, one might surmise that capital markets may have reasserted themselves as a source of funding for Japanese companies.

The data clearly indicate that news of the demise of indirect finance in Japan is exaggerated. According to the Bank of International Settlement,[4] the proportion of loans in all corporate funding in Japan has fallen from 74.2 percent in 1989 to 63.8 percent in 2002. This compares with 95.5 percent in Germany in 2001 and 41.2 in the United States in 2002.

The move in Japanese numbers represents a 14 percent drop, but almost two-thirds of Japanese corporate funding still comes from banks. The decline may also prove temporary. The recession reduced the need and ability to borrow for new investment especially for the large number of domestically-bound firms that continue to be highly dependent on banks. At the same time, banks for sometime found themselves with inadequate capital cover to extend new loans, leading to a credit crunch (*kashi shiburi*). Now that Japanese banks have disposed of most of their troubled loans and the economy is shaping up, business loans may regain lost ground.

I conclude that Japan's financial system continues to be bank-led despite some decline in the role of indirect finance since 1989.

Human capital

An evaluation of the institutions of human capital in the Redding model involves assessments of three areas: (1) education and training, (2) unions, and (3) the labor market.

The education system has undergone various structural reforms since 1990 (Goodman 2005; Ministry of Education 2002a). Much of the effort seems to have gone into making the extant system more flexible and decentralized. The 1998 School Education Law revision introduced "secondary education schools" (*chuutou kyouiku gakkou*) that combine junior and senior high school and created the possibility for second and third-year high school students to enter college without graduating from high school. College students entering from 2000 onward can graduate in 3 years, and it has been possible since 1999 to enter graduate school without graduating from college. Decentralization

---

[4] Graphical representation published in 73rd Annual Report of the Bank of International Settlement, 30 June 2003. I subsequently obtained the raw time series data from the Bank.

has aimed to give more autonomy to individual schools, for instance, by abolishing the approval system for appointments to superintendent in 2000. Further reforms introduced information technology to the classroom from 1994, instituted support for home education from 1999 onward, and removed the public university system, which accounts for about 20 percent of all students (Goodman 2005), from direct state control.

Participation in the education system is high and has been rising. Advancement rates to high school have been stable at around 95 percent since 1980, and an upward trend in advancement to graduate school has been evident at least since 1980 (Miyawaki 2005). What has changed considerably is advancement rates to college, which have risen by almost 50% from 24.6 percent in 1990 to 42.4 percent in 2004 after having been fairly flat in the 1980s (Miyawaki 2005). This development may reflect a premium placed on higher qualifications in today's knowledge society as well as the increased willingness of parents to educate their daughters through college, as discussed earlier. At the same time, it is highly likely that college enrolment rates rose as jobs for high school graduates became scarce during the economic downturn of the 1990s and postponement of entry into the labor market looked like a wise choice.

In terms of measurable quality of output, the Japanese education system continues to compare favorably internationally. The International Mathematics and Science Studies have for decades found Japanese achievement to be at world-leading levels. The Third International Mathematics and Science Study (Martin, Mullis, Gonzalez and Chrostowski, 2004; Mullis, Martin, Gonzalez and Chrostowski, 2004), with measurements taken in 1995, 1999, and 2003, shows virtually no change during these years. Science scores are 554, 550, and 552, respectively, while mathematics scores are 581, 579, and 570. The proportions of students answering identical questions right have also tended to remain stable over time (Table 2.3).

Evidence from the Program for International Student Assessment (PISA) studies undertaken by the OECD (2003, 2004a) in 2000 and 2003 is somewhat more mixed. In 2003, Japan scored sixth for mathematics (534 points), second for natural sciences (548 points), and fourteenth for reading (498 points) among 40 nations. While this continues to place Japan far ahead of the United States (483, 491, and 495 points) and Germany (503, 502, and 491 points), raw scores in

Table 2.3. Time series of Japanese scores on identical question groups in the Three Waves of the International Math and Science Survey

Subject	Year	Question Group A	Question Group B	Question Group C
Math	1964	64.4		
	1981	63.6	59.9	
	1995	65.4	61.4	78.1
	1999			77.6
Science	1983	71.7		
	1995	71.2	70.0	
	1999		70.2	

Note: "Question Group" is a set of the same questions used more than once. Numbers indicate percentages of examinees answering correctly
Source: Ministry of Education 2002b

mathematics and reading dropped considerably from the 2000 PISA study, by 23 and 24 points, respectively. The public soul-searching that promptly ensued publication of the latest results quickly pointed to recent educational reforms as the culprit, and it seems possible that some aspects of the reforms will be rolled back.

Much of vocational training in Japan has tended to occur within the firm (Dore and Sako 1989; Ito 1992), which makes its extent difficult to capture in statistics (cf. Estevez-Abe, Iversen, and Soskice 2001). Survey evidence reported by Inagami and Whittaker (2005) suggests that both on-the-job and off-the-job training organized by the firm continue to be widespread. In 2000, three-quarters of employees considered skill formation a company responsibility, and almost as many, 69 percent, opined that training would also in future remain a company responsibility. While not longitudinal in nature, these data suggest that company-based training in Japan is still common.

The primary vehicle of labor organization in Japan has been labor unions, predominantly at the company level (Allinson 1993; Kawanishi 1992; Kume 1998; Tachibanaki and Noda 2000). The OECD labour Market Statistics database indicates that labor union density hit a peak of about 35 percent in the mid-1970s and has been falling since at fairly constant rates, reaching 25.4 percent in 1990 and 20.3 percent in 2002. The decline of the unions in Japan mirrors that in Germany (31.2 in 1990, 23.2 in 2002) and the United States (15.5

in 1990, 12.6 in 2002), which suggests as the underlying cause global developments such as structural shifts from manufacturing toward service industries.

The nature of industrial relations in Japan appears to have remained amicable. The LABORSTA database of the International Labor Organization (ILO) shows that the number of days lost to strikes has dropped to negligible during the 1990s, with an average of 16,030 days lost annually from 2001 to 2003. The numbers for Germany and the United States are 166,754 and 1,962,767. The placidity of Japanese labor is striking given that the economic crisis did necessitate some restructuring, albeit mostly upon consultations with the unions. My own interviews with Japanese executives mentioned earlier revealed that most see unions as partners, as expressed in statements such as, "In the case of virtual any company in Japan, the labor unions are now leading an existence close to being partners of management." Further evidence of continued good relations comes from Inagami and Whittaker (2005), who report that 46 percent of executives disagree with the notion that unions will become irrelevant, with only 16 percent agreeing.

Turning to characteristics of the labor market, I find that lifetime and long-term employment seems to continue to refuse to give in to predictions of its demise. Lifetime employment has traditionally been a preserve for male employees. Kato (2001) finds that ten-year retention rates for male employees have changed only marginally from 1977 to 1997 (Figure 2.3), and the older the employee, the less change. Analysis of the Basic Survey on Wage Structure suggests that employment tenure for males actually increased over the past two decades, rising from 10.8 years in 1980 to 12.5 years in 1990 and 13.3 years in 2000 (Inagami and Whittaker 2005).

One reason of continued long-term employment is likely to be that employment protection–barriers to layoffs–remains high. The OECD Labor Market Statistics database provides an index of the overall strictness of protection against dismissals on a scale from 0 (no protection) to 3 (high protection). The index for Japan declined moderately from 2.7 in 1990 to 2.4 in 1998 and remained stable thereafter. With this, Japan remains in roughly the same league as Germany (2.7 throughout), in which headcount reductions are notoriously difficult, and far remote from the relatively hire-and-fire United States (0.2 throughout).

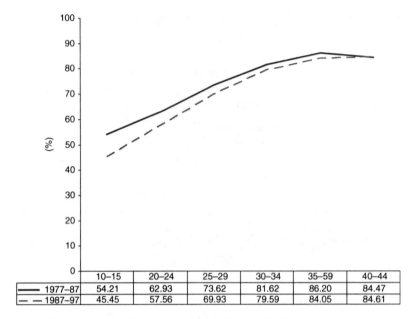

	10–15	20–24	25–29	30–34	35–59	40–44
—— 1977–87	54.21	62.93	73.62	81.62	86.20	84.47
— — 1987–97	45.45	57.56	69.93	79.59	84.05	84.61

Figure 2.3. Ten-year job retention rates, 1977–87 and 1987–1997
X axis shows age groups, y axis the percentage of employees retained over a ten-year period
Source: Kato 2001

Long-term employment and high employment protection are coupled with relatively low unemployment protection. This is visible in the proportion of public expenditure in labor market programs, including unemployment benefits, to GDP (Figure 2.4). Even if we correct for the fact that unemployment rates in Germany are about two-thirds higher in Germany following unification in 1990 than in Japan and in the United States, outlays on labor market programs are much higher in Germany. This reflects not only fairly generous unemployment benefits, but also active labor market programs such as job creation schemes and retraining. In Japan and in the United States, the state is much more hands-off. In both cases, the development of outlays tracks the business cycle – upward throughout the 1990s in Japan, and falling in the United States from 1991 till 1999 before rising again as the Internet bubble burst. The underlying mechanisms keeping outlays low have not changed in either country: In Japan, firms are expected to bear much of the burden of structural adjustment, keeping surplus labor on the job through mechanisms

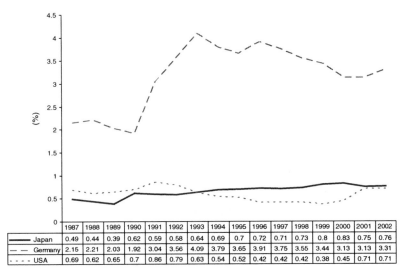

	1987	1988	1989	1990	1991	1992	1993	1994	1995	1996	1997	1998	1999	2000	2001	2002
Japan	0.49	0.44	0.39	0.62	0.59	0.58	0.64	0.69	0.7	0.72	0.71	0.73	0.8	0.83	0.75	0.76
Germany	2.15	2.21	2.03	1.92	3.04	3.56	4.09	3.79	3.65	3.91	3.75	3.55	3.44	3.13	3.13	3.31
USA	0.69	0.62	0.65	0.7	0.86	0.79	0.63	0.54	0.52	0.42	0.42	0.42	0.38	0.45	0.71	0.71

Figure 2.4. Public expenditure in labor market programs as percentage of GDP, 1987–2002
Source: OECD Labor Market Statistics database.

such as universal pay cuts, reduced working hours, and transfers to lower-paying subsidiaries. In the United States, the burden of the adjustment rests to a relatively large extent on the individual.

In sum, the data suggest little transformational change in the area of human capital. While education has seen some structural changes and increases in advancement rates to college, the impact on the business system as a whole, if any, is not yet manifest. Despite a recent drop in one international ranking, the Japanese education system remains highly competitive internationally. Unions are in decline as elsewhere in the world, but industrial relations continue to be amicable despite restructuring in the 1990s. Employment continues to be lifetime or long-term, employment protection measures have eased relatively little, and the state does not show any signs of becoming more involved in labor market programs.

Social capital

The Redding model reserves the term "social capital" for the extent of trust in society, both between persons and in the institutional fabric. A major source of social capital, both interpersonal and institutional, lies in the existence and strength of voluntary nongovernment associations (Putnam 1993a; Schwartz 2003). By bringing together individuals and firms across social boundaries and cleavages, associations allow the building of trust and cooperation among them (Putnam 1993a). Viewed from this perspective, the potential for the building of social capital in Japan seems to have increased between 1986 and 1996 – by 12.8 percent overall (1986: 33,668 associations; 1996: 37,982) and 10.0 percent for business associations (1986: 13,386; 1996: 14,728) (Tsujinaka 2003). This generally mirrors a rise in associations in the United States over the same period (total: 1986: 84,989, 1995: 93,754; business: 1986: 12,077, 1995: 14,643) (Tsujinaka 2003). Correcting for population size, density of associations in general remains lower in Japan than in the United States, but density of business associations in 1996 was more than twice as high in Japan, at 11.8 associations per 100,000 inhabitants, than in the United States, at 5.6 associations per 100,000 inhabitants (Tsujinaka 2003). For Germany, the comparative number for 2004, the only year available, is a total of 13,941 associations (Deutsches Verbändeforum 2005). Of these, 7,594 were business associations, yielding a density of 9.2 per 100,000 inhabitants. Overall, this suggests very high, and still rising, potential for the building of trust and cooperation among Japanese firms.

Neither interpersonal nor institutional trust appear to have changed decisively over recent decades. Expressions of interpersonal trust show, if anything, a slight improvement compared with 1983, though a worsening compared with 1993. On balance, the number of Japanese who believe that one must be careful rather than trust people exceeds that stating the reverse by 26 percentage points in 2003, as compared with 30 points in 1983 and 17, in 1993 (Institute of Statistical Mathematics 2004). At the same time, a majority rejects the notion that people will opportunistically take advantage of them given a chance with a margin of 37 percentage points in 2003, as compared with 30 points in 1983 and 40 points in 1993 (Institute of Statistical Mathematics 2004).

Measures of institutional trust overall draw a fairly stable picture. The one major exception is the perception of society as unfair, with the number of respondents seeing society as unfair exceeding that of respondents considering society to be fair by 38 percentage points in 2003, up from 16 points in 1993 but down from 47 points in 1998 (Institute of Statistical Mathematics 2004). At the same time, talent and effort are seen as much as the basis of success in society as in 1988, with majority margins of 14 percent in both 1988 and 2003 (Institute of Statistical Mathematics 2004). Further, the proportion of Japanese expressing "a great deal" or "quite some" confidence in the legal system in the World Value Surveys rebounded sharply to almost 79.6 percent in 1995, the latest available data point, after some decline in the 1980s, with a low in 1990 at 62.4 percent. It continues to stand considerably higher than in Germany (53.7 percent in 1997) and the United States (36.3 percent in 1995). Transparency International Corruption Perception Index values indicate that the perception of corruption in Japanese society has improved somewhat from 6.72 in 1995, the first year of the survey, to 7.3 in 2005. However, Japan still trails Germany (8.2 in 2005) and the United States (7.6 in 2005) on this count.

In sum, indicators of social capital in Japanese society do not suggest radical change in social capital in the Japanese business system. While the potential for the creation of social capital through associations is overall somewhat lower than in the United States, the considerably higher density of business associations in Japan suggests ample breeding ground for inter-corporate social capital.

Business system

The top layer of the Redding business systems model consists of ownership, inter-corporate networking, and management.

Ownership

The analytical work in the "ownership" box involves assessing three characteristics: (1) ownership patterns, (2) corporate governance, and (3) horizontal and vertical integration. No empirical data seem available concerning the latter point, so my analysis will focus on the questions of ownership and corporate governance.

Most major Japanese enterprises are corporations. Their shareholder structure has undergone considerable change since the 1990s (Figure 2.5). The largest shareholders in Japanese listed companies are still financial institutions, followed by corporations, individual shareholders, and foreign shareholders. While corporations and individual shareholders have seen only small changes in the proportion of shares they hold, financial institutions have reduced their holdings by about one-third since 1990. By contrast, foreign

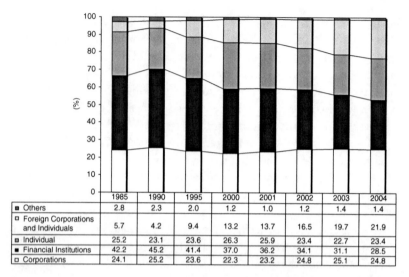

Figure 2.5. Ownership of companies listed on the Tokyo Stock Exchange, unit shares, 1985–2004
Source: Miyawaki 2005

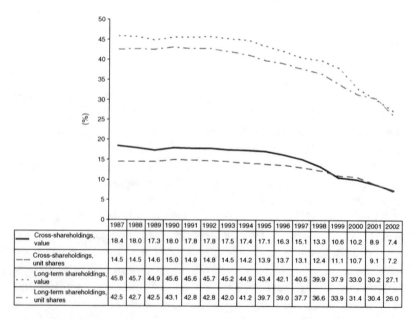

Figure 2.6. Cross-shareholdings and long-term shareholdings as percentages of the general market, 1987–2002
Source: Kuroki 2003

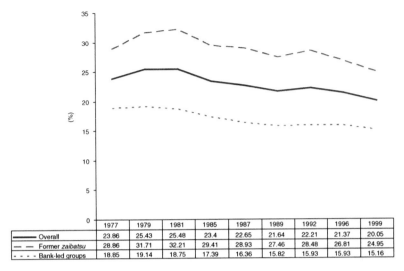

	1977	1979	1981	1985	1987	1989	1992	1996	1999
Overall	23.86	25.43	25.48	23.4	22.65	21.64	22.21	21.37	20.05
Former *zaibatsu*	28.86	31.71	32.21	29.41	28.93	27.46	28.48	26.81	24.95
Bank-led groups	18.85	19.14	18.75	17.39	16.36	15.82	15.93	15.93	15.16

Figure 2.7. Cross-shareholdings within business groups, 1977–1999
Source: Japan Fair Trade Commission 2001

shareholders have expanded their proportion about five-fold, and about a fifth of corporate Japan is now foreign-owned.

One accompanying effect has been that cross-shareholdings and long-term shareholdings in the Japanese economy have seen a marked decline since the early 1990s (Figure 2.6). Cross-shareholding in the general market is now down to less than half the levels seen in 1990 at about 7 percent. Long-term shareholding has also declined drastically, down about 40 percent from levels in 1990 to now around 27 percent.

However, the unwinding trend of cross-shareholding seems to have largely bypassed the six major business groups. The latest available data from the Japan Fair Trade Commission (2001) indicate that compared with 1989 levels, cross-shareholding within the business groups, excluding life insurance companies, fell only slightly, from 21.6 percent in 1989 to 20.1 percent in 1999 (Figure 2.7). The former *zaibatsu* groups – Mitsubishi, Mitsui, and Sumitomo – showed larger declines than the bank-led groups – Daiichi Kangyo, Fuyo, and Sanwa. These data suggest a high degree of resistance to change. At the same time, a recent spate of mergers of firms across group boundaries may have affected the picture, though it is not yet clear how: While these mergers can be seen as a sign of weakening of the groups, they may also indicate a reconfiguration, and perhaps even reinforcement, of the business groups. Empirical research on this question is needed.

Change in the area of corporate governance has remained limited. While several legal reforms came into effect (Jackson 2003a), the optional character of many of them means that only a relatively small number of firms has introduced tangible reforms in their corporate governance structures. Jackson and Miyajima (2004) report that of 721 firm examined, only 14 percent had instituted a considerable degree of corporate governance reforms. Common denominator among these firms seems to be a high proportion of institutional and thus foreign investors. Similarly, Inagami and Whittaker (2005) report that by early 2004, only thirty-six listed companies, out of about 3,500, had taken advantage of the option to reform their board structure along Anglo-Saxon lines as made possible by changes in the Commercial Code in 2002. Again these tended to be companies with relatively high international exposure.

Perhaps the clearest indication of relative continuity in corporate governance in Japan is that a market for corporate governance – hostile takeovers – is still virtually absent from Japan. According to one estimate in 2001, about a tenth of Japan's 3,500 listed companies had break-up values more than twice their market capitalization (*Economist* 2001). In a system with a functioning market for corporate governance, these companies would need to take urgent measures to increase their market valuation to prevent being taken over and restructured.

In Japan, hostile takeovers remain a rarity. The Thomson One Bank Deals database indicates that from 1990 until the end of 2004, only 4 hostile takeovers were attempted in Japan, 3 of which were completed. This is even fewer than in Germany, another country highly averse to hostile takeovers, with 7 attempted and 4 completed. It is a small fraction of the takeover activity in the United States, where the same period registered 335 attempts and 75 completions. All four Japanese attempts occurred after 1998, which may indicate a development toward more takeover bids. It is unlikely, though, that any such trend would last: Fears of hostile takeover bids has prompted the Ministry of Economy, Trade, and Industry (METI) to set up an advisory panel "to study whether Japan can introduce typical defensive measures such as the so-called poison pill and employee stock ownership plans under the current legal framework"

(Nakata 2004). The prospects for a sea change in the Japanese corporate governance structure seem consequently slim.

In sum, the data show that ownership patterns have changed a good deal, with foreign ownership increasing rapidly. However, while cross-shareholdings and long-term shareholdings in the general market have been unwinding, the latest available data suggest that the six major business groups have by and large maintained their cross-shareholding ties. Options for firms to adopt more Anglo-Saxon-style corporate governance mechanisms have become available, but only a relatively small proportion of firms, mostly those with large foreign ownership, seem to have taken advantage of them. The main ingredient of a shareholder-oriented corporate governance structure, a market for corporate governance, is still virtually absent and unlikely to grow much in the near future.

Networks

Most research on corporate networks in Japan has focused on two types of networks: business groups, also known as horizontal *keiretsu*, and supplier networks, also known as vertical *keiretsu* (e.g., Dore 1986; Gerlach 1992; Lincoln and Gerlach 2004; Sako 1992). I will discuss this literature in more detail and in comparative perspective in Chapter 4. In addition, informal networking in intra-industry networks involving firms and other organizations is pervasive in the Japanese economy. I will explore these networks in Chapters 4 through 6.

The available statistical evidence on business groups is mixed. On the one hand, there are some signs that links within groups are weakening. Interlocking directorates are becoming less common, showing a decline from 6.34 in 1989 to 4.17 in 1999 (Japan Fair Trade Commission 2001). Intra-group purchasing has fallen as well, though relatively little, from 7.75 percent in 1992 (no 1989 data points available) to 6.44 percent in 1999 (Japan Fair Trade Commission 2001). On the other hand, the amount of lending from each group's banks to group members increased slightly from 3.13 percent in 1989 to 3.53 percent in 1999 (Japan Fair Trade Commission 2001), and there is some evidence that equity ties within business groups strengthened during the 1992–1997 period (McGuire and Dow 2005). Similarly, the number of member firms in the six groups' presidents' councils (*shachoukai*), arenas of regular meetings of the presidents of group member firms that is sometimes taken as definitive of group membership (cf. Miwa and Ramseyer 2002), increased from 156 in 1981 and remained virtually unchanged in the 1990s at 193 firms in 1991 and 192 firms in 1999 (Japan Fair Trade Commission 2001; Lincoln and Gerlach 2004). In addition, a majority of 52.8 percent of group member firms expressed the expectation that their groups would be maintained in the present state or deepened. Only 18.4 percent anticipated that their groups could be coming to an end (Japan Fair Trade Commission 2001). As remarked earlier in this chapter, recent mergers across groups may have affected this picture since, though it remains unclear how.

Empirical evidence on change in vertical *keiretsu* appears to be very limited. Nissan famously slashed the number of its suppliers, but no other major Japanese firm seems to have pursued a similarly radical line. Ahmadjian and Lincoln (2001) have found that *keiretsu* ties were eroding as early as the mid-1980s, and that ties were reconfiguring away from networks mostly toward more arms-length contracting. At least in the case of Toyota, however, there also seems to be the opposite pattern of integrating suppliers even more closely in order to prevent them, or their products, from falling into the hands of competitors (Ahmadjian and Lincoln 2001). More empirical research on the state of the vertical *keiretsu* is needed.

We also have no time-series data on the third type of networking common among Japanese firms, intra-industry networks, as this phenomenon has received almost no attention in the prior literature (cf. Omori and Yonezawa 2002; known exceptions are Henry 1992; Watanabe, Irawan, and Tjahya 1991). I will discuss these networks in detail from Chapter 4, but here suffice to say that intra-industry networks are facilitated by, if not formally attached to, industry associations. Since the number of business associations has increased over recent years, a drop in the prevalence of intra-industry networks seems unlikely. Here, too, time-series research on the development of these networks is needed.

Overall, the available evidence suggest some loosening, but not a radical departure from the networked nature of the Japanese business world.

Management

The Redding model asks for analysis of two aspects: employer-employee interdependence, and delegation to employees. I will add to this a third element I consider to be important, namely the accepted means of establishing hierarchy within the organization.

The key metric for employer-employee interdependence is employment tenure. I have already discussed these data as part of the discussion of human capital, with the result that tenure lengths have, if anything, extended during the 1990s. This would suggest a strengthening of employer-employee interdependence.

No recent data are available for the extent of delegation to employees. Prior research suggests that delegation is considerable and decision-making, highly participatory, at least at the management level (Lincoln and McBride 1987; Marsh 1992). However, to my knowledge, the last published empirical evaluation of the *ringi* mode of decision-making, in which proposals circulate until a consensus is reached, dates to 1992 (Marsh 1992). I consequently have no indication of the extent to which this system has undergone changes over the past 15 years.

In terms of hierarchy, there has been much ballyhoo over a shift from the traditional seniority system (*nenkou joretsu*) to a more performance-based system. At least as of 2000, the data do not bear this out. Age-wage statistics computed by Inagami and Whittaker on the basis of the Basic Survey on Wage Structure (Inagami and Whittaker 2005) show the same basic profile for 2000 as for 1990– or 1980 and 1975, for that matter. Wage levels still rise with age, peak in the employment group of 50–54-year-olds, and then fall off as employees retire. The difference between entrance and peak wage levels fell somewhat for male university graduates, but increased slightly for manufacturing workers. It is possible that the performance-based systems purportedly introduced over the past years will show results only with considerable lag. Conceivable, though, is also that firms may have announced a move toward performance-based systems, but for a variety of reasons have not actually implemented them.

Overall, I find no hard evidence of a major shift in Japanese core management practices. Employer-employee interdependence remains high, and the seniority system is still clearly evident in the data.

Linkages and tensions

Figure 2.8 summarizes the key findings of the discussion so far and also shows some of the main linkages between system elements and

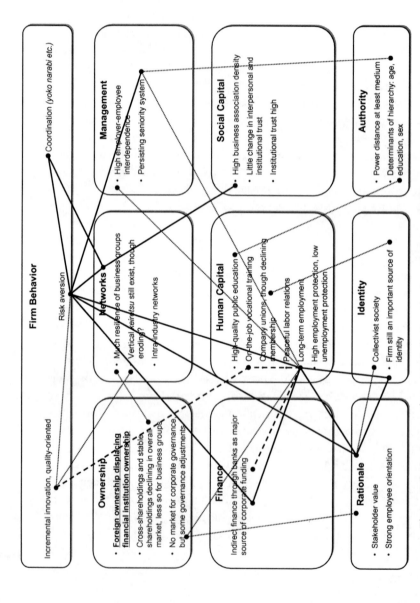

Figure 2.8. Summary of empirical findings and main linkages between elements

Firm Behavior

Incremental innovation, quality-oriented

Risk aversion

Coordination (yoko narabi etc.)

Management

- High employer-employee interdependence
- Persisting seniority system

Social Capital

- High business association density
- Little change in interpersonal and institutional trust
- Institutional trust high

Authority

- Power distance at least medium
- Determinants of hierarchy: age, education, sex

Networks

- Much resilience of business groups
- Vertical keiretsu still exist, though eroding?
- Intra-industry networks

Human Capital

- High-quality public education
- On-the-job vocational training
- Company unions, though declining membership
- Peaceful labor relations
- Long-term employment
- High employment protection, low unemployment protection

Identity

- Collectivist society
- Firm still an important source of identity

Ownership

- **Foreign ownership displacing financial institution ownership**
- Cross-shareholdings and stable shareholdings declining in overall market, less so for business groups
- No market for corporate governance but some governance adjustments

Finance

Indirect finance through banks as major source of corporate funding

Rationale

- Stakeholder value
- Strong employee orientation

behavioral patterns at the firm level in graphical form (cf. Redding 2005). To keep the figure from becoming too complex, I show only the main linkages, and I do not include linkages among items within boxes (with one exception). The linkages marked with dashed and solid lines form complementarities that I will explore in more detail as I move on.

The figure shows that major change in the Japanese business system over the past fifteen years is evident mostly in the ownership box. The share of foreign ownership is increasing, cross-shareholdings and long-term shareholdings are unraveling outside business groups, and pressure for adjustments in corporate governance toward the interests of (foreign) shareholders is rising. Counter to conventional wisdom, changes in financial markets appear to have little to do with these developments. Nothing in the structure of the capital markets in 1990 de jure prevented foreign shareholders from taking a significant stake in a Japanese company. The obstacle to doing so was typically that the requisite shares were not available, as they were in the hands of stable shareholders such as banks and affiliated corporations. What changed the picture were not the Big Bang reforms and financial globalization, but the recession and banking crisis of the 1990s. Financial institutions had to sell shares to shore up their capital basis, and with neither domestic investors nor domestic firms willing or able to buy them, the door opened to foreign portfolio investment.

Rising foreign ownership is increasing pressure to restructure the Japanese business system along more shareholder-friendly, and thus possibly Anglo-Saxon, lines. While the Japanese shareholders of old were usually happy with, or resigned to, firms paying them dividends while virtually ignoring them otherwise, foreign shareholders demand attention to the creation of shareholder value and thus also corporate governance mechanisms. Longtermism may give way to short-term thinking geared toward "making the numbers" for the next quarterly report, with possible knock-on effects on other elements of the system, such as longterm employment. The complementarities in the Japanese business system may begin to unravel.

Counteracting this impetus for structural change are at least three major sources of rigidity in the Japanese business system evident in Figure 2.8: vested interests expressed in the existing rationale, complementarities as a source of competitive advantage, and the coordinated nature of the Japanese business system.

First, there appears to be a preference in favor of maintaining the existing institutional structure. The discussion of rationale in the business system reveals that both large parts of the general public and many top managers are supportive of the status quo rather than of institutional change away from the present stakeholder-oriented structure. Indeed, when I asked the executives I interviewed for their views of the ideal economy, many described the present Japanese economy, though with less influence from the bureaucracy and a healthy banking system. In the words of one executive, "If we reform the bureaucracy and the banks, an ideal economy may come into being." Background of this high level of support is likely to be the former ability of the system to produce desirable economic outcomes for most Japanese, with the effect of establishing the system as legitimate and creating broad-based vested interests in it (cf. Yamamura 2003).

Second, some of the present complementarities seem to be a source of competitive advantage. Hall and Soskice (2001) have argued that competitive advantage in high-quality products relying on incremental innovation, typical of Japan, is contingent on the concurrent presence of workers developing firm-specific skills, long-term employment, and patient capital. The willingness of workers to develop firm-specific skills requires there to be long-term employment, otherwise workers would be better off to develop general, fungible skills that can be put to use for any employer, as is the case in the United States. Long-term employment, in turn, tends to be dependent on capital being patient, because only then can staffing levels be maintained during business downturns.

This institutional configuration is, or at least was, present in the Japanese system (Figure 2.8, dashed lines), and to the extent that managers are aware of it, they may seek to maintain it. The cardinal question is whether increased foreign ownership may threaten it by pressuring firms to improve profitability in the short-term by reducing headcount and increasing labor flexibility. To the extent that Hall and Soskice are correct, this would cause the institutional complementarities underlying Japanese production strategies to unravel and may undermine the viability of Japanese business in the long term. This would not be in the interest of shareholders, but it is not clear, either, to what extent investors are aware of the institutional linkages of competitive advantage.

Third, the coordinated nature of the Japanese business system (Hall and Soskice 2001; Whitley 1999) is inimical to rapid and radical change, as I will argue in detail in the following chapter. Japanese firms have a well-known penchant for coordinating with their peers. Firms often mimic each other's actions, a practice known as *yoko narabi* (lining up side by side) (cf. Okimoto 1989), and major investment announcements by one firm are often followed by similar announcements by all other major players in the industry. This undifferentiated corporate behavior has led scholars of strategic management to suggest that most Japanese firms in effect had no strategy (Porter and Takeuchi 1999).

Viewed from the perspective of the firm, the incentives for coordinating, and doing what everyone else is doing, are linked to risk aversion. Risk aversion is the consequence of at least two factors. First, Japanese society in general seems to be highly risk-averse (Hofstede 1997), in part because of conformity pressures not to take risks lest the entire group find itself in a position to have to share responsibility for any unfortunate outcomes (Lincoln 2001). Second, the stakeholder rationale of the Japanese business system puts a premium on firm survival, which militates against risk-taking (Figure 2.8, solid lines). This is clearest in terms of long-term employment: With employees having nowhere else to go in case of bankruptcy, there is a strong incentive for taking conservative decisions. The interests of other stakeholders – suppliers, customers, lenders, and shareholders – would likewise suffer in case of bankruptcy, which again suggest treading carefully.

Coordination helps firms reduce uncertainty and thus risk in at least three ways. First, coordination typically involves information exchange, which broadens the basis of empirical data available to the firm for decision-making. As we know from statistics, on average and all else equal, more data mean less uncertainty about actual conditions.

Second, coordination often involves the sharing of interpretations of data, which may yield more carefully deliberated decisions. Sharing of interpretations can occur overtly in what one might call *direct* coordination, in which two or more actors jointly undertake the processes of sense making and decision making. It can also occur in a more *indirect* fashion through information sharing alone, as such information will tend to be shaped by social construction processes such as uncertainty absorption that point toward some possible interpretations and tend to rule out others (cf. Weick 1979).

Third, should a given decision prove flawed, coordination may make it easier for firms to obtain help from lenders and government. Having engaged in coordination enables an individual firm to argue that it took all efforts to make the right decision by getting as much data as possible and take others' opinions into account. The firm may also argue that the adoption of similar measures by other firms suggests that its own decisions were in line with widely shared consensus. To the extent that other firms took similar decisions, adverse consequences are also likely to affect multiple players, which may increase the likelihood that government will pay attention and provide help.

Key mechanisms of coordination and uncertainty reduction are networks and associations (Hall and Soskice 2001; Oliver 1991). I have already discussed the persistence of business groups and supplier networks, and evidence shows that information exchange and coordination are important ingredients in these relationships (Dore 1986; Gerlach 1992; Japan Fair Trade Commission 2001; Lincoln and Gerlach 2004). Intra-industry loops, as will become clear, fulfill similar information collection and coordination functions, with the added benefit that firms within one's own industry tend to have the most pertinent information and represent the benchmark group against which any bailout decisions will be judged. Coordination with the government bureaucracy occurs mostly through the almost 15,000 industry and trade associations in Japan, which typically employ a retired bureaucrat in a leading position (Schaede 2000). Industry associations cover on average about 90 percent of the firms in their industry and thus provide a forum for industry-wide self-coordination and information exchange (Schaede 2000). I will explore these mechanisms from Chapter 4 onward.

3 | Coordination and institutional adjustment

T HE ANALYSIS in Chapter 2 has suggested that despite poor economic performance, institutional change in the Japanese business system since 1990 has been limited. My argument in this chapter is two-fold. First, on average and all else equal, the rate of institutional adjustment in the present era tends to slow with the degree of societal coordination in the business system and thus in adjustment processes. Formally defined, societal coordination represents the organizing of economic activity and the building of economic institutions through non-market interaction and cooperation of actors (cf. Hall and Soskice 2001; Streeck and Yamamura 2003). Societal coordination is more encompassing than formal regulation in that it also occurs voluntarily, without the involvement of government, and often informally. For instance, the phenomenon of *yoko narabi* already discussed represents voluntary informal coordination of activities such as investment. No regulations are involved, except in the sense that no regulations exist that prevent this type of behavior.

All advanced economies feature at least some degree of societal coordination. Government rules and regulations, for instance, are typically the result of coordinated action to erect or revise institutions. There is a difference, however, in degree, with some countries leaving relatively more room for market forces while others prefer higher degrees of coordination. In keeping with the literature (Hall and Soskice 2001), I refer to the former as liberal market economies (LMEs) and the latter as coordinated market economies (CMEs), though I am conscious of, and will take into account, considerable variation in coordination within these categories.

This chapter is partially based on a joint paper with Arie Y. Lewin, The Fuqua School of Business, Duke University. His permission to draw on this work for this book is acknowledged with much gratitude.

Second, the rate of progress in societally coordinated adjustment processes is at least partially contingent on pressure for adjustment emanating from actions of micro-level actors such as individuals and firms. These actions can be political in nature and aimed at coordinated adjustment process, but many of them may contribute to building pressure even though they are autonomous, apolitical, and undertaken without intention to induce systemic institutional change. Societally coordinated institutional adjustment is thus a two-track process: an official, coordinated process, and an unofficial, mostly non-coordinated one in which apolitical autonomous actions contribute to building pressure for change that feeds back into the official, coordinated process.

I begin by demonstrating in broad comparative perspective that in the present times of dynamic environmental changes, higher degrees of societal coordination are negatively correlated with indicators of economic performance. Second, I elucidate the mechanisms underlying the relatively slower rate of adjustment of CMEs, as compared with LMEs, by exploring the different dynamics of autonomous versus coordinated adjustment. I find that under the present conditions, coordinated adjustment is more prone to delay. Third, I explore how micro-level actors generally respond to institutional misalignments – that is, divergence between their needs and the constraints of the extant institutional structure – and how their actions contribute to building pressure on the coordinated adjustment process. Fourth, I introduce societal coordination as a contingency in micro-level action and adduce empirical evidence that suggests that CMEs tend to show higher levels of micro-level action conducive to building pressure for coordinated adjustment than LMEs.

I close by considering the implications of the discussion for the Japanese business system. My prognosis suggests little prospect for radical or rapid institutional adjustment. Not only is the societal coordinated adjustment process of Japan structurally vulnerable to delay and deadlock, the evidence also suggests that the generation of pressure through micro-level action is functioning at relatively low levels. I trace the causes of this latter phenomenon to three elements: geography, which forestalls some of the kinds of actions suitable for building pressure; legitimacy of the present system; and illegitimacy of taking autonomous action even in the face of adversity, with group dynamics and especially the social networks pervading the Japanese business system serving as enforcement mechanisms.

Performance and adaptation

There is no direct method of measuring the degree of adaptive fitness of the institutional structure in a given business system. However, economic performance and unemployment measures can serve as proxies, as the institutional structure has a direct impact on them (e.g., Blanchard and Wolfers 2000; Nickell et al. 2003; North 1990, 1994; OECD 2005). Institutions affect economic performance through their impact on transaction costs (North 1990; Williamson 1985). By lowering the transaction costs of some forms of economic activities and increasing them for other kinds, the institutional structure of the economy enables and supports some types of economic activities while discouraging others (Hall and Soskice 2001). As the economic, political, social, and technological context of business evolves over time, institutions must change alongside to provide support for the right kinds of economic activities. To the extent that they do not, economic performance is likely to suffer.

For instance, the institutional structure of Japan with patient capital, long-term availability of labor, and high levels of firm specific skills is taken to be conducive to patterns of incremental innovation, but inimical to radical innovation (Hall and Soskice 2001). All else equal, the Japanese economy is thus likely show relatively higher levels of performance if the economic, social, and technological context of economic activity favors incremental innovation strategies. Conversely, it will exhibit relatively worse performance if the context favors radical innovation strategies, as is arguably the case during the present transition to the next industrial age.

If societal coordination is indeed linked to slower rates of institutional adjustment as argued, then countries with higher levels of societal coordination should, all else equal, have performed relatively worse in recent years in terms of economic growth and unemployment. To explore this argument in comparative perspective, I extend the empirical scope of the bulk of this chapter to 20 OECD countries (Table 1). These 20 countries are the full sample for which there is a reliable measure of the degree of coordination in the business system. This measure comes in the form of the coordination index developed by

Table 3.1. Societal coordination index scores

Country	Societal Coordination Index
Australia	0.36
Austria	1.00
Belgium	0.74
Canada	0.13
Denmark	0.70
Finland	0.72
France	0.69
Germany	0.95
Ireland	0.29
Italy	0.87
Japan	0.74
Netherlands	0.66
New Zealand	0.21
Norway	0.76
Portugal	0.72
Spain	0.57
Sweden	0.69
Switzerland	0.51
United Kingdom	0.07
United States	0.00

Source: Hall & Gingerich, 2004

Hall and Gingerich (2004), which is based on factor analysis of six variables that are indicative of the extent of coordination in the economy: shareholder power, dispersion of control (widely held or controlling shareholders), size of the stock market, level of wage coordination (national, intermediate, firm), degree of wage coordination, and labor turnover. The factor score, standardized to vary between 0 and 1, indicates the degree of coordination in a given economy, with higher values indicating more coordination (Table 3.1).

Higher coordination is associated with relatively lower economic growth. Figure 3.1 plots societal coordination index values against average real GDP growth rates from 1993 through 2003. As the regression line indicates, there is a tendency for higher societal coordination to be linked with lower growth rates. The correlation coefficient of index values and average real growth rates is -0.48. Ireland

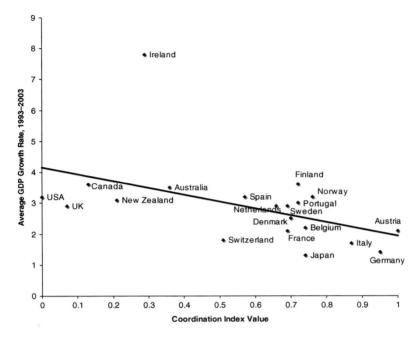

Figure 3.1. Societal coordination and average GDP growth rates, 1993–2003
Sources: Hall & Gingerich, 2004; OECD 2004b

emerges as an influential point (outlier) as the consequence of unique factors such as an EU-induced economic boom (cf. *Economist* 2004). Eliminating the outlier point for Ireland makes the strong negative relationship between societal coordination and average GDP growth rates even clearer, with the correlation coefficient changing to −0.56.

There is a positive relationship between the degree of coordination and change in unemployment rates between 1993 and 2003. Figure 3.2 plots societal coordination index values against the difference between OECD standardized employment rates in 2003 and 1993, again with linear regression line. The figure shows that unemployment rates increased from 1993 to 2003 in four economies, remained stable in one case, and fell in all other economies. There is a positive relationship between the degree of coordination and the difference of 2003 and 1993 employment rates: LMEs on average tend to show marked drops in their unemployment rates, while CMEs on average tend to show smaller drops or even increases. The correlation coefficient is +0.38. Spain (0.57; −11.5) emerges as most influential point; eliminating it

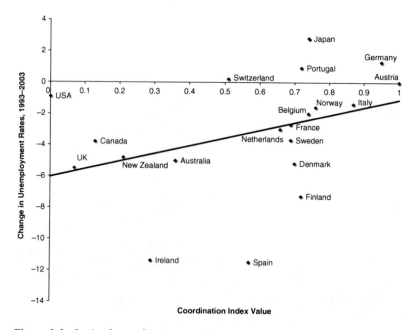

Figure 3.2. Societal coordination and change in unemployment rates, 1993–2003
Sources: Hall & Gingerich, 2004; OECD 2004b

increases the correlation coefficient to +0.44. Ireland (0.29; −11.4) seems like a second influential point, but eliminating it as well actually would actually reduce the correlation coefficient to +0.40.

These numbers suggest that on the arguably two most important dimensions of economic performance, growth and employment, CMEs have lately tended to lag behind LMEs. This is a striking departure from the state of affairs up until the late 1980s, when CMEs paired at least comparable growth with lower unemployment rates than their liberal brethren (Hall and Soskice 2001). Given the linkage between these measures and institutional adaptation, this suggests that LMEs have been able to maintain relatively greater fit between their institutional structures and changing environmental conditions than have CMEs.

Coordinated and autonomous adjustment

What are the underlying causes of this divergence? One line of reasoning is that CMEs may be victims of their success in the previous industrial age:

> The *socio-institutional framework* adapts to each paradigm and, in turn, shapes the preferred direction in which the technological potential will be deployed and how its fruits will be distributed. But, this deep adaptation eventually becomes an obstacle for the introduction and diffusion of the next technological revolution. A society that had established countless routines and habits, norms and regulations, to fit the conditions of the previous revolution, does not find it easy to assimilate the new one. (Perez 2002:153f.; italics in the original)

Past success spawns at least three mutually related effects that delay adjustment processes. First, success means legitimacy (e.g., Yamamura 2003). The more successful an institutional system has been, the longer it will take for actors within it to call the system into doubt. Second, the more successful a system has been, the more actors have to lose through structural reform if change in environmental conditions turns out to be temporary in nature. This increases the propensity of actors to adopt a wait-and-see attitude. Third, success contributes to path dependency and thus institutional lock-in (North 1990; Pierson 2004; Thelen 2004). A successful institutional arrangement can create strong positive feedback by inducing economic actors to build their expectations and strategies around the prevailing institutional pattern, thus reinforcing the institutional structure. Similar to technology lock-in (Arthur 1994a; David 1985), this may prevent the adoption of an alternative structure even if that alternative proves more efficient.

Related to lock-in is another common explanation for institutional inertia in CMEs, namely, the delaying influence of vested interests (e.g., Katz 2002; Lincoln 2001; Sakakibara 2003; Yamamura 2003). As mentioned in Chapter 1, vested interests exist in many quarters, including labor unions, firms, bureaucrats, and the general public. The mere presence of vested interests, however, cannot account for differences in adjustment behavior between CMEs and LMEs. Any institutional structure, whether liberal or coordinated, creates vested interests (North 1990; Pierson 2004). The presence of vested interests is thus a constant across systems, so it cannot be a source of variation.

There are two ways to rescue the argument: First, vested interests in CMEs may possess greater bargaining power relative to challenging forces than in LMEs. The key distinction between CMEs and LMEs is that CMEs are more willing than LMEs to draw on nonmarket forms of coordination and thus institutions to supplement and supersede coordination by market forces alone. Institutions, especially those built through political processes, have distributional consequences that typically favor their creators (Knight 1992). The more coordinated an economy, the more such institutional arrangements are likely to exist, and thus the greater the likely power differentials between vested interests and challengers.

Second, there may be structural differences explaining why vested interests have greater influence in institutional adjustment processes in CMEs than in LMEs. In what follows below, I argue that the extent to which adjustment occurs through societal coordinated as opposed to autonomous adjustment represents such a structural variation, with far-reaching effects that go beyond bestowing greater influence on vested interests.

Societally coordinated adjustment by definition involves the cooperation of a number of actors toward changing institutions. Societal coordination in this mode typically occurs through bargaining among organizational actors such as employer associations, labor unions, interest groups, and government (Hall and Soskice 2001). These actors are operating at the *aggregate level*, in the sense that they aggregate and represent the interests of firms, workers, or other recognized constituents on a broad basis, such as entire industries, sectors, regions, or nations. The outcome of the process is a commonly agreed-to institutional innovation or change whose implementation is often undertaken collectively.

By contrast, *autonomous adjustment* in my definition occurs when actors introduce institutional innovations without involving active societal coordination, cooperation, or bargaining with external actors, typically through nonconformity with the informal institutional structure. These actions usually take place at the *micro level*, in the sense that actors are individuals or individual organizations whose degree of interest aggregation does not exceed the boundaries of the individual organization. Diffusion of institutional innovation and institutionalization in this mode takes place through isomorphic and evolutionary mechanisms (cf. DiMaggio and Powell 1983; Greenwood, Suddaby, and Hinings 2002; Meyer and Rowan 1977; Williamson 1985), and if the actor is an organization, internally through coordinated implementation.

I stress the absence of *external* coordination and bargaining because I recognize that organizations such as firms internally tend to be coordinated through their own social and political dynamics with shifting coalitions and actors of varying interests (e.g., Cyert and March 1963; Greenwood and Hinings 1996). I thus distinguish between internal and external coordination, with autonomous adjustment referring to the absence of the latter. For example, assume a firm wants to adjust the rules governing working hours for its employees. Internally, this change will show some elements of coordination in decision-making and implementation, for instance, by involving representatives of management and labor. Externally, however, the firm has at a maximum two mutually exclusive choices: it can pursue coordination by bargaining for new rules with various outside parties such as other firms and unions, a process that may also involve different constituencies within the firm building coalitions across organizational boundaries; or it can introduce changes autonomously by designing and implementing new rules independently of other actors. In the discussion of autonomous adjustment, I assume that organizations will pursue the latter option, and I will disregard dynamics within the organization.

The differentiation between societally coordinated and autonomous adjustment is distinct from the familiar theme of centralization and decentralization in the literature (for an extensive review, cf. Volberda 1998). It is true that highly centralized states such as France show higher levels of societal coordination than highly decentralized ones such as the United States. However, the most highly societally coordinated countries, such as Austria and Germany, tend to exhibit only medium levels of centralization, in the sense that policy-making on institutional change does not occur within a relatively isolated policy elite on top, but within a broader network-like decision-making structure incorporating both the state as well as aggregate-level organizational actors such as associations, unions, and interest groups. A highly societally coordinated decision-making structure thus resembles a network of multiple alliances of organizations rather than a single hierarchy.

The differences in prevalence of societally coordinated vs. autonomous adjustment have important implications for the characteristics of the adjustment process on at least three dimensions: uniformity of adjustment, riskiness of adjustment, and rate of adjustment.

LMEs tend to produce a greater variety of adjustment outcomes (cf. Kitschelt 2003). In LMEs, the greater prevalence of autonomous adjustment means more room for each actor to socially construct and interpret its environment differently and devise a solution congruent with this analysis. Only at a later stage, when it becomes apparent that some solutions are more successful, evolutionary and isomorphic mechanisms induce actors to converge on a dominant practice or a small set of competing solutions (DiMaggio and Powell 1983; Meyer and Rowan 1977; Williamson 1985).

CMEs, by contrast, tend to seek and implement universal, system-wide solutions. This tendency is inherent in the principle of societal coordination: There is no point to societal coordination if in the end, after incurring the costs of bargaining, each actor proceeds with its own institutional innovation. One risk associated with the proclivity for universal solutions is that there may be conditions where one solution does not fit all. Small firms, for instance, may require different labor regulations than large firms. Under these conditions, societally coordinated adjustment may lead to suboptimal compromise solutions.

Further variation arises in terms of riskiness of adjustment decisions. In LMEs, especially under uncertainty about the desirable path of institutional adjustment, autonomous institutional adjustment implies some risk for each actor, but relatively little risk for the system as a whole. The greater the complexity of the issue, the more likely actors will have only partial information, and their analytical capabilities may be insufficient for finding the right solution. This implies a risk of inadequate adjustment responses at the level of the micro actor, though this risk is tempered by the freedom to engage in further problemistic search (Cyert and March 1963) until an adequate solution emerges. From the perspective of the nation, however, the multitude of emerging solutions represents a hedge against uncertainty about appropriate adjustment responses to a changed environment. The variety of institutional innovations initially produced by autonomous adjustment represents a population of experiments that increasingly evolve more concrete information about their feasibility and consequences. The overall outcomes achieved through such a process are initially likely to be neither optimal not disastrous, but could result in multiple equifinal superior solutions.

For CMEs, by contrast, the tendency to seek and agree upon universal solutions leaves little room for experimental evolution of new institutional structures. Getting the initial response wrong could have an adverse impact on the entire institutional structure, and the error may be difficult to correct because actors may be reluctant to engage in renegotiations for fear of loss of political credibility or face. This places a premium on developing an accurate picture of the situation and interpreting it correctly.

There are potential obstacles to both. First, there are pathologies associated with information flow that originates at the micro level, where institutional misalignment problems first manifest themselves, to the CME decision-making level. The ability to perceive an institutional misalignment is patterned by a shared, socially constructed view of reality that grows out of social interaction among the individuals and organizations involved in coordinated decision-making processes (cf. Weick 1979). This socially constructed reality is "embedded, preserved, and legitimized in a 'cultural web' of organizational actions, myths, rituals, and symbols" (Volberda and Lewin 2003:2123) and thus highly resistant to change and new interpretations (cf. Barr and Huff 1997; Johnson 1988). The result is an asymmetry between information flows that reinforce stability and dominant orthodoxies and those that destabilize the status quo. The encompassing nature of policy making in some highly coordinated market economies, which involves a multiplicity of channels conveying information to policy-makers (cf. Berger 1981; Schmitter and Lehmbruch 1979), may be able to mitigate these issues partially by increasing the probability that discordant information will reach the relevant group of decision-makers.

Second, cognitive limitations and group dynamics may have an adverse impact on decision-making, especially in small and cohesive groups. In principle, group decision-making should benefit from the presence of multiple perspectives and the attendant increase in pertinent power and analytical capacity. In practice, the ability of groups to "get it right" seems most strongly developed when members analyze the issue and devise solutions independently. In many cases, the average of the proposed solutions tends to be close to the optimum one – thus the notion of the "wisdom of crowds" (Surowiecki 2004).

Policy-making deviates considerably from this ideal process. One likely reason for limited debate is that decision-makers are prone to share similar backgrounds and worldviews, be it through self-selection (e.g., choice of schools and careers) or the selection criteria of the elite itself for admitting new members. This will probably place a limit on the range of options decision-makers are willing to consider (Hall and Taylor 1996; March and Olsen 1989). Furthermore, there is considerable potential for pressures to conform, as decision-makers do not want to jeopardize their position by challenging what appears to be the group consensus (Janis 1982). Where the decision-making group is hierarchically organized, there is also pressure to follow the revealed or presumed preferences of the leader (Janis 1982).

In terms of rate of adaptation, LMEs are likely to be more timely in their *initial* response than CMEs. In LMEs, actors affected by institutional misalignment are also the ones who tend to have autonomy to effect an adjustment. The "man on the spot" (Hayek 1945:524) makes his decision based on his knowledge of the "particular circumstances of time and place" (Hayek 1945:522). Since the decision is independent of other actors, vested interests do not come to bear on this process. Institutional adjustment at the level of the individual or the organization can thus be nearly instantaneous. However, since institutional innovations in this adjustment mode spread through isomorphic and evolutionary processes, the emergence of one or a small number of dominant system-wide solutions may require some time.

By dint of the unitary and consensual nature of the adjustment process in CMEs, system-wide implementation of institutional adjustment, *once decided upon*, can be quick. However, institutional adjustment decisions in CMEs, especially those involving major or radical kinds of institutional change, tend to take considerable time to reach, if they then are reached at all. At least five factors conspire to produce this effect. First, information about the consequences of institutional misalignment needs to diffuse or be communicated to the appropriate aggregate decision-making level. In addition to the pathologies of information transmission already discussed, all else equal, such a process is less time-efficient, as communication takes time. Other factors also contribute to delays, including collective action (Olson 1965) and free-rider problems, which reduce the incentive for the individual to report a given misalignment, as well as the effects of garbage can processes (Cohen, March, and Olsen 1972).

Second, all else equal, policy-making processes in CMEs are usually more involved. Typical of decision-making processes in CMEs are group processes involving representative actors such as employer associations, unions, and government, but also other interest groups such as environmentalists and churches. Group sizes range from a relatively small in more centralized ("statist;" cf. Boyer 1997) systems to very large in more encompassing ("corporatist;" cf. Berger 1981; Schmitter and Lehmbruch 1979) systems. The larger the number of actors involved in decision-making, the more difficult the process of arriving at an agreement (cf. Olson 1965; Tsebelis 1995). This effect is especially pronounced if decisions require consensus, as is often the case in many CMEs.

Third, in CMEs, the greater the perceived risk associated with a given institutional adjustment, the slower the decision-making process. Compared with LMEs, in which the variety of initial adjustment responses represents a hedge against faulty adjustment decisions, decision-makers in societally coordinated systems depend on negotiating uncertainty through deliberation, discussion, and thought experiments. Not only does this take time, the attendant uncertainty stemming from the absence of empirical evidence tends to hinder swift adoption of a possible institutional remedy.

Fourth, decision-making processes in CMEs can be slowed by the need to take into account institutional complementarities. CMEs tend to show higher levels of complementarities for two reasons. First, it is easier to build complementarities when the major actors governed by them are involved in the process of designing them. Second, by definition, CMEs tend to feature higher levels of formal institutionalization – as will be illustrated later in this chapter – around which actors' expectations can converge to form complementarities. The implication is an increased probability that decision-makers in coordinated adjustment processes need to devise adjustment solutions not only for individual misaligned institutions, but for entire sets of mutually dependent institutions. All else equal, this is likely to be more time-intensive.

Fifth, decision-making processes in CMEs give vested interests greater opportunity to delay, water down, or block institutional adjustment. The actors that are called upon to make institutional adjustments are often the same that were involved in the creation of the present postwar institutional structure. Since institutions have distributional consequences that favor their creators (Knight 1992), these actors tend to have a vested interest in the persistence of the system, or at least in those parts that bestow special privileges upon them. This is less of an issue as long as adaptation involves incremental changes, which may entail some loss of privileges, though rarely a large part or all of them. However, when more radical adjustments are needed, the attendant shifts in privileges are likely to lead to increased propensity for delay and deadlock.

Micro-level action and pressure for adjustment in cmes

The discussion so far suggests that CMEs are likely to proceed with institutional adjustment at a relatively slower rate than LMEs. Yet there are also countervailing forces that may help the adjustment process move forward. First, at least some vested interests will see their preferences changed and their power eroded by exogenous changes in the environment. Labor unions, for example, have increasingly been losing support and membership, which has tended to reduce their ability to resist change and increase their willingness to compromise.

Second, and more importantly in the context of this chapter, official bargaining at the aggregate level is only aspect of adjustment processes in CMEs. The official, coordinated adjustment process is complemented by an unofficial, mostly noncoordinated one in which micro-level actions contribute to building pressure for change that feeds back into the official, coordinated process. Many of these actions are at least initially autonomous (no other actors are involved), apolitical (power does not matter), and without intention to effect systemic institutional adjustment (relief at the level of the individual actor suffices). However, their overall effect is to build pressure on aggregate-level actors to effect adjustment by introducing positive feedback into the system (cf. Baumgartner and Jones 2002). These dynamics are an important underexplored component of institutional adjustment processes, especially in CMEs. While prior work on institutional change has recognized micro-level action as a factor in institutional change processes (cf. Van de Ven and Hargrave 2004), the focus there has been on action intended to effect institutional change, typically through political processes involving coordinated mechanisms such as bargaining and collective action (e.g., Aoki 2003; Barley and Tolbert 1997; Buchanan and Tullock 1962; Commons 1950; Knight 1992; Niskanen 1990; North 1990;

Seo and Creed 2002; Streeck and Thelen 2005; Thelen 2004; Tullock, Seldon, and Brady 2002; Van de Ven and Hargrave 2004). I agree that this form of action can play an important role in institutional change, but I argue that additional, though often unintentional, pressure for institutional change can emerge from actions that are at least initially autonomous, apolitical, and undertaken without intention to induce systemic institutional change.

Micro-level actors such as individuals and firms come into play in CMEs because lack of institutional adjustment not only reduces aggregate economic performance, as argued earlier, but also inflicts economic pain in form of real costs and opportunity costs on micro-level actors. For example, firms and their employees will feel the pain if flawed labor regulations weaken competitiveness. Firms may see their margins or revenues reduced, and employees may lose their jobs. What are their options if coordinated adjustment is too slow in providing relief?

A number of works have attempted to define the universe of responses micro-level actors can adopt in unpalatable situations. Evaluating how firms, organizations, or states could discern a deterioration in their ability to serve the needs of their customers, members, or citizens, Hirschman (1970) suggests two signs of discontent: exit or voice. The construct of exit bases on the idea of customer refusal to keep buying goods whose quality has worsened or whose price has increased. It has tended to be interpreted and used as a catch-all category encompassing virtually any kind of opting out from existing institutional arrangements (cf. Dowding, John, Mergoupis and van Vugt 2000). Voice relates to political pressure mechanisms including collective action (Olson 1965) designed to obtain either change in a given institutional misalignment or compensation, for example, through subsidies.

Oliver (1991) proposes that organizations retain the option of taking strategic action in response to institutional pressures that are incompatible with organizational goals and requirements. Reviewing empirical findings, she identifies five generic strategies: acquiescence, compromise, avoidance, defiance, and manipulation. Each of these strategies in turn involves three tactics. Acquiescence implies conformity with the institutional context. Compromise denotes an attempt to reduce the need to conform to extant institution through balancing conflicting expectations, pacifying the source of conformity pressure while mounting minor resistance, or bargaining for exemptions. Avoidance means noncompliance with the institution through concealed nonconformity, avoidance of outside scrutiny, or exit from the activity governed by the institution. Defiance involves active resistance by ignoring the institution, openly challenging it, or attacking it. Manipulation, finally, is defined as "the purposeful and opportunistic attempt to co-opt, influence, or control institutional pressures and evaluations" (Oliver 1991:157). The notion of strategic action as embodied in these five options has become established in the literature and is often referred to in the context of deviance from institutional norms (e.g., Fiss and Zajac 2004) or action aimed at changing institutions (e.g., Beckert 1999; Henisz and Zelner 2005).

Closer consideration and empirical observation suggests that in terms of accounting for the possible range of micro-level responses, both models can be elaborated further, as illustrated by the following three examples. For one, it is not clear whether either model allows for autonomous adjustment. The notion of addressing the problem at hand autonomously seems absent from Hirschman's approach under any stretch of imagination of the meaning of "exit." Similarly, Oliver's definition of manipulation would not seem to encompass autonomous adjustment, as co-optation and control aim at lessening the enforcement of extant institutions, while influence is less direct than autonomous action that results in institutional change. Second, actors may comply with the offending institution, but seek to circumvent its effects, a possibility that fits neither model. This can, but need not, occur in a concealed way. For example, citizens exploiting loopholes in tax regulations can do so quite openly without fear of retribution. Or take the example of a baker in Germany who is discontent with laws preventing her from opening her shop on Sundays. She may legally do business on Sundays by supplying her wares to convenience stores attached to gas stations, which are allowed to open on Sundays to supply travelers. Third, actors may engage in self-compensation across different areas in the institutional structure of the economy. For example, citizens who are irate about utility fees they consider usurious may decide "to get even" by cheating on their taxes. Our citizens thus compensate their losses in one area by abusing the institutional structure in another area that, by itself, may not have stirred any micro-level action. Neither model seems to speak to this possibility.

Various strands of the institutional literature in different disciplines approach institutions in highly distinct ways, but they tend to concur that institutional configurations that are aligned with actors' needs lend an economic advantage through mechanisms such as bestowing legitimacy (DiMaggio and Powell 1983; Meyer and Rowan 1977) or altering transaction costs (e.g., Keohane 1984; North 1990; Williamson 1985). Where institutions fail to meet the needs of actors, these benefits are diminished, eliminated, or even transformed into liabilities. In these cases, institutional misalignment imposes an economic cost on the actor relative to the outcome that would be obtained under a fully aligned institutional structure.

I propose that actors' responses in the face of such cost can lead to four possible outcomes (Table 3.2): the actor can (1) accept misalignment and cost as they are (acquiescence); (2) aim to eliminate or reduce the misalignment and thus its cost (abatement); (3) aim to reduce the cost of misalignment without affecting institutional misalignment (diminution); or (4) shift itself or its assets outside the system to avoid both misalignment and cost (exit). These choices are collectively exhaustive, but not necessarily mutually exclusive in the sense that some tactics may combine elements across categories.

To facilitate the discussion, I distinguish action aimed at these outcomes along two further dimensions (Table 3.2). First, actors can attain abatement or diminution either through their own action or by inducing third parties to take action. Many examples of the latter kind of responses, such as collective action in the form of social movements, are political and not autonomous in character and thus fall into the category of coordinated adjustment. However, there are also instances that are both autonomous and apolitical and thus pertinent to this discussion, such as the claiming of benefits without entitlement under established social security systems. Second, responses can be legal or illegal, where "legal" denotes formal compliance with the existing formal institutional structure. For instance, diminution by the actor itself can be legal in form of circumvention such as the exploitation of tax loopholes, but it can also be illegal in form of illegal claiming of social insurance benefits.

The actual choice of action from among the available options is contingent on the particular circumstances of time and place and the different types of micro-level actors (e.g., organizations, individuals). In general, however, one can make three predictions about the course

Table 3.2. Micro-level responses to misalignment between actors' needs and institutions

Behavioral Choice	Mechanism	Legal Examples	Illegal Examples
Acquiescence	Accepting the misalignment and its cost	compliance with the institution	–
Abatement	Reducing or eliminating misalignment and thus the cost	by own action: non-compliance with informal norm	by own action: breach of law or regulation
		by inducing action by others: collective action aimed at obtaining abatement	by inducing action by others: illegal demonstrations aimed at obtaining abatement
Diminution	Reducing the cost while leaving the misalignment untouched	by own action: circumvention	by own action: self-compensation
		by inducing action by others: collective action aimed at obtaining compensation	by inducing action by others: claiming of benefits not entitled to
Exit	Avoiding the misalignment and its cost altogether	emigration, FDI	illegal emigration, capital flight

of action that micro-level actors might take. First, all else equal, actors are likely to prefer lower-cost options. This suggests, all else equal, a bias against favoring voice and especially collective action unless group size is small and the attainable benefit has private-good characteristics (Olson 1965).

Second, all else equal, the more complex the institutional environment, the less likely that actors will on their own enact actions leading to legal abatement or diminution. This is in part a corollary of the previous point, because complexity implies high transaction costs by making it more difficult to navigate the institutional environment. At the same time, the multiplicity of institutions typical of a complex institutional environment makes it, all else equal, more likely that actors will, intentionally or inadvertently, engage in illegal action by violating one or more formal institutional rules.

Third, all else equal, actors will prefer legal to illegal options because the latter carry the risk of a penalty. The strength of the preference depends on the expected disutility of the penalty, that is, perception of its gravity and the probability that it will be incurred.

Autonomous micro-level action and pressure for institutional change

Most autonomous actions by micro-level actors do not grow to become forces that influence systemic changes. However, when micro-level actions become widespread, their cumulative effect may build pressure on higher-level policy-makers directly involved in formal institutional change. One effect likely to attract the attention of policy-makers is the cumulative social and economic consequences that may result from micro-level strategic action. For example, growing exit by firms and entrepreneurs and their assets can have an adverse impact in areas such as investment demand, employment creation, social welfare programs, economic output, and tax revenues. Illegal action, such as tax evasion or unregistered employment, typically tends to result in lower tax revenues while necessitating higher outlays for enforcement, such as the hiring of more tax inspectors and increase outlays for social benefits. Passive micro-level responses consistent with acquiescence can impose economic costs by perpetuating the lack of adjustment and its adverse effects on overall economic performance.

Positive feedback (cf. Baumgartner and Jones 2002) can induce a cascading effect across the system. Micro-level actions such as exit or illegal action tend to impose economic pain on other actors in the system. For example, exit by firms may hurt producers of investment goods, cost individuals their jobs, and increase the tax burden on present or future generation of citizens by depressing tax revenues. This can affect the inducement-contribution balance (March and Simon 1958) of other actors in the system, pushing some of them over the threshold to action. The result can be a vicious circle of mutually reinforcing economic pressures and micro-level actions.

Learning and legitimization may further encourage and reinforce the adoption of micro-level actions. Even where actors do not coordinate their actions, they learn from and imitate one another (Bandura 1977). Learning in the context of micro-level action may occur through informal contacts, but also through the media as well as specialized agents such as tax lawyers and investment advisors (cf. Abrahamson 1996; Abrahamson and Fairchild 1999). For example, the Swiss private banking industry has developed a full range of processes and services such as banking secrecy and clandestine cash courier services to meet the needs of micro-level actors seeking to minimize or evade taxes by shifting their wealth to Swiss banks. As these responses become widespread, they may themselves gain social legitimacy and take on the character of an informal institution, which will in turn hasten their diffusion in the system through isomorphic processes (DiMaggio and Powell 1983).

The rising economic costs of institutional misalignment and the emergence of informal and often illegal but increasingly widespread micro-level responses can pose a threat to the legitimacy of established institutions and thus contribute to a process of deinstitutionalization (DiMaggio 1988; Oliver 1992). By threatening the legitimacy of state institutions and of those involved in reinforcing and defending them, accumulating deviant micro-level action can contribute to placing discussion of change on the political agenda (cf. Kingdon 1984), and it gives policy-makers additional incentives to produce results.

Throughout the adjustment process, negative feedback mechanisms such as diminution through compensating social insurance benefits or cooptation of disaffected groups into the aggregate-level decision-making structure with concomitant benefits can contribute to decreasing felt pressure for institutional change and to maintaining the status quo (cf. Baumgartner and Jones 2002; Pharr 1990). However, when the state does not respond on a timely basis to building pressures or when the economic capacity to sustain negative feedback responses is exhausted, a point may be reached where pressures can no longer be contained and revolutionary processes sweep away the extant institutional structure (cf. Goldstone, Gurr, and Moshiri 1991; Gurr 1973; Keddie 1995; Skocpol 1994).

Societal coordination as contingency in micro-level action

As already discussed, the key difference between LMEs and CMEs is the extent to which LMEs allow and rely on autonomous adjustment. CMEs discourage actors from autonomous adjustment through a number of mechanisms including legality, legitimacy, and complexity. What constitutes legal autonomous action in LMEs is often illegal in CMEs. For example, the decision to keep one's retail shop open until midnight is managerial prerogative in the United States, but a breach of law in CMEs such as France and Germany. At the same time, the norm of societally coordinated adjustment in CMEs places social legitimacy constraints on deviants who seek to make autonomous adjustment decisions. And where legality and legitimacy leave room for autonomous adjustment, the complexity of the task is greater in CMEs than in LMEs. The preference for societal coordination in CMEs by definition implies a greater density of institutions compared with LMEs (Figure 3.3), with attendant increase in institutional complementarities (cf. Hall and Soskice 2001). All else equal, this higher institutional complexity makes it more difficult to devise adjustment responses that both reduce the misalignment and fit the existing or remaining institutional configuration.

This diverts actors in CMEs away from autonomous adjustment and toward the other possible responses. One likely outcome, at least initially, is a relatively higher incidence of acquiescence. The prevalent norm of coordinated adjustment in CMEs implies an expectation that adjustment is supposed to occur "on high" and thus reduces the legitimacy, and possibly also the motivation, of taking action in general. Collectivism will exacerbate legitimacy pressures by "hammering in the nail that stands out" (cf. Lebra 1976), and CMEs tend to be more collective than LMEs: the correlation coefficient of Hall and Gingerich's coordination index and Hofstede's individualism index is −0.56.

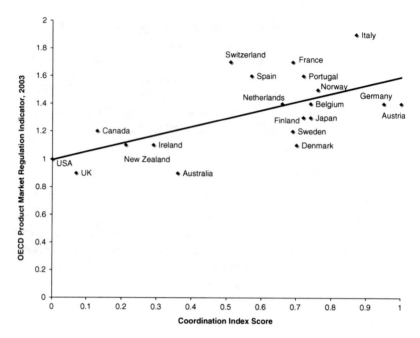

Figure 3.3. Societal coordination and product market regulation, 2003.
Correlation coefficient is +0.64.
Sources: Conway, Janod, and Nicoletti 2005; Hall & Gingerich, 2004

Higher collectivism means higher conformity pressures (Hofstede 1997), which is likely to increase the incidence of acquiescence.

However, as the dysfunctional effects of institutional misalignments accumulate and their costs mount, acquiescence is likely to give way to some form of autonomous action at the micro level. Since CMEs discourage autonomous adjustment, micro-level actors will seek to induce others to provide abatement or will themselves pursue illegal abatement, legal or illegal diminution, or legal or illegal exit (Table 3.2). As these responses spread through the system, pressure for societally coordinated adjustment is likely to build through the mechanisms laid out earlier.

Empirical validation of these effects is difficult because much of them are unobserved. In addition, multicausality renders many aggregate-level data unusable for our purpose. For instance, migration patterns *prima facie* appear to be a good indicator of exit behaviors by individuals. However, differences in legal regulations of migration make a meaningful comparison of numbers within the OECD impossible, as most European Union citizens enjoy complete freedom of movement within the Union. Bankruptcy and firm closing numbers similarly at first look like a plausible measure of exit responses. However, the data do not differentiate between intentional withdrawal from business activity, the measure of interest, and involuntary withdrawal in which actors may want to continue their business activities but cannot, for instance, because of a downswing in the business cycle. The picture is further confounded by the relative social acceptability of bankruptcies in LMEs as opposed to the social stigma associated with bankruptcies in CMEs (cf. Lewin and Kim 2004).

Two types of aggregate-level measures that could serve as proxy variables for micro-level action are (1) the size and growth of a country's shadow economy and (2) the growth of a country's outward FDI position. The former is indicative of illegal abatement and diminution as already discussed, while the latter represents one form of exit that, contingent on the specific circumstances, may be legal or illegal. There seem to be no reliable, publicly available comparative measures of actions representing legal abatement and diminution.

The shadow economy, also known as the parallel economy, is the sum of illegal economic activity that occurs outside the official institutional framework (Enste 2003; Schneider and Enste 2000b). Most important contributor to the shadow economy in advanced economies is illegal labor markets, with concomitant tax evasion and noncontribution to mandatory social insurance schemes as well as abuses of social insurance benefits (Enste 2003). The causes of the shadow economy are taken to lie in "faulty, nonmarket-conforming and performance-distorting state intervention" (Schneider and Enste 2000a:101) that results from formal institutional actions such as specific legislation, administrative rules, and regulations. Similarly, FDI outflows can represent a response by firms to institutional misalignments as previously discussed in the context of the German example.

Consistent with my proposition, shadow economy and growth in outward FDI stocks are positively correlated with societal coordination. The data show a clear positive relationship between the degree of societal coordination and both, the size of the shadow economy in 2003 – the latest year for which there are final data (Schneider 2005) – as well as the increase in the size of the shadow economy from 1989–90, the first available data point for the full sample, to 2003.

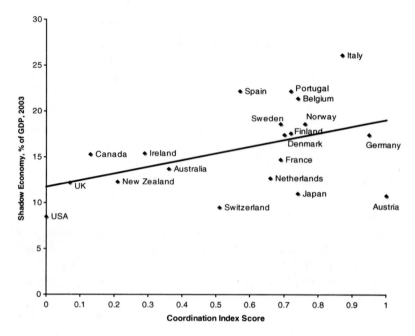

Figure 3.4. Societal coordination and shadow economy as percentage of
GDP, 2003
Sources: Hall & Gingerich, 2004; Schneider, 2005

Figure 3.4 plots the societal coordination index values against the size
of the shadow economy as estimated for 2003. There is a clear trend
for more societally coordinated economies to be associated with a
larger shadow economy, with the correlation coefficient at +0.45.
Figure 3.5 plots the societal coordination index values against the
cumulative increases in the shadow economy, expressed in percentage
points of GDP, between 1989–90 and 2003. It indicates that CMEs
have tended to experience a higher increase in the size of the shadow
economy than LMEs. The correlation coefficient is +0.41.

A limitation of the shadow economy measure is that it may exhibit
upper boundary effects. Since LMEs tend to be less densely regulated
than CMEs, as previously shown, it may be possible that LMEs
cannot reach the same levels of activity in the shadow economy as
CMEs. It is not clear where this boundary may lie, but the example of
Canada illustrates that LMEs may reach levels similar to those of
CMEs such as Germany in terms of size of the shadow economy
relative to GDP. Lower boundary effects do not appear to exist, as a

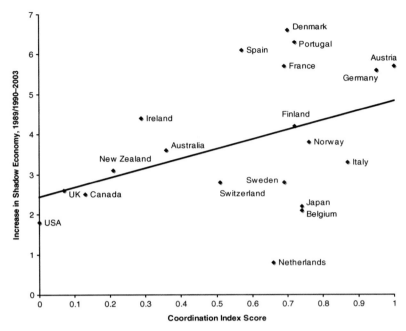

Figure 3.5. Societal coordination and increase in shadow economy as percentage of GDP from 1989/90 to 2003
Sources: Hall & Gingerich, 2004; Schneider, 2005

number of CMEs and LMEs showed similar sizes of the shadow economy in the 1970s (Schneider and Enste 2000b). This implies that the higher regulatory density of CMEs does not automatically translate into relatively larger shadow economies.

Figure 3.6 plots the societal coordination index values against changes in outward FDI stock from 1993 through 2002. I operationalize the change in outward FDI stock as the ratio of 2002 outward stock, standardized by 2002 home country GDP, to 1993 outward stock, standardized by 1993 home country GDP. All FDI and GDP data are obtained from the OECD, with 1993 FDI stock data unavailable for Belgium, Ireland, Norway, and Portugal. The correlation coefficient of societal coordination index values and ratio of outward FDI stock is +0.45. Excluding the Spanish outlier data point, which shows an extreme increase in outward FDI stock likely as a consequence of the Spanish investment boom in Latin America (cf. *Economist* 2000), raises the correlation coefficient further to +0.54.

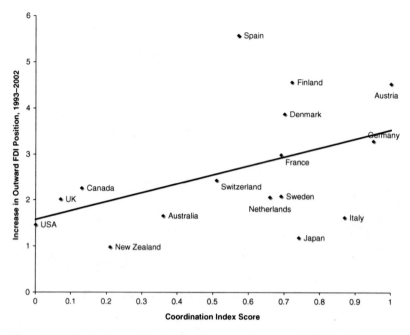

Figure 3.6. Societal coordination and increase in outward FDI Position, 1993–2002. Time-series FDI data not available for all OECD countries. Sources: Hall & Gingerich, 2004; OECD 2004b

The relatively higher growth of FDI among CMEs seems to be neither the result of temporal effects, nor of European integration, nor of a concerted effort by CMEs to globalize their firms. Temporal effects may be present if societal coordination had in the past resulted in a more domestic orientation, leading firms to move quickly as globalization gathered steam so they would not miss out on opportunities abroad. This does not seem to be the case: The data show that in 1993, both LMEs and CMEs on average had almost identical ratios of outward FDI stock to GDP, with the LME average ratio at 0.153 and the CME ratio at 0.147. By 2002, the LME average ratio had increased to 0.274, but the CME ratio had almost tripled to 0.396.

The effect I describe does not appear to be related to a possible FDI boom following the introduction of the EU Common Market in 1992. The observed positive relationship between societal coordination and stock of outward FDI still holds if only the EU nations in the sample are analyzed. However, the correlation coefficient as indicator of fit decreases as a consequence of the relatively higher dispersion within this sample as compared with the full sample. Much of this is due to the Spanish data point (a special case as already discussed). With Spain included, the correlation coefficient is to +0.22; without it, the correlation coefficient is +0.41.

Concerted efforts at FDI also seem to be absent. There have indeed been cases of concerted internationalization in the past. For example, the Japanese bureaucracy in the 1980s orchestrated an almost complete relocation of the Japanese aluminum industry to countries with lower energy prices. There is no evidence, however, to support the notion of a societal coordinated exit in the outward FDI data presented here. On the contrary, governments and labor unions, who are often also partners in societal coordination, have been actively fighting outward FDI.

In sum, micro-level responses to institutional misalignments are an important component of institutional adjustment in both, LMEs and CMEs. LMEs draw more on autonomous adjustment to shape up their institutions, while CMEs can rely on pressure emanating from the micro-level to keep the coordinated adjustment process moving.

Implications for Japan

The implications of this discussion for change in the Japanese business system are unfavorable. That Japanese politics is highly coordinated, vulnerable to blockage by vested interests, and slow to produce institutional change is well documented (e.g., Katz 2002; Lincoln 2001). Indeed, Hall and Gingerich's index is likely to underestimate the degree of coordination in the Japanese business system because it does not take account of the numerous networks-based means of often informal coordination in the business system such as corporate networks, the penetration of trade associations by the bureaucracy, and the deliberation councils (*shingikai*) organized by the ministries (Lincoln and Gerlach 2004; Schaede 2000; Schwartz 1998).

In addition, micro-level forces with the potential to drive forward the process seem to be comparatively weak. This is evident both in the discussion of the size of the shadow economy and of changes in outward FDI stock.

As any country today, Japan has a sizeable shadow economy (*chika keizai*). Estimates put its size at 11 percent of GDP in 2003 (Schneider

2005), and a burgeoning popular literature in Japan delights in shedding light on the phenomenon. Especially tax evasion seems to be common, with small business and farmers allegedly not declaring, respectively, 40 and 60 percent of their incomes (DeWit 1999). Much of the popular allure of Itami's hit movies "Taxing Woman" and "Taxing Woman 2" lay in the fact that they were as much documentary as comedy, paying homage to the creativity of the Japanese tax evader who fools the tax man by founding (tax-exempt) religious organizations or buying winning lottery tickets to launder undeclared profits.

Despite these attainments in the discipline of tax evasion, the Japanese shadow economy is not only relatively small, but has also grown less since 1989 than in comparably coordinated economies. If one defines a peer group of countries with coordination index values within ±10 percentage points, we find that these countries on average have a shadow economy the size of 17.9 percent of GDP. The value for Japan is 11.0 percent, or about five eighths of the peer group average. Similarly, the increase in the size of the shadow economy from 1989–90 to 2003 comes to an average of +4.0 percentage points for the peer group, but only +2.2 percentage points or slightly over half for Japan.

OECD data on outgoing foreign direct investment (FDI), a measure of exit responses by firms, draw a similar picture. Again Japan does not fit the general pattern. The average ratio for its peer group is 3.1, while Japan's is only 1.2, or less than 40 percent. Since this measure corrects for GDP size, growth differentials are not a plausible explanation. It also seems unlikely that Japan was suffering from FDI indigestion after having binged in the 1980s: Standardized for economic size, Japan's outward position in 1993 was about one-third the average of the sample and smaller than that of all but Austria and Spain, both of which subsequently registered above-average increases.

What are the reasons for less shadow economy and exit via FDI in Japan and, by extension, probably also less micro-level action in general? There are two possible interpretations: First, Japan's economic structure may have been more adaptive than those of its peers. In the light of the previous chapter and the weak performance of the Japanese economy since 1990, this would appear highly implausible.

The alternative is that given the same degree of adjustment need, the Japanese economy produces less shadow economy activity and exit, and possibly micro-level action in general, than its peers. Several factors support this interpretation. First, the insular geography of Japan is likely to have a dampening influence especially on the shadow economy. Disgruntled Europeans who earn money in the shadow economy can take the proceeds to tax havens such as Switzerland, as discussed on the German example earlier. Japan's position as an island country without similarly trustworthy tax havens within easy reach is likely to reduce the incentive to engage in shadow economy activities.

Second, as we have concluded from the discussion of rationale in the previous chapter, the institutional structure of the postwar Japanese business system still enjoys high legitimacy. This is likely to dampen the perception that taking action is necessary.

Third, deviant action in general remains socially illegitimate. As we have seen, Japan continues to be a highly collectivist society, and the spirit of hammering in the nail that stands out remains pervasive. As Lebra (1976:28) puts it in her classic study of Japanese behavioral patterns, "*conspicuous* idiosyncrasy and dissension are avoided or suppressed, and *acquiescence* is upheld as a main mechanism for maintaining consensus" (emphases added). Deviance, such as unwelcome innovation in business practices that upset the competitive status quo, is punished through ostracism, harassment, and at times violence (cf. Upham 1991) toward both firm and employees.

Conformity pressures can only work if deviant behavior can reliably be detected. A key enabling mechanisms for detection is the extensive social networks (cf. DiMaggio and Powell 1983; Galaskiewicz and Wasserman 1989; Meyer and Rowan 1977; Oliver 1991, 1992) that I have pointed out in Chapter 2 and that I will explore in detail for the remainder of this book. These networks are a means of coordination and information exchange, and as such they make the actions of individuals and organizations easier to follow. For example, the presence of "old boy" bureaucrats in virtually every major industry association means that through the associations and the intra-industry loops attached to them, government can keep much better appraised of industry developments than otherwise possible (cf. Schaede 2000). Indeed, the organizational precursors of today's industry associations were aptly named "control associations" (*touseikai*), with the explicit objective of helping the government bureaucracy monitor industry behavior during the Pacific War (Murakami and Rohlen 1992; Nakamura 1995; Okazaki 1994; Schaede 2000). Networks thus not only allow for higher coordination in the system, they also represent a control mechanism that prevents micro-level action by increasing the probability that it will be detected and sanctioned.

The social networks pervading Japanese business thus have adverse implications for the rate of institutional adjustment in the system. In Chapter 2, I argued that networks represent a tool for mitigating uncertainty. From the viewpoint of the Japanese firm, with its emphasis on stakeholder value, that is a good thing. The flipside, however, is that these same networks represent a conduit for conformity pressures and thus an obstacle to deviant micro-level action that could help build pressure for coordinated adjustment to advance. From the viewpoint of the Japanese business system, with its need to make itself fit for the future, that represents a major challenge.

4 | Coordinating networks in the Japanese business system

T HE PREVIOUS chapters have suggested that networks play a key role for coordination in the Japanese business system. In this chapter, I summarize and extend our knowledge of the extensive arsenal of social networks available to Japanese firms. I proceed in two steps. First, I describe the workings of the main mechanisms previously described in the literature: business groups, vertical *keiretsu*, R&D consortia, and the state-associations-firms nexus. Second, I introduce intra-industry loops, an industry-based form of informal social networks that despite its pervasiveness in the Japanese business system has largely eluded systematic exploration. Intra-industry loops represent an immediate source of industry information available to firms, and to the extent that coordination tends to occur with reference to actors that are proximate and similar, they are likely to constitute a key source of coordination and conformity pressures. To underline that Japanese firms not only have access to numerous forms of social networks, but also draw on them at relatively high levels of intensity, I conclude with a brief comparison of the prevalence of the identified kinds of networks in Japan, Germany, and the United States.

Major networks in the Japanese business system

Perhaps the best-known networking phenomenon in the Japanese business system is the business group (*kigyou shuudan*), also known as "horizontal *keiretsu*." Scholarly interest in these networks has been intense (Caves and Uekusa 1976; Dore 1983; Gerlach 1992; Granovetter 1994; Hoshi 1994; Imai 1982, 1992, 1994; Ito 1992; Johnson 1982; Lincoln 1999; Lincoln and Gerlach 2004; Lincoln, Gerlach, and Ahmadjian 1996; Miwa and Ramseyer 2002; Nakamura 1995; Nakatani 1984; Schoppa 1997). Business groups link firms in unrelated industries such as banking, trade, textiles, steel, and transportation, ideally with only one member firm representing each significant industry ("one-set principle") (Ito 1992:182). Many of Japan's major companies are a member of one (or, in some rare cases such as Hitachi, more than one) of the six major business groups: Fuyo, Ikkan, Mitsubishi, Mitsui, Sanwa, and Sumitomo. These six groups together in 1999 accounted for about 13.2 percent of capital, 11.2 percent of assets, and 10.8 percent of sales in the Japanese economy (Japan Fair Trade Commission 2001).

A number of recent mergers of firms and banks across the traditional boundaries of these groups has raised questions about the emerging shape and future direction of the groups. As the impact of these developments is as of yet unexplored in the scholarly literature, the mergers can equally be interpreted as a weakening of the groups, as efforts aimed at reconfiguration, or even as attempts to strengthen the groups. Especially the later two options could imply a reinforcement of coordination, as the merged entities may act as bridges connecting formerly mutually isolated networks.

Business groups have come in two types: former *zaibatsu* and "bank-led" (Ito 1992:180) groups. The *zaibatsu* type, comprising the Mitsubishi, Mitsui, and Sumitomo groups, has its origin in the prewar and wartime *zaibatsu*, which were holding companies that controlled vast conglomerates of firms in unrelated industries. U.S. occupation forces moved to dissolve the holding companies as a threat to competition in 1947 and sold off their stakes in the individual firms to the public (Nakamura 1995). However, this did not spell the end of the groups as intended, as *zaibatsu* member firms maintained informal ties reinforced by business and equity ties, and the banks in each group informally replaced the abolished holding companies as the center of group coordination (Ito 1992; Nakamura 1995). On the other hand, the bank-led business groups – Fuyo, Ikkan, and Sanwa as well as some smaller groups – coalesced around banks only after the war. Partially forced together by what was then the Ministry of International Trade and Industry (MITI) (Johnson 1982), they are less closely knit than the former *zaibatsu*, as evident in the data shown in Chapter 2.

The incentives for these groups to form and stay together have changed over time. For the *zaibatsu*, adding more firms was a means of risk diversification and an opportunity to grow further (Amsden and Hikino 1994). As for risk, spreading an investment over several unrelated businesses is to follow the proverbial advice not to have all of one's eggs in the same basket. The diversified holding will still feel the pain if business turns bad for some of its firms, but firms in other industries that do better can compensate for the losses and allow the suffering conglomerate to survive through cross-subsidies. As for growth, investing in new, rising industries represented a way for the *zaibatsu* to keep growing even when growth in its existing industries leveled off. At least until recently, the Korean equivalent of the *zaibatsu*, the *chaebol*, exhibited exactly this kind of investment behavior (Amsden 1989).

With the demise of the holding firm, the growth aspect from the perspective of a single owner lost its significance. However, the risk diversification function survived, augmented, in the immediate post-war period, by preferential access to scarce resources such as credit. As regards risk, it is now the individual group member firms that spread their entrepreneurial risk through mechanisms such as stable cross-shareholding in other group firms, which are active in unrelated industries (Ito 1992; Lincoln and Gerlach 2004; Sheard 1994). This has several effects on member firms: First, having a stake in one another helps firms cooperate and coordinate. Firms in business groups regularly share market and business information, for example at the regular Presidents' Club meetings (*shachou-kai*) and through the exchange of board members (Dore 1986; Hoshi 1994; Imai 1992; Japan Fair Trade Commission 2001; Lincoln and Gerlach 2004). This information exchange reduces uncertainty in corporate planning (Imai 1992). Group linkages also facilitate resource allocation in line with the promotion of collective welfare of the group (Lincoln and Gerlach 2004). They further provide an incentive for stable, long-term lending and mutual trading relations (Gerlach 1992; Hoshi 1994), which protect firms from the vicissitudes of short-term economic development but have induced foreign trade negotiators to brand business groups a structural trade impediment (Lincoln 1999; Schoppa 1997). Second, dividend income from cross-shareholding can help stabilize firms' balance sheets. Third, should a group firm fall on hard times, other group members have an incentive to help it recover (Hoshi, Kashyap, and Scharfstein 1991; Lincoln and Gerlach 2004) – often better to prop up an investment than to see it fail altogether. The overall effect of these interdependencies seems to be that group firms on average have lower profits than nongroup firms, though with less variability (Nakatani 1984) and better prospects for a speedy recovery from a downturn in business (Lincoln, Gerlach, and Ahmadjian 1996).

In addition to this stabilizing function, membership had the privilege of access to scarce resources in the immediate postwar period. The government bureaucracy relied heavily on business groups for reconstruction, not only because they brought together the biggest firms, but also because their central coordination made policies easier to implement. Group member firms thus enjoyed access to benefits such as financial capital, available in the form of directed lending through the group banks, and import licenses for raw materials and capital goods (Johnson 1982; Nakamura 1995).

Closely related to business groups is a second type of networks, vertical *keiretsu*. These networks come in three general varieties:

The first are the *sangyō keiretsu*, or production keiretsu, which are elaborate hierarchies of primary, secondary, and tertiary-level subcontractors that supply, through a series of stages, parent firms. The second are the *ryūtsū keiretsu*, or distribution keiretsu. These are linear systems of distributors that operate under the name of a large-scale manufacturer, or sometimes a wholesaler. ... A third – the *shihon keiretsu*, or capital keiretsu – are groupings based not on the flow of product materials and goods but on the flow of capital from a parent firm[.] (Gerlach 1992:68f.)

Of the three, production *keiretsu* have received by far the most attention (e.g., Ahmadjian and Lincoln 2001; Asanuma 1994; Dore 1983; Fruin 1992; Gerlach 1992; Imai 1992; Imai, Nonaka, and Takeuchi 1985; Lincoln 1999; Lincoln and Gerlach 2004; Miwa 1994; Nakamura 1995; Sako 1992; Saxonhouse 2000; Schoppa 1997; Westney 1996). Linking suppliers and buyers in a long-term relationship, production *keiretsu* have received credit as one source of success of the Japanese automobile industry (Miwa 1994), though they are by no means limited to the automobile industry: With production *keiretsu* having formed around most major manufacturers in most Japanese industries, their total number is at least in the hundreds, if not thousands.

As so many aspects of the contemporary Japanese economy, production *keiretsu* have their historical origin in the wartime economy. Having originally produced all parts in-house, large firms in the military industries started subcontracting parts to smaller firms "as an emergency measure to facilitate production increases" (Nakamura 1995:18). The system initially survived the end of the war because firms were able to maintain a wage differential between large and small firms – an aspect of Japan's "dual economy" – that made it cheaper for large firms to buy parts from subcontractors than to produce them themselves (Nakamura 1995). Only later did the system evolve away from exploitative "ordering externally on unequal terms" (Nakamura 1995:167) to the kinder supplier-buyer networks we know today.

The benefits for production *keiretsu* are, for the most part, mutual. First, being in a long-term cooperative relationship reduces uncertainty by decreasing the need to renegotiate contracts as well as by enabling open information and technology exchange (Dore 1983; Imai 1992; Sako 1992). Firms in such a relationship can expect to resolve issues more quickly (Dore 1983), and they stand to gain from coordination in research and development (Imai, Nonaka, and Takeuchi 1985). Long-term contracting also reduces short-term competitive pressures by making it extremely difficult for outside firms, even those with a distinct competitive advantage, to enter in a business relation with the buyer (Lincoln 1999; Schoppa 1997; Westney 2001).

Second, in exchange for offering the supplier a stable source of income that will not suddenly run dry when business conditions weaken, the buyer expects the supplier to accept lower margins and help keep stocks of parts – and thus the costs of financing them and building expensive warehouses in land-scarce Japan – at a minimum through consistently high quality,[1] just-in-time (JIT) delivery, and quick reaction to contingencies (Sako 1992). In addition, especially when the buyer owns part or all of the supplier, *keiretsu* allow the buyer to shift the costs of adjustment to its suppliers, for example, by passing on surplus personnel to suppliers (Ito 1992). In sum, production *keiretsu* are beneficial for both sides, though overall, they still seem to bestow a greater advantage on the buyer.

A third type of firm networks to have received considerable attention in the literature is R&D consortia (e.g., Aldrich and Sasaki 1995; Branstetter and Sakakibara 1998, 2002; Hage and Alter 1997; Imai 1988, 1992; Imai, Nonaka, and Takeuchi 1985; Lincoln 2001; Okimoto 1989; Okimoto and Nishi 1994; Sakakibara 1997; Saxonhouse 1986; Westney 1994; Witt 2001b). Owing their existence to specific, often state-sponsored research projects, these networks link large firms in the same industry together for the duration of the project – typically 5–10 years. Estimates of their number are difficult, since different government ministries and agencies sponsor projects independently of each other, not all projects are registered, and some private consortia exist. For instance, Aldrich and Sasaki (1995) report that

---

[1] The more faulty parts, the more of them the buyer has to keep in stock to ensure a certain supply of usable parts.

between 1950 and 1992, 128 consortia had been officially registered, out of which 81 still existed in 1992. By contrast, Branstetter and Sakakibara (2002) indicate having access to data from 145 consortia in the period from 1980 through 1994. My own conversations with government officials suggest that the actual number may be even higher than that reported by Branstetter and Sakakibara.

Japanese R&D consortia were inspired by the British Research Associations of World War I. The first research cooperative in Japan emerged in 1956, when a group of automotive air filter manufacturers formed a private consortium. The first government-sponsored consortium appeared in 1959, and in 1961, the Engineering Research Association Act officially recognized research cooperatives (Aldrich and Sasaki 1995). Until about 1980, projects focused on catching up technologically with Western competitors by producing commercially viable products within about five years. As Japan reached the technology frontier, the emphasis shifted toward basic research. Project duration has increased to about ten years on average to allow for the increased time demand of basic research. The funding scheme changed from loans that had to be repaid if the project was declared a success (*hojokin*) to nonrepayable reimbursements for commissioned research (*itakuhi*). However, under the present scheme, all patents remain with the government, which subsequently licenses out the technology. One implication of this licensing scheme is that firms have an incentive not to share patentable information with the consortium as the project expiration date draws close, but to hold back until the project has been terminated and then to register the patent in their own name. Patent registration numbers related to R&D consortia show a consistent pattern, with applications dropping in the final years of a consortium but rising markedly immediately after project termination (Branstetter and Sakakibara 2002).

While public money is an important element of Japanese R&D consortia, the amounts involved have been more modest than often assumed. The sum of public funding from 1960 to 1991 amounted to about 0.47 percent of GDP, with the average project receiving about ¥8.4 billion out of public coffers (Sakakibara 1997). By contrast, public funding in the United States in the same period reached about 1.32 percent of GDP, and the U.S. consortium SEMATECH alone had received US$850 million from the U.S. government by 1996 (Sakakibara 1997).

The coordination benefits of research consortia come in at least three forms. First, consortia have a signaling effect on firms and banks (Okimoto 1989; Saxonhouse 2000). Since project decisions are based on extensive consultations involving bureaucrats, scholars, and firm representatives – typically in the context of a government ministry-based deliberation council (*shingikai*) (Schwartz 1998) – firms can interpret a research project as a sign that that particular field may be commercially viable. That the government is willing to put money down for at least partial funding of the project, a practice known as "pump priming" (*yobimizu o suru*), gives credibility to the signal. Second, as I will argue in Chapter 6, consortia seem to help create social capital and thus social networking among their participants.

Additional benefits accrue if the pooling of the resources of firms and state allows research otherwise considered too basic, and thus unprofitable, to take place while at the same time avoiding the waste of resources associated with each firm having to develop the same technology by itself (Branstetter and Sakakibara 2002; d'Aspremont and Jacquemin 1988; Hage and Alter 1997; Imai 1988; Katz 1986; Okimoto 1989; Spence 1984). However, with Japanese firms no longer worried about catching up with the West, this only works if the underlying technology is truly basic: When firms feel the technology is too close to production for them to share information with competitors, lackluster support is bound to render the project a failure. For example, firms that feel compelled to take part in a project against their will, which can happen when they fear that the ministry in charge would otherwise sanction them – for instance, by preventing their participation in future, more promising projects – may dispatch only second-rate researchers.

The state-associations-firms nexus is another form of networks that has received considerable attention in the Japanese context, though often in explorations of its constituent parts rather than as a whole and rarely from the perspective of the firm (e.g., Amyx 2004; Curtis 1988; Doner 1997; Dore 1986; Johnson 1982; Lincoln 2001; Lynn and McKeown 1988; Okazaki 1994; Okimoto 1989; Sakakibara 2003; Samuels 1987; Schaede 2000; Schwartz 1998; Tilton 1996; Upham 1991; Vogel 1996). Present throughout the Japanese business system, this nexus represent a conduit for coordination and information flow between the private sector and the state.

The historical origins of the nexus in its present shape appear to lie mainly in government efforts to increase coordination in industries as a response to the Great Depression, which had hit the Japanese economy hard. In 1931, the Japanese government reacted with a series of laws that made it easier for firms to form cooperatives and associations, with the intention of establishing a mechanism through which firms could coordinate price and market share agreements. These laws, known as the Cooperative Law (*Kougyou Kumiai Hou*) and the Important Industries Control Law (*Juuyou Sangyou Tousei Hou*), increased the number of manufacturing cooperatives (associations of smaller firms) from 82 in 1929 to 850 by 1936 and the number of associations of larger firms from an initial 31 in 1931 to 1,172 by the end of 1937 (Schaede 2000).

Further proliferation and close integration with government activity ensued during the war. Faced with the question of how to coordinate the activities of firms to support the war effort, the Japanese government experimented with various forms of centralized planning. In 1941, this led to the formation of a new three-tier system with government ministries on top, control associations (*touseikai*) with compulsory membership in the middle, and firms on the bottom (Murakami and Rohlen 1992; Nakamura 1995; Okazaki 1994; Schaede 2000). These *touseikai*, of which about 1,500 existed by the end of the war (Lynn and McKeown 1988), collected information such as production capacity figures from member firms for the ministries (Schaede 2000). The ministries, in turn, used the industry associations to implement the economic plan by coordinating production and distribution (Schaede 2000). The allied occupation (1945–52) moved to abolish the control associations as a threat to competition in 1947, but many control associations escaped dissolution by recasting themselves as industry associations (Lynn and McKeown 1988).

Present-day Japan features a highly complex association landscape with about 15,000 organizations (Tsujinaka 2003) that in any given industry bring together an estimated 90 percent of all firms active in that line of business (Schaede 2000). Associations vary in their level of aggregation, which ranges from industry-specific associations to the very peak level associations that represent, in theory, the interests of Japanese business as a whole (Schaede 2000; Tilton 1996). In practice, average size of member firms tends to increase with level of aggregation of the association, with the result that the activities of the top level associations tend to be aligned with the interests of big business. Best-known, and probably still most powerful, among the top level associations is the Japan Federation of Economic Organizations (*Keidanren*).

With most political activity outlawed during the war, politicians were not part of the original three-tier structure of state, associations, and firms. After the war, coordination between the long-ruling Liberal Democratic Party (LDP) and peak level associations, especially *Keidanren*, tended to be close. But while *Keidanren* in the 1950s and 1960s was so influential that it could make or break prime ministers, its role seems to have diminished in recent years (Curtis 1999). In its stead, lower-level associations seem to have taken on a more prominent role in liaising with politicians and the bureaucracy (Curtis 1999). However, political interest in individual industries has tended to be limited to specific industries such as agriculture, transportation, defense, or telecommunications, typically for political rather than economic reasons. For these industries, Diet members of the LDP form interest groups known as *zoku* ("tribes"), which then may exert considerable influence on policy making in these industries (Curtis 1988).

Coordination effects from the state-associations-firms nexus have come in several forms. First, the nexus has been instrumental for coordination of post-war industrial policy (Calder 1993; Okimoto 1989; Samuels 1987). The evidence suggests that industrial policy in Japan is not imposed by the bureaucracy in a top-down fashion, but coordinated in a process of "reciprocal consent" (Samuels 1987). Industry associations aggregate individual company interests and opinions and act as conduits for information and requests from industry to government, which in turn uses the associations for administrative guidance and to distribute information and money to industry (Okimoto 1989; Schaede 2000; Tilton 1996; Upham 1991).

Personnel interlocks and numerous meeting opportunities facilitate these processes. A prominent example of interlocks is the practice of *amakudari* ("descent from heaven"), in which firms or associations hire retired bureaucrats in order to reinforce their ties with the bureaucracy. In many associations, for instance, the bureau chief in charge of daily operations (*senmu riji*) is a retired bureaucrat (Schaede 2000). This gives the bureaucracy a trusted source in the association, but also provides the association a direct connection to government. Interlocks are also evident in form of seconding of firm personnel to associations and the bureaucracy, though the latter is relatively less common. Meeting opportunities include formal meetings at associations and policy deliberation councils (*shingikai*) (Schwartz 1998) located in ministries. Common are further informal consultations between firm representatives and government bureaucrats attached to the bureau responsible for the respective industry (*genkyoku*).

While there is considerable disagreement whether the system of reciprocal consent has produced desirable outcomes in terms of industrial policy (Beason and Weinstein 1996; Calder 1993; Friedman 1988; Imai 1988; Johnson 1982; Komiya 1988; Noble 1988; Okimoto 1989; Pekkanen 2003; Samuels 1987; World Bank 1993), government and business appear to perceive it as beneficial. In general, one of the first steps in a new industry is still for the ministry to create an association[2] (Dore 1986) or for firms to request one. Indeed, the Japanese government has come to rely on this system to such an extent that it has at times required the creation of Japanese-style industry associations in countries receiving Japanese developmental aid in order to facilitate the distribution of funds to local firms (Doner 1997).

Second, membership in industry associations allows firms to coordinate among themselves (Lynn and McKeown 1988; Okimoto 1989; Schaede 2000). First, associations facilitate information exchange among their members (Lynn and McKeown 1988; Okimoto 1989; Schaede 2000). This should allow firms to negotiate uncertainty about developments in their industries. Second, associations help firms to self-regulate (Schaede 2000; Tilton 1996). Expressions of this form of coordination can range from benign steps designed to facilitate trade in the industry, for example through standard setting or quality inspections, to collusive measures like price-fixing, the erection of entry barriers, exclusive trade ties, or boycotts. Third, associations enable coordination of collective action such as lobbying of government and politicians (Okimoto 1989; Schaede 2000). This may happen in concert with the bureaucracy when parliamentary agreement is

---

[2] Given that the bureau chief (*senmu riji*) of associations is generally a retired bureaucrat, cynics might say the motive behind this practice is less to facilitate communications than to create another cushy position for retirement ("*amakudari*").

necessary for some measures upon which the industry and the respective ministry in charge have agreed (Okimoto 1989). It may also occur, however, in an adversarial fashion when an industry and its ministry fail to agree on a common platform for action, though the possibility that the association may need the help of the ministry in the future generally discourages this kind of lobbying (Okimoto 1989).

Intra-industry loops

Most of the work on the state-associations-firms nexus has approached the topic either from the vantage point of the state or, less commonly, of the industry associations. Viewed from the perspective of the Japanese firm, however, the state-associations-firms nexus as described in the literature is only part – albeit an important one – of a larger networking phenomenon: intra-industry loops. Despite the prevalence of intra-industry loops in the Japanese economy and despite hints at their existence in works on the nexus (e.g., Okimoto 1989; Schaede 2000; Tilton 1996), they have gone largely unexplored in the literature (known exceptions are Henry 1992; Watanabe, Irawan, and Tjahya 1991). What are these loops, and how are they different from other forms of firm networks present in Japan?

Broadly speaking, one can conceive of three "pure" theoretical types of firm networks (Figure 4.1) (cf. Sako 1992):

- Type I: horizontal inter-industry networks
- Type II: vertical inter-industry networks
- Type III: intra-industry networks

As the name implies, type-II networks connect firms of one industry with firms or organizations[3] in unrelated industries, where "unrelated" means that the actors in type-I networks are not involved in the same value-creation chain. Business groups, also known as "horizontal *keiretsu*," fall into this category. Type-II networks, by contrast, connect firms of one industry with firms or organizations of related

---

[3] Note that the usage of "organizations" is generic in the sense of "groups of individuals bound by some common purpose to achieve objectives" (North, 1990:5). Among others, organizations as conceptualized here include government, the press, and universities.

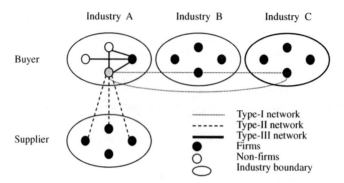

Figure 4.1. A typology of firm networks

industries, where "related" indicates that the network members are involved in the same value-creation chain. An example of this type would be the (vertical) *keiretsu*. Type-III networks, finally, connect firms of one industry with firms or organizations engaged in the same industry. Research consortia and other alliances among competitors are well-known examples of this type.

Intra-industry loops are a variety of type-III intra-industry networks. They facilitate the exchange of information important to their respective industries (Henry 1992; Watanabe, Irawan, and Tjahya 1991), and thus coordination within them. The defining characteristics of these loops are:

- **Ubiquity:** Almost all Japanese industries have their own, distinct loop.
- **Comprehensiveness:** Loops include all firms and nonfirm actors (e.g., associations, government, universities, banks, politicians, and the press) in the same industry.
- **Permanence:** Loops exist as long as their industries do.
- **Multiplexity:** Actors use loops to transmit all kinds of information relevant to the industry; examples are data about trends, technology, regulations, and pertinent economic policy.

These characteristics set information loops apart from research consortia, which exist mostly in a few high-technology industries targeted by industrial policy, focus chiefly on firms, expire at the end of the underlying project, and exchange almost exclusively research-related information. (However, as we will see, R&D consortia play an important role as catalysts in the development of intra-industry loops in new industries.) At the same time, these characteristics illustrate that from the perspective of the firm, the state–associations–firms nexus is only part of a larger picture. It is true that Japanese firms are engaged in networking with associations and government, and these relations are extremely important. However, they also network with one another outside the confines of the associations, and they maintain industry-related ties with additional kinds of actors such as universities, the press, and banks.

Central actor in a given intra-industry loop, and seed of its development, tends to be that industry's main industry association. Industry associations are "nonprofit membership organizations whose members are primarily business firms rather than individuals and which perform a variety of activities for their member firms" (Lynn and McKeown 1988:6). In Japan, the most common and important of these activities are:

- providing a forum for meetings and information exchange,
- collecting and disseminating information,
- acting as a conduit for communication with the bureaucracy and politicians,
- coordinating collaborative research, and
- coordinating collective action (Lynn and McKeown 1988; Okimoto 1989; Schaede 2000).

Virtually all Japanese industries have one main association that serves most or all of these functions.

In doing so, associations provide crucial ancillary support for intra-industry loop networking. Social networks such as intra-industry loops do not appear out of thin air; they need an organizational basis that enables them by providing opportunities for contact (Friedland and Robertson 1990). Academic conferences are a good example for illustrating this need: By assembling a large number of scholars, conferences facilitate information exchange and networking in the scientific community and provide direction – coordination – for future research. Similarly, by bringing together more than 90 percent of the major firms in their industries (Schaede 2000) as well as academics, bureaucrats, bankers, and reporters with an interest or involvement in the industry, Japanese industry associations provide contact opportunities crucial for successful intra-industry loop networking (cf. Tilton 1996).

Intra-industry loop networking is highly institutionalized. An indication of this is that many Japanese firms dedicate personnel specifically to loop networking. Networkers, known as *"madoguchi"* (window) to the industry, are typically male and around 40 years of age. As mid-level managers – most of them are section or division chiefs (*kachou, buchou*) – with a technical or product-related background, they are ideally positioned for their task: Having risen through the ranks of their prior departments, they have learned the ropes of the industry and know who in their companies is engaged in industry-related activities. On the other hand, they have not been in management long enough to lose touch with the nitty-gritty realities and requirements *sur place*, as sometimes seems to happen higher up in the hierarchy. Persisting status sensibilities dictate that any departures from the *kachou* or *buchou* level be rare and almost always on the upper side. Where they occur, they often involve smaller firms in which executives take loop networking in their own hands, though I have encountered a few major firms with a preference for executive-level loop networking.

Often, the *madoguchi* belong to the firm's planning department (*kikaku bu*). However, some firms maintain a separate "external affairs" (*shougai katsudou*) department just for the purpose of networking. Virtually all loop networking occurs through the *madoguchi* and to the extent that other employees network, the *madoguchi* are expected to know – "you must know everything," as one interviewed *madoguchi* put it.[4] Functionally, external affairs departments represent the opposite of the public relations departments (*kouhou bu*): While personnel in the latter hand out information about company activities to the public, networking personnel work constantly to bring information in.

Even though it is by necessity individuals who perform the actual networking, loop networking is ultimately an inter-organizational phenomenon. Long-term employment implies that the connections on which *madoguchi* draw de facto become those of their firms. The *madoguchi* are thus agents of their respective firms and organizations

---

[4] This and the following quotations are drawn from interviews with *madoguchi*. The details of data collection are laid out in the Appendix, notes on Chapters 5 and 6.

who utilize connections belonging to their principals. In other words, there may well be some underlying friendship when Mr. Takahashi of Firm A exchanges information with Mr. Yamada of Firm B. However, the effect is that Firm A is trading data with Firm B. When Mr. Takahashi and Mr. Yamada rotate to their next assignment some years later, as is the custom in Japanese firms, their successors will tend to carry on the dialogue, personal affinity permitting. This is similar to the practice of journalists who, on receiving a new assignment, may pass on their contacts to their successors. But it is very dissimilar from the inter-personal forms of networking manifest for instance, in Silicon Valley networks and Chinese *guanxi*.

Contact is established in various fashions. One source of the social capital needed for loop networking seems to be common membership in association committees, which enables the *madoguchi* to sniff out the representatives of other firms and organizations during and after meetings as well as in breaks. Another approach is to draw on established contacts to receive introductions, thus establishing the necessary trust by having the introducer vouch for the probity of the introduced. Further opportunities for networking arise out formal events and the informal barhopping (*nijikai*) that often follows them:

This may be typically Japanese, but when one piece of work is done, all the people in the association come out to a party. Since they are throwing a party for us, while one is drinking alcohol, well, my own company is doing this sort of things, the company of the other is also doing this sort of things, you end up exchanging that kind of information.

The importance of alcohol in the process finds its expression in the term "nomination" – a wordplay that combines Japanese "*nomu*" for "to drink" with English "communication." Nomination seems to facilitate the exchange of information that would normally not be shared in a more formal context:

If you drink, there are some cases in which no secrets come out, but there are also cases in which secrets do come out as information, by the power of the alcohol ... information that would not come out in a normal meeting.

Given the Japanese social norm that (most) things said or done under the influence of alcohol cannot be held against the individual, such lapses of secrecy tend to constitute a misdemeanor at worst.

The ground rules for information trade in intra-industry loops are simple: The currency of exchange is information, and a norm of extended reciprocity applies. Networkers use information they have as a currency to obtain information they want; no money ever flows. The acquirers may choose to settle their informational debt in the future, but settle they eventually must: By the rule of extended reciprocity, each actor must repay each piece of information received with an adequately valuable piece of information, either now or sometime in the future. The use of nondisclosure agreements or other legal safeguards in the context of loop networking is uncommon.

This can work because even when there are incentives to cheat, the incentives not to cheat are often even bigger (Granovetter 1985; Gulati 1995). First, there seems to be a social norm that information exchange, to the extent that it occurs, must be truthful. Lying is seen as incompatible with the social responsibilities of firms, and where information cannot be shared for mutual benefit, the appropriate response is not to say anything. Membership in the same industry association seems to amplify this sense of moral obligation and thus, by implication, the potential for the building of social capital. By contrast, doubts whether foreign firms will play by the same rules are likely to make it more difficult for foreign concerns in Japan to engage in loop networking.

Should cheating occur and be detected, the deceived party will no longer be available as a source of information in the future. From a rational choice perspective, this deters cheating if each party concludes that the present expected value of all future information combined exceeds the benefits from the single act of deception under consideration. Typically, this will be the case where both parties expect to be dealing with each other indefinitely or at least many years hence, have a sufficiently low discount rate for future information, and have sufficient reason to fear that cheating will be detected and sanctioned (cf. Axelrod 1984).

One implication is that fledgling or floundering companies should be considered relatively unattractive networking partners. Interviewees indeed suggested that successful engagement in the loop requires signaling that one's firm is there to stay. A common method seems to be to join the respective industry association: Since annual membership fees can reach upper five-digit dollar amounts, depending on firm size and association, a company's ability to afford them can be interpreted as a signal of vitality that increases the probability that it will be around long enough to value the future.

In addition, there is a distinct risk that third parties, too, will no longer be available as sources of future information. Deceived parties may spread news about the cheater's opportunistic behavior among other actors in the network, be it to warn friends or just to get even with the cheater. With their reputation ruined (cf. Greif 1993, 1994; Hall and Soskice 2001; Kreps 1990), cheaters may find themselves cut off from information by other actors in the loop as well. The associated costs are additional to those of losing the cheated party as an information source and can amount to a multiple of them.

Third, some parties are capable of direct, painful retaliation whose costs may exceed the benefits of deception. For example, in Japan, crossing METI, the press, politicians, or banks is seldom a good idea. METI today may have renounced much of its regulatory power, but it is far from powerless. Apart from the withholding of information, sanctions could include the denial or delay of permits or subsidies as well as the refusal to include a cheater in government-sponsored projects.[5] Irate journalists might well get even by publishing critical articles about the cheater. This is especially effective against firms, which may see their share prices plummet in response to negative news. Crossed politicians may use their influence to make life for the cheater miserable, for example, by instigating tax audits. And banks may get even by refusing future financial transactions with the cheater or, if the target is a firm, by issuing, or having an affiliated brokerage issue, an unfavorable assessment of the firm's performance. Again, the costs these sanctions inflict on the cheater are additional to, and potentially larger than, the costs of just losing an information source.

Conclusion

Japanese firms can thus draw on at least four different major forms of social networks to achieve coordination: business groups, *keiretsu*, R&D consortia, and intra-industry loops (subsuming the state-associations-firms nexus). However, for Japan to qualify as a

---

[5] Cf. Upham (1991) for an account of how METI (formerly MITI) can use informal means to thwart entrepreneurs who pursue interests running counter to METI's orchestration efforts.

true "network economy," it is not enough for its business system to feature these mechanisms; it must also be the case that firms draw on them more heavily than those in LMEs such as the United States and at least at similar levels as those seen in other CMEs such as Germany. What is the evidence that this is indeed the case?

Comparison of networks across national boundaries is difficult. Different national business systems evolve distinct forms of networking whose one-of-a-kind character defies direct comparison, and where comparison is in principle possible, the data are often unavailable. Japanese-style business groups in which coordination occurs in the absence of a holding firm, for instance, only exist in Japan, and networking involving government, associations, and firms is highly dependent on historical developments, as illustrated by the *touseikai* experience in Japan. As for data availability, I am not aware of comparative quantitative data on the prevalence of supplier networks and of public R&D consortia across the economies of Japan, Germany, and the United States.

One can, however, make partial comparisons in some areas by disaggregating larger phenomena and using proxy measures. As evident from the discussion in Chapter 2, cohesion among Japanese business groups is in part expressed through interlocking directorates. An interlock occurs where one person occupies board seats in more than one firm. This phenomenon occurs among noncompeting firms in the United States and in Germany as well, and since the interlocking directors share their social construction of reality with the board members of several firms, interlocking directorates are a likely source of coordination.

The evidence suggests that Japan occupies an intermediate position with 4.2 interlocks as compared with 6.3 in Germany and 3.0 in the United States (Table 4.1). For the purpose of this comparison, I compute the average number of interlocks among the 30 largest listed firms in Germany and the United States (those in the DAX and the DJIA). I compare this with the average number of interlocks within business groups in Japan, which on average comprise 32 firms (see Chapter 2). This is not a perfectly matching sample, but defensible in that German and US firms can in principle share directors with any noncompeting firm they want. Japanese business group members, by contrast, typically do not share directors across business group boundaries. Since the top-30 Japanese stocks are distributed across

Table 4.1. *Comparative network statistics for Japan, Germany, and the United States*

	Japan	Germany	United States	Sources
Formal existence of business groups	yes	no	no	Whitley, 1999
Interlocking directorates	4.2 (business group average, 1999)	6.3 (DAX average, 2005)	3.0 (DJIA average, 2005)	Japan Fair Trade Commission, 2001; German Stock Exchange; company web sites
Nonfinancial corporate ownership of listed shares	21.5% (2003)	32.5% (2003)	≤2.6% (3Q 2002)	Deutsches Aktieninstitut; New York Stock Exchange; Tokyo Stock Exchange
Financial corporate ownership of listed shares (banks and insurances)	29.4% (2003)	22.2% (2003)	7.8% (3Q 2002)	Deutsches Aktieninstitut; New York Stock Exchange; Tokyo Stock Exchange
Existence of supplier networks	common	some	few	Gerlach, 1992; Orrù 1997; Whitley, 1999
Business association density per 100,000 inhabitants	11.8 (1996)	9.2 (2004)	5.6 (1995)	Deutsches Verbändeforum; Tsujinaka, 2003

Note: Shareholder structure data are by market value. Japanese financial corporate ownership excludes investment trusts and annuity trusts held by trust banks. U.S. statistics on shareholder structure include no category for corporate ownership, the 2.6 % listed is the value for the "other" category various groups, the number of interlocks computed on the basis of this sample would be artificially low.

Another indicator of cohesion in business groups is cross-shareholdings. As discussed in Chapter 2, business group members in Japan on average hold 20.1 percent of the group's equity. Comparable numbers are not available for Germany and the United States. One can, however, obtain a rough gauge of the potential for cross-shareholdings by comparing how much of outstanding stock is in the hands of financial and nonfinancial corporations. The data suggest that 50.9 percent of outstanding shares in Japan are held by other corporates. This is about the same as Germany at 54.7 percent, but about five times the level in the United States at 9.4 percent (Table 4.1). Japan-style reinforcement of networking through mutual capital ties thus seems unlikely in the United States, but is distinctly possible in Germany.

In terms of supplier networks, the available evidence suggests that supplier networks are more common in Japan than in both Germany and the United States. In Germany, firms tend to have integrated their suppliers, though some regional supplier networks exist especially in southern Germany (Orrù 1997). Supply chain integration is also common in the United States, and purchases from independent suppliers occur more at arm's length than on an interdependent long-term basis (Whitley 1999). Supplier networks akin to the Japanese *keiretsu* do exist elsewhere, such as in the coordinated business districts of Italy or in Chinese capitalism (Redding 1990; Whitley 1999). Within the sample of the leading three industrialized nations, however, extensive supplier networks seem to be a distinctly Japanese characteristic.

One can use the density of business associations as a proxy of the relative prevalence of intra-industry loop networking. As argued earlier, industry associations help firms create social capital and are thus important facilitators of intra-industry loop networking. To the extent that business associations elsewhere play similar roles, a comparison of association density can represent a proxy measure of the ability of firms to engage in informal intra-industry networking.

The data show that Japan has the highest density of business associations among the three countries (Table 4.1). Japan in 1996 featured 11.8 business associations per 100,000 inhabitants, as compared with 9.2 for Germany in 2004 and 5.6 for the United

States in 1995. Assuming that the other nations do not organize more firms per association, this seems to suggest more contact opportunities and higher potential for the formation of social capital among Japanese firms, and thus more networking and coordination within industries.

Overall, these data suggest that Japan does indeed feature relatively high levels of firm networking, even when compared with a highly coordinated CME such as Germany. This implies high coordinative capacity, but by extension also relatively slow rates of institutional adjustment of the Japanese business system.

5 | Intra-industry loop networking

UCH OF THE social network literature has relied on publicly available records of networking activities to construct large datasets amenable to statistical and structural networking analysis. This reliance on public records means that informal networks are likely to receive relatively less attention, which may explain why intra-industry loops in Japan have experienced little empirical exploration to date.

This and the next chapter are about intra-industry loops, and thus about informal networking. Main objective of this chapter is to offer an explorative description, based on field research involving interviews and questionnaires, of the networking patterns evident within these loops. In addition, I present industry life cycle stage as one possible contingency mediating networking characteristics in intra-industry loops. To these ends, I explore and compare loop networking in three industries: micromachines, semiconductor equipment, and apparel.

Following a discussion of the case selection criteria and brief information about data collection, I describe the most salient characteristics of each industry, including products, history and economic status, as well as major firms, associations, government agencies, universities, and media. I then present my findings about the characteristics of firm networking, both at the level of the entire network and broken down by category of networking partner (associations, government, etc.). The results suggest that Japanese firms may draw most heavily on intra-industry loop networking, in rising and declining industries. This implies that Japanese firms may coordinate most within their industries when uncertainty is highest and variety in solutions and supporting institutions would be most beneficial to the Japanese economy as a whole.

Case selection criteria

Primary selection criterion of the three case industries was variation in the stage in the industrial life cycle. I further selected the industries to be constant across a second possible contingency, the government ministry overseeing their activities, and I chose industries featuring a relatively large number of firms. This section explains the underlying rationale for these criteria.

Industrial life cycle

The literature has identified the industrial life cycle as an important contingency variable for in firm-level phenomena (e.g., Hambrick and Lei 1985; Miles, Snow, and Sharman 1993; Robinson and McDougall 1998; Smith and Cooper 1988; Strebel 1987; Van de Ven and Poole 1995). Models of the industrial life cycle have varied in the number of stages they include. The classical life cycle model used in the political science literature, and adhered to in this chapter, features three stages, rising, mature, and declining (Okimoto 1989). Business scholars have tended to add further stages to gain a more finely grained picture. For instance, Shepherd (1975) has proposed that industries go through the stages of introduction, growth, maturity, and decline, and Kunkel (1991) extends the six-stage model by Hofer (1977) to distinguish development, growth, shakeout, maturity, saturation, decline, and rejuvenation. The life cycle literature focusing on technology (Abernathy and Utterback 1978; Klepper 1997; Tushman and Anderson 1986; Utterback 1994) tends to distinguish between initial, intermediate, and mature stages (Klepper 1997), with declining industries included only implicitly in form of advanced mature industries within a given nation that are continuously shrinking in sales. Regardless of the number of stages and the various labels attached, common denominator of industrial life cycle models tends to be that output tends to follow a characteristic pattern, starting from low levels in rising industries, growing quickly to level off as the industry matures, and then entering secular decline as the industry phases out within the given national context (Klepper 1997; Okimoto 1989).

Several streams of literature suggest that the characteristics of firm networking at the level of the individual business unit may vary with stage in the industrial life cycle of the respective industry of the business unit. Perhaps best-known in the Japanese context is the industrial policy literature (Calder 1993; Johnson 1982; Komiya 1988; Okimoto 1989; Pekkanen 2003; Samuels 1987; Uriu 1996). A central objective of industrial policy is to accelerate economic development by hastening the move into more advanced, rising industries while orchestrating the retreat from internationally uncompetitive, declining industries. To this end, the industrial-policy model envisions a relatively heavy state role in rising and declining industries. Mature and thus internationally competitive industries, by contrast, require little attention and support from government (Okimoto 1989).

Though industrial policy outlived its raison d'être when Japan caught up with the West in the 1980s (Callon 1995), the underlying thinking of nurturing rising industries and phasing out declining ones has survived. Some protective measures such as import restrictions are no longer possible under WTO terms, but the coordination structure for orchestrating moves into new industries is still functional. Deliberation councils (*shingikai*) continue to play an important role in forging consensus among academics, bureaucrats, and businesspersons about what appears to be the most promising next-generation industries, and government still provides funding and signaling through mechanisms such as publicly funded R&D consortia. Similarly, declining industries continue to experience, and may collectively ask for, industrial policy measures such as government subsidies and government-supervised reductions in output levels.

There is considerable evidence that industrial policy requires high degrees of coordination with the private sector to be effective in steering economic development. In the Japanese case, industrial policy was not a top-down, centralized process in which the bureaucracy was able to boss around the private sector, but a coordinated process of give and take governed by "reciprocal consent" (McKean 1993; Samuels 1987; Tilton 1996). In a broader context, this is consistent with the argument by Evans (1995) that government policy needs to be "embedded" in the private sector to be effective, though not to the extent that government policy becomes captured by narrow private interests. One would consequently expect coordination around industrial policy to be highest in the early and late stages of the industrial life cycle.

The new institutionalism in sociology offers a consistent prediction. Rising and declining industries operate under higher levels of environmental uncertainty than mature industries in the sense that anticipation and prediction of future states of the world is more difficult for them (cf. Pfeffer and Salancik 1978). Business invariably involves some degree of uncertainty. Firms in rising and declining industries face additional uncertainties about broad strategic questions such as their ability to establish themselves in a new industry or their ability to reorient their strategy to survive in a moribund industry. Under these conditions of uncertainty, institutional theory predicts an increased propensity for organizations to mimic each other (DiMaggio and Powell 1983; Galaskiewicz and Wasserman 1989; Oliver 1991). Social networks facilitate imitation by providing relational channels for the diffusion of information, norms, and values (DiMaggio and Powell 1983; Meyer and Rowan 1977; Oliver 1991). One would consequently expect higher levels of loop networking activity in rising and declining industries relative to mature industries.

A similar expectation arises from work on networks in strategic management. Social networks are recognized as an important tool for acquiring resources necessary for firm survival and growth (Gulati 1998; Hite and Hesterly 2001; Martinez and Jarillo 1989) such as technological know-how (Bouty 2000; Hamel 1991; Sakakibara 1997; Von Hippel 1987). Since resource needs and resource acquisition challenges vary with life cycle stage (Bhide 1999; Churchill and Lewis 1983; Hite and Hesterly 2001), the resources exchanged through a firm's networks and the importance firms attach to these exchange relationships may vary with life cycle stage (Tripsas 1998). In particular, social networks have been found to represent a tool for managing resource needs in environments that are more dynamic and thus likely to experience higher uncertainty (e.g., Baker 1992; Eccles and Crane 1987; Powell, Koput, and Smith-Doerr 1996). Higher levels of uncertainty should thus be accompanied by greater use, and higher perceived value, of social networking.

To the extent that intra-industry loops represent a coordinating mechanism as contended in Chapter 4, it therefore stands to reason that networking characteristics may vary with life cycle stage. Specifically, one would expect firms in early and late stages of the life cycle to make greater use, and attach greater significance, to loop networking than firms in mature industries. The overall expectation is

Coordination

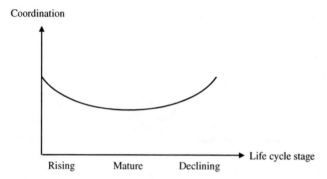

Figure 5.1. Variation of the degree of coordination in industries with life cycle stage

thus that network characteristics roughly follow a U shape as an industry progresses through the life cycle: relatively high networking activity in the rising and declining stages, and relatively low activity in the mature stage (Figure 5.1).

An exploration of the linkage between life cycle stage and loop networking can essentially follow two kinds of research design: longitudinal or cross-sectional. For the present task, a longitudinal design is not feasible. The time required for any single industry to go through all stages of the life cycle typically exceeds the remaining life expectancy of most researchers, which rules out first-hand observation over time. Given the informal nature of loop networking, one can also not turn to public records to reconstruct loop networking characteristics in past periods.

I consequently adopt a cross-sectional design using data from three industries – micromachine, semiconductor equipment, and apparel – that occupy different positions in the industrial life cycle: rising, mature, and declining. This general approach is common across disciplines, such as political science (e.g., Uriu 1996) and strategic management (e.g., Miles, Snow, and Sharman 1993; Robinson and McDougall 1998; Smith and Cooper 1988). The implicit risk is that at least some of the variation observed in the data may be due to industry characteristics rather than life cycle stage. Keeping the government ministry in charge constant across industries partially mitigates this risk, as elaborated below, though it does not eliminate it. I will return to this issue in the discussion section of this chapter.

Demand is a common criterion for judging where an industry stands in the industrial life cycle (Okimoto 1989). If demand is operationalized as sales volume, the micromachine industry seems to be at the very beginning of the cycle. At the time of field research for this chapter, the industry was so new that it was not registering any sales at all. The industry should consequently offer a good picture of networking in an infant industry. The semiconductor equipment industry represents a mature industry. This classification is less clear-cut than it may seem, as an industry with growing sales can in principle be either rising or mature. Precedent and heuristics, however, both point to a classification as mature. As for precedent, the semiconductor industry has been considered a mature industry in earlier studies (Okimoto 1989). Since the semiconductor equipment industry has developed roughly in parallel, it is reasonable to categorize it likewise. In terms of heuristics, one can deduce from the life cycle model that industries with large sales volume are likely to be mature industries. In the late 1990s, the semiconductor equipment industry weighed in at total sales of about 13 billion dollars, an amount considerably larger than one would expect of a fledgling industry. The apparel industry, finally, is an industry in decline. The total sales volume of Japanese firms has been deteriorating since the 1980s in the face of fierce international competition. In the eight years leading up to the field research for this chapter, the total Japanese sales of Japanese producers diminished by 14 percent, and the value of domestic production contracted by more than 34 percent. A reversal of these trends is not in sight.

Government ministry

All three industries have in common that they are under the aegis of what now is the Ministry of Economy, Trade and Industry (METI). This eliminates an important possible source of industry-specific variation in networking patterns, which I would expect to vary by government ministry in charge. Different government ministries in Japan are differently active in regulating and "guiding" the industries under their jurisdiction, which could lead firms and other players in different industry to network differently. Holding constant for ministry jurisdiction consequently eliminates a potential source of variation.

Number of firms

All case industries consist of a relatively large number of firms. The semiconductor equipment industry features more than 400 firms, and estimates put the number of apparel firms at 20,000, though only about 200 of them are major players. With initially about 25 firms, the micromachine industry looks small in comparison, but is fairly large for a Japanese start-up industry. The Japanese semiconductor industry, for example, started out with only five firms (Fujitsu, Hitachi, Mitsubishi Electric, NEC, and Toshiba) participating in the now famous VLSI (Very Large-Scale Integration) semiconductor project (Imai 1988).

There are two advantages to surveying industries with many firms. First, the larger a firm population, the more data one can obtain. Provided respondents are truthful, more data allow a clearer and less uncertain picture to emerge. Second, examining a large population of firms reduces the risk that observed networking activity is related to illegal collusion rather than to legal coordination through information exchange. By the logic of collective action (Olson 1965), collusion becomes more difficult the more actors are involved. Both apparel and semiconductor equipment industries have too many firms for cartels to function effectively (cf. Tilton 1996). A cartel could in principle form in the micromachine industry, but given that there were very few products in the industry at the time of my research, the industry had little to collude on.

Data and method

I obtained information about loop networking in the case industries through a total of 101 interviews and 78 questionnaire replies, mostly from firms, but also from other actors involved in each industry's loop. In the questionnaire replies, which form the main empirical basis of this chapter, respondents indicated for each networking partner the frequency of contact (5-point Likert scale), the perceived importance of information exchange with that particular partner (4-point Likert scale), the direction of information flow (5-point Likert scale), and the kinds of information exchanged (technology, market and trends, politics, other).

All data were collected in 1997 and 1998. A second wave of data collection in the micromachine industry in 2004 – analyzed in Chapter 6 – has yielded data suggesting that the fundamental characteristics of loop networking have not changed since. This is also consistent with our finding in Chapter 2 of high structural inertia preventing quick change in the Japanese business system. Further details about data collection can be found in the Appendix.

Formal analysis involves the comparison across industries of medians of the number of ties reported (outdegree), of the relative proportions of ties dedicated to each of the four kinds of information exchanged, and of means of the values reported for information balance, perceived importance, and contact frequency. These comparisons are complemented with means difference tests where appropriate. Further structural network analysis (cf. Wasserman and Faust 1994) is not meaningful in the present case because it requires nearly complete samples, with neither semiconductor equipment nor apparel reaching the requisite level of completeness.

The networkers

In this section, I describe the inner makeup of the case industries, proceeding from the youngest to the oldest industry. For each industry, I define its products, very briefly delineate its history and economic status at the time of the field research, and introduce the major players, focusing on leading firms, associations, government agencies, universities, and the press.

Two constants across industries involve politicians and financial organizations. As for politicians, they do not appear to be involved in any of the three industries. The micromachine and semiconductor equipment industries have no need for succor from politicians such as state subsidies. Even in the apparel industry, which as a declining industry should be conducive to intervention by politicians, field work uncovered no hard evidence for it. This is probably the result of two factors. First, as interviewees pointed out, the apparel industry is too small, and not rich enough, for politicians to care much about its decline. Second, there is a consensus that the Japanese textile industry in general is at a point where further efforts to prop it up are pointless, which discourages firms from lobbying politicians (Okimoto 1989) and politicians from getting involved. As for financial organizations, to the extent that they play a role in these industry's networks, their lineup is entirely predictable and typically includes the major Japanese banks ("city banks," cf. Witt, 2001a) as well as the major Japanese and foreign investment houses.

Micromachines

A micromachine is an "extremely small machine comprising very small (several millimeters or less) yet highly sophisticated functional elements that allow it to perform minute and complicated tasks" (Micromachine Center 2005b). The concept is easiest to grasp with the help of concrete examples from the micromachine national research project that helped create the industry in 1991. Research in the project involved three kinds of machines: power plant maintenance systems, microfactories, and intraluminal diagnostic and therapeutic devices.

Common research on maintenance machines for power plants focused on three varieties of devices:

- a system for internal tube inspection, which moves through power plant tubes and notifies maintenance personnel of problems like cracks in tube walls;
- a system for the inspection of the exterior walls of heat exchange tubes consisting of multiple micromachines able to couple and uncouple so as to adjust to varying tube circumferences;
- a snake-like system for the inspection and repair of narrow, "complex" areas such as the space between rotor blades (Micromachine Center 2005a).

Ultimately, self-propelled machines of this sort may make it possible to conduct continuous inspections and maintenance even while power plants are running. Cost savings from the deployment of such technology could be enormous: Nuclear power plants, for example, currently have to be shut down for weeks in regular intervals for inspection and maintenance.

The work on microfactories aimed to create table-sized assembly sites for small industrial devices. Though none of my interviewees could tell me what exactly such factories would produce, the notion has much appeal to Japanese firms because of the high cost of land necessary for conventional factories.

The third strand of work strove to devise minuscule catheters and therapeutic devices attached at their tip. The idea was to make catheters, balloons, and lasers small enough for cerebrovascular diagnostics and therapeutics, for example, to diagnose and treat aneurysms and strokes that are not amenable to invasive procedures. In the very long run, researchers are hoping to produce minuscule machines that make surgery obsolete by floating freely through the human body and doing repair work where necessary – not unlike the pipe inspection machines for power plants.

At the time of my research, all three kinds of devices still faced considerable technological obstacles. Micromachine components derived from the research project, however, were beginning to find their way into practical applications such as ink jet printers.

The micromachine industry is one of Japan's youngest. After years of discussions among academics, especially at the University of Tokyo, first mention in the general press was in the *Nihon Keizai Shimbun* in February 1989 (Nihon Keizai Shimbun 1989), followed by a whole series of articles in the same and other papers. In August 1990 the Industrial Technology Council (*shingikai*) of then MITI announced its decision to spend 25 billion yen (about $250m) on a ten-year micromachine research project running from 1991 to 2000 (Nihon Keizai Shimbun 1990).

Central to the industry's efforts to get off the ground through collaborative research has been its industry association, the Micromachine Center (MMC). Founded in 1992, it coordinated on behalf of METI the research activities in the projects mentioned before of 26 "Research Supporting Members." This category consisted of 22 major Japanese firms (Table 5.1), the U.S. Stanford Research Institute (SRI), the Australian Royal Melbourne Institute of Technology, the Japan Electrical Safety & Environment Technology Laboratories (JET), and the Japan Power Engineering and Inspection Corporation (JAPEIC).

As a consequence of the slew of public funding the industry received, government involvement was considerable for the duration of the project. Like all other Japanese industries, the micromachine industry had a home bureau at METI, namely the Industrial Machinery Division in the Machine and Information Industry Bureau. In charge of handling the project itself were the former Agency of Industrial Science and Technology (AIST) and the New Energy and Industrial

Table 5.1. Firms participating in the "Micromachine Technology" national research project

Aisin Cosoms R&D Co.	Murata Manufacturing
Fanuc	Nippondenso
Fuji Electric	Olympus Optical
Fujikura	Omron Corporation
Hitachi	Sanyo Electric
Kawasaki Heavy Industries	Seiko Instruments
Matsushita Research Inst. Tokyo	Sumitomo Electric Industries
Mitsubishi Cable Industries	Terumo
Mitsubishi Heavy Industries	Yaskawa Electric
Mitsubishi Materials	Yokogawa Electric

Source: MMC

Technology Development Organization (NEDO). In addition, the former National Research Laboratory of Metrology, Mechanical Engineering Laboratory, and Electrotechnical Laboratory supported the research consortium technologically.

The field attracted considerable attention from university researchers. Especially at the University of Tokyo, where the idea of a national micromachine project originated, engineers were keenly working on micromachine technology, with at least 5 laboratories (Fujita, Higuchi, Kurosawa, Miura, and Nakajima) involved. Nagoya University (Ikuta and Sato) and Touhoku University (Esashi) also seemed to play an important role in the industry.

Articles about micromachines appeared in papers such as the *Nihon Keizai Shimbun, Nikkan Kougyou Shimbun,* or the *Nihon Kougyou Shimbun*. Given the general audience these papers target, the contents of these articles is probably of limited use to firms.

Semiconductor equipment

The semiconductor equipment industry supplies the machines necessary for the production of semiconductors. Common in the field is the distinction between front-end and back-end equipment: The former refers to machinery used in the actual production process of semiconductors including mask/reticule manufacturing equipment, wafer-manufacturing equipment, and wafer processing equipment. Back-end equipment relates to the machines used for packaging and testing semiconductors, so-called assembly equipment and test/inspection equipment. Generally speaking, the front-end process is extremely capital-intensive, while the back-end process is relatively labor-intensive and consequently often performed at separate production sites in low-labor-cost countries.

Historically, the semiconductor equipment industry has developed roughly in tandem with the semiconductor industry. For a few years after Intel brought the first mass-produced integrated circuit to market in 1971, semiconductor producers designed and manufactured their own equipment. This approach was everything but efficient: Firms ended up researching and developing independently a large variety of equipment – a typical production line today employs about 25–40 different kinds of machines – only to produce a few machines of each type to meet their own needs.

The plight of the semiconductor producers was the business opportunity for the specialized suppliers that began to appear in the late 1970s. By focusing on narrow ranges of equipment, specialists were able to realize cost advantages in production and speed up the pace of innovation. The new division of labor proved successful, and of the major semiconductor makers in Japan, only Hitachi continued to build equipment, though in an independent division that also sold to other manufacturers.

Economically, the semiconductor equipment industry mirrored the success of the semiconductor industry. In nominal terms, sales more than quadrupled between 1987 and 1997, and the industry was poised to continue to achieve on high growth rates. However, with its demand derived from the semiconductor industry, the semiconductor equipment industry has proved susceptible to what is known as the "semiconductor cycle," a pattern of overinvestment in semiconductor production capacity resulting in a glut of semiconductors and predictably followed by a slump in prices and cuts in new investment. The first such slump occurred in the early 1990s, followed by a second one in the second half of the 1990s coinciding with the Asian Economic Crisis of 1997–98.

The semiconductor equipment industry in Japan consisted of about 400 firms, many of which were small or medium-sized enterprises and not publicly listed. Unlike their U.S. competitors, which tend to cluster in Silicon Valley, Japanese semiconductor equipment manufacturers were generally quite dispersed geographically. Industry leaders in Japan were Tokyo Electron, Nikon, Canon, Hitachi, and Advantest.

Unusual by Japanese standards is that the industry had two main associations: the Semiconductor Equipment Association of Japan (SEAJ) and the Japanese branch of Semiconductor Equipment and Materials International (SEMI). SEMI began operations as an international organization as early as 1970, organized its first exhibition in Japan in 1977, and established its permanent Japan office in 1985. By contrast, efforts to organize SEAJ just began in 1985, and only in 1995 did the government elevate it to an official industry association by conferring on it the status of a nonprofit juridical person (*shadan houjin*). By the time SEAJ finally got rolling, SEMI had firmly established itself as the hub of conference and trade fair activity, and it was no secret that SEAJ was not happy about having been preempted in these activities by a foreign "invader."

Noteworthy is also an organization known as the Semiconductor Leading Edge Technologies (SELETE). SELETE is an association in the guise of a corporation (*kabushiki gaisha*) that the ten largest Japanese semiconductor manufacturers set up in 1996 with a two-fold mission: evaluating next-generation semiconductor equipment on behalf of its members, and developing key advanced semiconductor technologies. Ironically, SELETE was founded as the Japanese response to the highly successful Semiconductor Manufacturing Technology (SEMATECH) in the United States, an association that U.S. manufacturers conceived of in 1986 whilst U.S. trade negotiators were pressuring the Japanese side into abolishing their semiconductor research cooperatives.

Other associations more or less involved in the semiconductor equipment industry included:

- the Association of Super-Advanced Electronics Technologies (ASET), a government-supported research association developing basic technology for future production;
- the Electronic Industry Association of Japan (EIAJ), the association in charge of semiconductors;
- the International Semiconductor Cooperation Center (INSEC), a low-key organization that sponsored international symposia, exhibitions and the like for users, suppliers and distributors and researches industry trends through surveys;

- the Japan Electronics Industry Development Association (JEIDA), covering computers and office equipment;
- the Japan Society of Newer Materials (JSNM), the association organizing the suppliers of raw silicon;
- the Semiconductor Industry Research Institute Japan (SIRIJ), a research association of the 11 largest Japanese semiconductor producers;
- the Semiconductor Technology Academic Research Center (STARC), an organization set up by the same 11 Japanese semiconductor producers involved in SIRIJ seeking to foster cooperation between semiconductor manufacturers and academia by commissioning university research; and
- J300, a loose federation of EIAJ, JEIDA, JSNM, SEAJ and SIRIJ to facilitate and coordinate the adoption of the 300 mm wafer size standard.

Government involvement in the industry centered on METI and its research facilities. In charge of the industry was the Industrial Machinery Division in the Machine and Information Industry Bureau of the ministry. Through its New Energy and Industrial Technology Development Organization (NEDO) and national research laboratories, the ministry also underwrote part of the activities of ASET.

Among the Japanese universities undertaking semiconductor and equipment-related research, leading research laboratories were located at Hiroshima University (Hirose), Touhoku University (Ohmi), and Touyou University (Horiike). Most other universities seemed to lag behind.

Finally, important players among the press were mostly trade papers and journals such as the *Denpa Shimbun*, the *Handoutai Sangyou Shimbun*, the *Nikkei Electronics*, the *Nikkei Microdevices*, and the *Semicon World*.

Apparel

The apparel industry produces clothing. In general, the field distinguishes among men's wear, women's wear, children's wear, undergarments, socks, and stockings.

Given Japan's long history in textiles and the infatuation of the Japanese youth with fashion, it is difficult to imagine that an apparel industry worthy of the name has existed in Japan for only about

50 years. Textiles soon became a mainstay of Japan's industrial development after the Meiji Restoration of 1868. By 1925, they accounted for as much as two-thirds of Japanese exports, though they thereafter declined rapidly in relative importance as the Japanese economy underwent its shift from light to heavy manufacturing (Ito 1992). Clothing, however, continued to be home- or custom-made for many years. Only the 1950s witnessed the first stirrings of what was to become today's apparel industry when textile wholesalers began to expand their businesses by designing their own ready-to-wear collections or licensing foreign brands. Many of today's large apparel firms used to be such wholesalers, and the widespread practice of subcontracting out large parts or all of production is a remnant from these earlier days.

But not all of Japan's approximately 20,000 apparel firms used to be wholesalers. The enormous proliferation of apparel firms stems from the development of the apparel industry into one of Japan's favorite industries for start-ups – as one interviewee quipped, US entrepreneurs found high-technology ventures, Japanese entrepreneurs open apparel businesses. With minimal capital requirements, many of these firms operate as family businesses from the living room, with designs often copied from those of the larger firms.

If the Greeks were right to say that the gods let die young those whom they like the most, the Japanese apparel industry must be a favorite. The industry has been considered in decline since the 1980s, and in the 8 years from 1991 to 1998 alone, domestic production contracted by about one third. During the same period, domestic apparel sales registered a – probably recession-related – decline of about 14 percent. A permanent recovery was not in sight, and METI seemed to have all but given up on the industry. The main reason for the decline of the industry is that firms had come under pressure from competitors abroad: Within the same eight-year period from 1991 to 1998, the value of imports increased by about 68 percent. Firms were responding to the challenge on the lower end of the price spectrum by shifting production abroad, but many of them had all but lost the battle for the high-price, high-margin end of the market because of a cardinal mistake in the past: Instead of building their own top brands, many apparel firms licensed foreign brands such as Dior, Polo, or Versace. With these well-established in the extremely brand-conscious

Japanese market, their foreign owners increasingly realized that it could be more profitable to cancel the license agreements and market their brands themselves, leaving their former licensees out in the rain.

The major firm players in the industry were mostly the about 165 firms organized in the Japan Apparel Industry Council (JAIC). Even though they represented a mere 0.8 percent of the total number of firms in the industry, these firms in 1998 accounted for about 45 percent of total industry sales. However, even among this select group, most firms were privately held. Industry leaders were Renown, Onward Kashiyama, Sanyo Shokai, and Naigai. Geographically, the larger apparel firms represented here are mostly clustered in and around Tokyo and Osaka.

As one would expect, the myriad firms in the industry were organized in countless industry associations. First among these was the Japan Apparel Industry Council (JAIC) mentioned earlier, bringing together apparel firms of all product categories. In addition, each clothing category had its own national association and a plenitude of regional associations, sometimes down to the level of individual districts or wards. A large women's wear producer in Tokyo would consequently find itself under the auspices of JAIC, the All-Japan Women's and Children's Clothing Industry Association (*Zen Nihon Fujin Kodomo Fuku Kouren*), the Tokyo Women's and Children's Clothing Industry Association (*Toukyou Fujin Kodomo Fuku Kouren*), and perhaps another association organizing producers in the respective Ward of Tokyo.

Besides JAIC, the most important among the Japanese apparel associations were:

- the All-Japan Men's Clothing Industry Association;
- the All-Japan Shirts Association;
- the All-Japan Women's and Children's Clothing Industry Association;
- the Japan Apparel Sewing Industry Association;
- the Japan Body Fashion Association;
- the Japan Cloth Central Wholesale Association;
- the Japan Clothing Industry Association;
- the Japan Knit Central Wholesale Trade Association;
- the Japan Knit Industry Association; and
- the Japan Socks Association.

As in the other cases, government involvement in the industry centered on METI. Formally overseeing the apparel industry was the Textile Division of the Consumer Goods and Service Industries Bureau. Most of the actual handling of the industry, however, for many years lay in the hands of the Textile Industry Restructuring Agency (TIRA), an independent government agency founded in 1967 to implement government policies related to the textile and clothing industry. In the course of administrative reform, the Small and Medium Enterprise Policy Planning Office within METI's Small and Medium Enterprise Agency absorbed TIRA in July 1999.

Universities and fashion schools played a very limited role in the Japanese apparel industry; the equivalent of Western fashion schools such as the Fashion Institute of Technology (FIT) at the State University of New York (SUNY) did not exist. Traditionally staffed by personnel that did not make it into any of the more prestigious industries, the industry had only recently begun to build the infrastructure for the education of first-rate employees. The results of these efforts was the Institute for the Fashion Industries (IFI) in Tokyo, founded in 1992 and intended to become Japan's FIT.

As in the West, a vast array of fashion publications existed. Most important for the trade were the *Senken Shimbun*, the *Nikkei Ryuutsuu*, and the *Nihon Sen'i Shimbun*.

Overall network characteristics

The total number of networking partners, or outdegree (cf. Wasserman and Faust 1994), reported by the median firm in the case industries ranges from 10 in the apparel industry over 12 in the micromachine industry to 15 in the semiconductor equipment industry (Table 5.2). The range of total number of networking partners falls between 1 and 25 for micromachines, 1 and 45 for semiconductor equipment, and 4 and 37 for apparel. Firms in the semiconductor equipment industry thus have most connections as compared with firms in the other industries.

This does not imply that networking is most meaningful for semiconductor equipment firms. The number of possible network actors is constrained, among others, by the number of potential networking partners available. Micromachine firms may want to

Table 5.2. Median, minimum, and maximum number of ties (outdegree) of firms in the case industries

	All Ties	Firms	Associations	Government	Universities	Banks	Press
Micromachines	12 (1, 25)	7 (0, 18)	1 (1, 3)	2 (0, 5)	2 (0, 5)	0 (0, 0)	0 (0, 0)
Semiconductor Equipment	15 (1, 45)	3.5 (0, 29)	4 (0, 9)	1 (0, 7)	1 (0, 5)	0 (0, 6)	2 (0, 7)
Apparel	10 (4, 37)	2 (0,11)	2 (1, 6)	1 (0, 6)	0 (0, 4)	1 (0, 4)	3 (1, 6)

Note: Numbers in parentheses denote minimum–maximum range

network with more other firms, but their choice is limited by the relatively small size of their industry. Similarly, apparel firms have fewer university contacts to choose from than semiconductor equipment firms. Standardization by network size (i.e., dividing the outdegree by the number of possible ties) does not address this issue satisfactorily, as resource constraints and decreasing marginal returns on additional ties will probably lead firms to grow their own networks only to a certain size even as more potential partners become available. Apparel firms have about 1,000 times as many firms to choose from as potential networking partners as micro-machine firms. That their network will not be 1,000 times the size is obvious. Standardization by potential network size thus introduces additional distortions if the networks to be compared are vastly different in size.

The questionnaire data allow us to distinguish four general kinds of information exchanged: technical matters including research and development and standards, market information such as general trends and expected growth, political matters such as subsidies and economic policy, and a residual category of "other." Most firm networking in the micromachine industry focuses on technical exchange (74 percent of all ties; Table 5.3), which suggests a focus on strengthening the technological foundations of the new industry. Networking about market information, which one would expect to be mostly of a long-term strategic nature in this case as firms had yet to commence production, is at a relatively low level (17 percent). That political content plays no role at all is in line with expectations and was confirmed in my interviews. The basic political decision of which firms to include in the national research project is over at this point, and other political issues such as regulations arise mostly once firms actually enter production. The remainder of networking activity in the industry concerns "other" kinds of information (10 percent),[1] which in the present sample consist mostly of information about coordinating the work of the Micromachine Center (*jimu katsudou*).

The semiconductor equipment industry networks mostly about technical matters (44 percent) and market trends (49 percent), with politics assuming a low level of prevalence (5 percent) and other kinds

---

[1] Numbers in this and the next chapter may not add up to 100% because of rounding.

Table 5.3. Distribution of kinds of information firms exchange in intra-industry loops (percentage)

		All Ties	Firms	Associations	Government	Universities	Banks	Press
Micromachines	Technology	74	78	63	76	70	—	—
	Market	17	14	20	14	26	—	—
	Politics	0	0	0	0	0	—	—
	Other	10	9	18	10	4	—	—
Semiconductor Equipment	Technology	44	41	52	54	82	4	28
	Market	49	59	39	29	18	64	72
	Politics	5	0	5	11	0	32	0
	Other	2	0	5	7	0	0	0
Apparel	Technology	35	47	31	23	40	0	48
	Market	43	41	39	62	50	34	47
	Politics	14	2	19	15	10	49	3
	Other	9	11	12	0	0	17	2

Note: Categories in italics denote modal kind of information exchanged

of information exchanges rare (2 percent). The main focus of firms in this industry is to work out the timing and technical details of the industry's transition to 300 mm wavers. That politics matters at all in an industry at this stage seems related to the semiconductor-related trade frictions that have haunted U.S.-Japan relations (Flamm 1996; Lincoln 1990a, 1999; Prestowitz 1988; Schoppa 1997).

By comparison, the apparel industry places relatively more emphasis on market information (43 percent) and politics (14 percent) than the other industries, while more operationally oriented technical networking matters less than elsewhere (35 percent) and other issues retain a relatively marginal role (9 percent). That politics is more important than in the other case industries is consistent with the general notion that politics matters in declining industries. Firms in such industries in general have among their options exit from the industry or lobbying for government support, and in Japan, the role of government in both winding down industries or propping them up has been considerable (Johnson 1982; Okimoto 1989; Peck, Levin, and Goto 1987; Samuels 1987; Uriu 1996). Similarly, the increased importance of market information compared with technological information – market-related networking occurs at a level of 1.11 times that of technical matters in semiconductor equipment, but at 1.23 times the level of technical matters in apparel – may suggest that firms in this declining industry place a relatively greater premium on reducing uncertainty around future economic developments.

In terms of direction of flow, firms in all three industries believe that on average, they are receiving at least as much information as they are giving out. On a scale from −2 (only giving out information without receiving any) over 0 (giving out as much as receiving) to +2 (only receiving without giving out), the micromachine industry scores 0.02, the semiconductor equipment industry, 0.22, and the apparel industry, −0.03. (Table 5.4). The fact that firms perceive that they receive about as much information as they give out – or slightly more in the case of semiconductor equipment – is a positive indicator for the health of the network: If firms thought that they were giving out considerably more information than they were receiving, loop networking would probably grind to a halt.

The importance that firms on average ascribe to information loop networking is highest in the apparel industry, followed by the

Table 5.4. Average information trade balance for firms

	All Ties	Firms	Associations	Government	Universities	Banks	Press
Micromachines	0.02	−0.04	0.38	−0.10	0.16	—	—
Semiconductor Equipment	0.22	0.08	0.67	0.31	0.27	0.20	−0.23
Apparel	−0.03	−0.05	0.79	0.39	0.33	−0.10	−0.84

Note: A value of 0 denotes that firms receive as much information as they give out. A negative (positive) value means that firms give out more (less) information than they receive

Table 5.5. Average importance firms attach to their network ties

	All Ties	Firms	Associations	Government	Universities	Banks	Press
Micromachines	2.74	2.67	3.12	2.74	2.69	—	—
Semiconductor Equipment	2.55	2.53	2.62	2.29	2.83	2.40	2.38
Apparel	2.90	2.38	2.68	3.17	2.89	3.26	3.23

Note: 1 = unimportant, 2 = somewhat important, 3 = important, 4 = very important

Table 5.6. Average frequency with which firms use their network ties

	All Ties	Firms	Associations	Government	Universities	Banks	Press
Micromachines	2.49	2.70	3.09	1.74	2.06	–	–
Semiconductor Equipment	2.42	2.33	2.49	1.42	3.19	3.13	2.38
Apparel	2.75	3.24	2.61	2.23	2.44	3.10	2.55

Note: 1 = once every six months or less, 2 = quarterly, 3 = monthly, 4 = weekly, 5 = daily

micromachine and semiconductor equipment industries (Table 5.5). Specifically, the mean importance on a scale from 1 (*unimportant*) to 4 (*very important*) of all the information loop ties of all firms in the samples is 2.90 for apparel, 2.74 for micromachines, and 2.55 for semiconductor equipment. These values translate roughly to *important* for apparel and *important minus* for the other cases.

Figures for the frequency of contact firms report for their ties present a similar picture (Table 5.6). In general, one would expect importance and frequency to be positively correlated, as firms should contact their networking partners more often when their demand for information is high. This is indeed the case: The mean contact frequency firms reported on a scale from 1 (*less than once every three months*) to 5 (*daily*) is 2.75 for apparel, 2.49 for micromachines, and 2.42 for semiconductor equipment, which roughly translates to an average contact frequency of once every 6 weeks for apparel, once every 8 weeks for micromachines, and once every 9 weeks for semiconductor equipment.

Networking with other firms

The number of ties firms maintain with other firms within the industry ranges from a median value of 7 in the micromachine industry to 3.5 in semiconductor equipment and 2 in apparel (Table 5.2). In each industry, some firms do not network with other firms at all. On the other hand, some firms network much more, with the maximum number of ties at 18 for micromachines, 29 for semiconductor equipment, and 11 for apparel.

In terms of information exchange among firms, technology and market information tend to play a lead role (Table 5.3). Micromachine firms use their ties mostly to exchange information about technology (78 percent). Market and "other" information play a very limited role at 14 and 9 percent, respectively. This contrasts with semiconductor equipment, in which most information exchange among firms concerns market developments (59 percent). Technology still plays a considerable role at 41 percent. In apparel, technology again becomes the most common topic at 47 percent, closely followed by market information at 41 percent. Little information exchange occurs concerning politics (2 percent), which is consistent with the view that firms prefer to organize collective action at the level of industry association rather than among themselves.

The data about the direction of information flow suggests that firms carefully guard their information trade activities to ensure that they receive about as much information as they give out. In all three industries, the balance is virtually 0, with micromachines at −0.04, semiconductor equipment at 0.08, and apparel and −0.05 (Table 5.4).

In terms of importance, firms rate networking with their peers least important in apparel, while micromachine firms rate their information exchange activities most important. Specifically, micromachine and semiconductor equipment firms rate firm-to-firm networking roughly as *important minus* (2.67 and 2.53, respectively), while apparel producers consider it *somewhat important plus* (2.38) (Table 5.5).

Apparel firms contact other firms most often, followed by firms in micromachines and semiconductor equipment. Apparel makers contact their peers about every 3 weeks (3.24), micromachine firms, about every 6 weeks (2.70), and semiconductor equipment producers, about every 9 weeks (2.33) (Table 5.6). Why apparel firms would eagerly network with other firms if they do not consider contacting them all that important is not clear at this point. The most plausible explanation is that the importance scores were unduly influenced by the *unimportant* ratings one firm assigned to all of its relatively numerous firm contacts. Eliminating these scores improves the importance score to *important minus* (2.64), which appears more plausible. However, only further research can establish whether this or any other mechanism represents the cause of the observed discrepancy.

Networking with associations

Industry associations are the central actors in intra-industry loops. They play a privileged role in networking by providing a forum for meetings and information exchange, collecting and disseminating information on behalf of their members, acting as a conduit for communication with the bureaucracy and politicians, coordinating collaborative research, and coordinating collective action (Lynn and McKeown 1988; Okimoto 1989; Schaede 2000). Since associations organize on average about 90 percent of the firms in their industries (Schaede 2000), associations provide an ideal breeding place for coordination and the building of new network ties. Virtually all industries have one main association that organizes most industry members and performs most of the above tasks. In addition, industries may feature further, often more specialized associations. For example, high-technology industries some-times have additional associations that focus entirely on collaborative research.

Virtually all firms in the case industries are connected with associations. Median degree is 1 for micromachines, 4 for semi-conductor equipment, and 2 for apparel (Table 5.2). The range of connections is from 0 in semiconductor equipment and 1 in the other industries to 3 in micromachines, 9 in semiconductor equipment, and 6 in apparel. The high median number of ties in the semiconductor equipment industry is the result of the presence of two main associations, as previously discussed, as well as numerous other associations coordinating research and product standardization.

Technology and market information again emerge as the most salient kinds of information exchanged. 63 percent of information exchange in the micromachine industry concerns technology (Table 5.3). This high proportion is mostly a function of research coordination through the Micromachine Center and other associations involved in the industry. An important additional element, however, is that the Micromachine Center is acting as information conduit between firms and government about progress in the government-sponsored R&D consortium. Market information and "other" information take on relatively limited importance at 20 and 18 percent, respectively, with the latter mostly consisting of preparation of association work. Neither interviews nor questionnaires found any evidence of information exchange on political matters.

Technology is also dominant in the semiconductor equipment industry at 52 percent. Background is again coordination of technology research and development, here in the context of the transition to 300 mm wavers. Market information comes in second at

39 percent, followed in equal part by politics and "other" information at 5 percent each.

What stands out about apparel is the relatively high proportion of information exchange about politics: 19 percent of ties concern political issues. This is consistent with the expectation of collective action in declining industries and with the contention that associations provide a forum for collective action. Modal category for apparel is market information, with a share of 39 percent, followed by technology at 31 percent.

The data on flow direction suggest that associations are living up to their role as providers, rather than consumers, of information. In all three industries, firms solidly report receiving more information than they give out, with the balance at 0.38 in micromachines, 0.67 in semiconductor equipment, and 0.79 in apparel (Table 5.4). The balance in micromachines is somewhat lower than in the other cases because firms participating in the government-sponsored R&D consortium had a duty to report regularly to the Micromachine Center about their research activities.

The importance that firms ascribe to networking with associations is highest in the micromachines industry, followed by the apparel and semiconductor equipment industries. Firms in the micromachine industry rate their contacts with associations at 3.12, firms in apparel, at 2.68, and firms in semiconductor equipment, at 2.62 (Table 5.5), which one could transliterate as *important, important minus*, and again *important minus*, respectively. The observed difference between apparel and semiconductor equipment is smaller than one would expect given the centrality of associations in collective action in declining industries. As it turns out, the Japanese semiconductor industry had recently expanded its collaborative research considerably in order to improve competitiveness. As a consequence, the semiconductor equipment industry probably exhibits higher levels of coordination and information exchange than average at this stage of the industrial life cycle.

The frequency figures draw a similar picture. Firms in micromachines contact associations most often, and firms in semiconductor equipment, least often. The scores for the industry are 3.09 for micromachines, 2.61 for apparel, and 2.49 for semiconductor equipment (Table 5.6). In real-life terms, this means that firms in micromachines contact their associations on average about every month, those in apparel, about every 7 weeks, and those in semiconductor equipment, about every 2 months. Again, for the reasons laid out before, the difference between apparel and semiconductor equipment is smaller than one would expect in a generic case.

Networking with government agencies

Government in the context of this study comprises all bureaucratic government agencies involved in a certain industry. These agencies come in two general varieties: administrative agencies and research agencies. It is the former that assume the role one commonly associates with government: the drafting and enforcement of laws and ordinances. In addition, and more important in this context, these agencies have in Japan traditionally played a coordinating and guiding role for industry. Especially METI, which is in charge of all three case industries, has acquired a reputation for involvement in initiating and helping build up new, "sunrise" industries on the one hand and propping up and eventually phasing out old, "sunset" industries. In both cases, the ministry has traditionally relied less on money than on information and persuasion paired with occasional, more or less explicit, threats to accomplish its objectives (Johnson 1982; Okimoto 1989; Samuels 1987; Upham 1991).

In the case industries, government involvement is high in micro-machines and apparel. In the former case, the focus is on the R&D consortium already mentioned. In apparel, firms have been looking to METI for guidance and information how to extract themselves out of their predicament, for example by coordinating an attempt to introduce the quick-response system that succeeded in giving the U.S. apparel industry a brief breath of relief (Abernathy et al. 1999). In semiconductor equipment, the role of government has been much less active.

The second variety of government agencies comes in the shape of research facilities, many of which are located in Tsukuba, a research town north-west of Tokyo. In these institutes, government researchers work on basic research that may in the long term support the tech-nological infrastructure of Japanese industry. In the case industries, these facilities were involved in the micromachine consortium, in aiding apparel firms to rationalize their operations through the use of technology, and to a lesser extent in laying the technological foundations for next-generation semiconductor manufacturing.

Ties between firms and government tend to be relatively sparse. The median micromachine firm is connected to 2 government agencies, while the median firm in the other industries is connected to only 1 (Table 5.2). In all three industries, some firms have no ties. The maximum number of ties is 5 in micromachines, 7 in semiconductor equipment, and 6 in apparel. The relatively low number of ties is likely to be a function of a combination of factors, including power distance, the relatively small number of government agencies, and also fear – "anything with the word 'public' in it [like 'public servant'] is scary," as one interviewee put it.

The kinds of information exchanged with government roughly mirror the patterns seen for associations. Micromachine firms mostly exchange information on technology (76 percent; Table 5.3), both in the context of collaborative research with government laboratories and in the context of updating government agencies on their progress in the government-sponsored consortium. Market and other information play a limited role at 14 and 10 percent, respectively. Again, neither interviews nor questionnaires unearthed evidence of information exchange on political matters.

Semiconductor equipment firms similarly focus on technology at 54 percent, followed by market information at 29 percent, politics at 11 percent, and "other" at 7 percent. Apparel firms again focus on market developments at 62 percent, followed by technology at 23 percent and politics at 15 percent.

Striking is the apparent reversal between semiconductor equipment and apparel in willingness of firms to discuss politics with government as compared with associations: while the proportion of political content in apparel is higher for associations than for government, the reverse is true for semiconductor equipment. This is consistent with the different kinds of support these industries would be seeking from government. In apparel, the industry needs help from government to survive, or at least to wind down in an orderly fashion. As a dying industry, it cannot expect much sympathy from METI. In semiconductor equipment, by contrast, firms at the time needed support in case of renewed trade conflicts with the United States. The strategic importance of the industry for the Japanese economy as a whole gives METI a much greater incentive to extend a hand to firms in semiconductor equipment than would be the case in apparel.

Firms on average tend to receive more information from government than they provide. For both semiconductor equipment and apparel, the balance is positive at 0.31 and 0.39, respectively (Table 5.4). Micromachines are the exception to the rule, with a slightly negative balance at −0.10. This is likely a consequence of the reporting requirements attached to receiving government funds in the context of the micromachine R&D consortium.

In terms of importance, ties to government agencies are most important for apparel firms, followed by firms in micromachines and semiconductor equipment. In fact, apparel firms rate government ties considerably more important than their peers in micromachines, leave alone firms in semiconductor equipment: Apparel firms consider these ties as *important* (3.17), while micromachine firms give them an *important minus* (2.74) and semiconductor equipment firms, only a *somewhat important plus* (2.29) (Table 5.5). This is consistent with the role government is playing in these industries: best bet for survival in apparel, provider of research funds in micromachines, and backup force against trade issues and relatively minor research aide in semiconductor equipment.

Frequency patterns are similar, with apparel firms leading the pack, followed by micromachine and semiconductor equipment makers. Apparel firms contact government on average every 10 weeks (2.23), while micromachine firms and even more so semiconductor equipment makers on average wait more than 3 months between contacts (1.74 and 1.42, respectively) (Table 5.6).

Networking with universities

Broadly speaking, universities have two missions: research and education. Most information exchange between firms and universities focuses on the former. Universities were an important source of technological expertise for firms from the Meiji period on through the Pacific War but largely withdrew from commercially oriented research following Japan's defeat. Since the 1980s, however, Japanese universities have started to return from their largely self-imposed exile and provide firms commercially viable research results, often in exchange for research funds, equipment, and research personnel seconded from the firms. In doing so, universities have once again become an important source of technological information for firms (Branscomb, Kodama, and Florida 1999; Hicks 1993).

The interest of firms in educational matters, on the other hand, is limited. Education as such lies outside the core competence of most firms, so there is little incentive for firms to try to mine education-related data. Only in regard to hiring does some of this kind of networking occur: Firms rely on faculty to provide them with a steady supply of qualified graduates. Since the level of networking activity in this regard seems insignificant in comparison with that concerning technology – the issue never came up in interviews or questionnaires – I will disregard it in this analysis.

Despite the great number of universities in Japan, firms tend to be frugal with their ties to them. The median degree is 2 for micromachines, 1 for semiconductor equipment, and 0 for apparel (Table 5.2). Minimum scores are 0 all round. Maximum degrees are 5 for micromachines and semiconductor equipment and 4 for apparel. The relative reluctance to network with universities may in part be due to the still widely held belief that, in the words of an interviewee, universities "are useless in the real world."

Given the functions of universities, one would expect technology to be the leading content of information exchange. This is indeed the case for micromachines and semiconductor equipment, at 70 and 82 percent, respectively (Table 5.3). Strikingly, though, apparel firms mostly discuss market information with universities (50 percent). The number-two category in micromachines and semiconductor equipment is market information (26 percent and 18 percent, respectively), in apparel, technology (40 percent). Politics plays a role only for apparel firms at 10 percent, apparently in the context of receiving advice from university professors on effective lobbying.

The public character of universities shows in the reported direction of information flow. In all three industries, firms report receiving more information from universities than they provide them. The scores are 0.16 for micromachines, 0.27 for semiconductor equipment, and 0.33 for apparel (Table 5.4).

In terms of importance, firms in all three industries rate their networking with universities similarly, with the micromachine industry valuing university ties a little less than the other industries. Specifically, apparel and semiconductor equipment firms consider their ties to universities *important* at 2.89 and 2.83, respectively, while micromachine firms rate theirs *important minus* at 2.69 (Table 5.5).

In terms of contact frequency, however, there is more variation. Semiconductor equipment firms contact universities most often, namely about every 4 weeks (3.19), while apparel firms contact their sources about once every 8 weeks (2.44) and micromachine firms get in touch only about once about every 3 months (2.06) (Table 5.6). The cause of the unexpectedly high average contact frequency for semiconductor equipment is unclear.

Networking with banks

Banks are financial intermediaries that help match the demand for capital in one sector of the economy – usually firms – with the demand for investment opportunities in other parts of the economy – usually households. As such, banks from a firm's perspective represent first and foremost a source of capital. This has been especially true for Japanese firms, which have traditionally relied on "indirect financing" through banks rather than securities markets for capital.

But banks can also be a good source of planning information. First, through their lending to various firms in the same industries, banks are usually well informed about the economic state of the respective industry and can provide firms useful pointers what developments to expect in the future. Doing so is usually in the very interest of the banks, as they would like to see debtor firms thrive so they can repay their loans. This is likely to be especially true in Japan, where a pattern emerged for firms to obtain a large part of their capital from a single "main bank," which in turn would monitor firm behavior and performance closely and, in case of bankruptcy, tend to absorb losses larger than its share of outstanding loans to the failed firm (Hoshi 1994; Sheard 1989, 1994). A similar structure exists, for example, in Germany, where the "Hausbank" ("house bank") plays an important role in corporate governance (Grant, Paterson, and Whitston 1987).

Second, since banks normally spread their lending across a large number of industries and sectors in the economy, they are in a good position to keep their finger on the pulse of the overall economy – as indeed they must, since fluctuations in the business cycle influence the bankruptcy rate in the economy and thus the risk of bank lending to firms. In addition, banks generally also maintain economic and research departments to be able to gauge economic developments.

Third, in particular in Japan, banks have traditionally also been well informed about political developments that could have an impact on business. For many years following the war, the government bureaucracy used the large commercial banks to funnel scarce capital to those industries it considered vital for rebuilding the Japanese economy (Johnson 1982; Nakamura 1995). While the system of directed lending fell into disuse as Japan's economy caught up with the West, banks maintained their close ties with government in general and the Ministry of Finance as the locus of fiscal and, until 1998, monetary policy-making. Only since the banking scandal of 1998 do bank ties with government seem to have loosened somewhat.

Only few firms network with banks. The median degree is 0 for semiconductor equipment and 1 for apparel (Table 5.2). In both industries, some firms do not network with banks at all. The maximum number of banks ties is 6 in semiconductor equipment and 4 in apparel.

Not a single micromachine firm reported information exchange with banks, neither in interviews nor in the questionnaires. Firms in an industry at this stage generally need no bank funding, as they receive public money and, where they undertake additional research, can often finance the ongoing research out of the proceeds from their other businesses. Without lending to that industry, banks do not know about developments in it, so they do not represent a viable source of information specific to the micromachine industry. Since micromachine firms do not produce yet, they also care very little about the general state of the economy. And since firms are directly hooked into the political process through the public research consortium in which they participate, they require no political information from banks. The result is that banks appear to be truly out of the loop in this case. This might explain at least partially why two banks – Daiichi Kangyo and Daiwa – took the unusual step of joining the Micromachine Center as "special supporting members:" The information they obtain as association members may help them determine the ideal timing for lending to the new industry or investing in it.

Both semiconductor equipment and apparel use bank ties to obtain information about market developments, with 64 percent of semi-conductor equipment firms and 34 percent of apparel firms describing such use (Table 5.3). Striking is the high proportion of political content, which is the modal kind of information exchanged in apparel at 49 percent and still quite common in semiconductor equipment at 32 percent. Main concern in both industries was government policy to stabilize and revive the Japanese economy and firms' suitable response to the expected course of government action. In apparel, however, firms also discussed protection and subsidies with banks.

The information balance is positive for semiconductor equipment firms at 0.20, but slightly negative at −0.10 for apparel firms (Table 5.4). The likely background of this variation is that apparel firms are more likely to be in need of financial support from banks. Obtaining such support may require the furnishing of relatively more information than would be the case in the less dependent semiconductor equipment industry.

Apparel firms rate networking with banks considerably more important than their counterparts in semiconductor equipment. While apparel makers see their bank contacts as *important plus* (3.26), semiconductor equipment makers rate them merely as *somewhat important plus* (2.40) (Table 5.5).

In terms of contact frequency, however, the two industries are virtually identical: Firms in both industries on average contact banks every month (3.13 for semiconductor equipment, 3.10 for apparel) (Table 5.6). This is not consistent with expectations from the importance score. The reasons for this deviation are unclear.

A special case: Networking with the press

The relationship of firms with the press represents a special case in that the press is the only example in which firms consistently report giving out more information than receiving. The information balance comes to −0.23 for semiconductor equipment and −0.84 for apparel (Table 5.4); micromachine firms reported no ties with the press. Why would firms continue to network with an actor with whom they incur an information trade deficit?

Interviews suggest that firms view the press less as a partner from whom to obtain information and more as a tool for disseminating the kinds of information they want to reach the public. Firms' relationship with the press thus seems to be more governed by their customer base than by the stage in the industrial life cycle of their industry.

Generally speaking, firms produce either consumer or investment goods. As the names imply, consumer goods are sold to consumers, whereas investment goods normally go to firms that use them to produce other goods (Kuß, 1993). In the present case, apparel falls into the consumer goods category and semiconductor equipment, into the investment goods category. As of the time of my research, micromachines were not on the market, so the industry had not established a target market yet.

In general, one would expect firm-to-press contacts to be more intensive in consumer goods industries. Producers of consumer goods talk with the press because the media represent an efficient way for them to interface with consumers. In consumer goods markets, firms face a large number of anonymous and relatively poorly informed customers who shop relatively often, but mostly in small lots and frequently from different producers. This makes it difficult for firms by themselves to reach out to individual consumers to create product awareness and obtain feedback about preferences. Instead, firms in consumer goods markets need to rely on intermediaries. For information about customer needs, they turn to retailers and market research firms. For creating awareness, they rely on retailers as well as advertising and favorable coverage in the media. Producers of capital goods, on the other hand, have only a relatively small number of clearly identifiable, well-informed customers who make large and often repeated purchases. Direct communication with these customers is not only possible, it is a prerequisite for successful sales. The interface function of the press is therefore less necessary.

Firms' reporting on their ties with the press is consistent with this picture. First, it is consistent with the absence of press ties among micromachine firms. Since no firm was in production at the point of this research, there was no product to advertise and no market trends to discuss. Press relations in connection with the government-sponsored R&D consortium were handled by the Micromachine Center. The other industries reported ties, with the median degree for semiconductor equipment is 2, that for apparel, 3 (Table 5.2). The range of connections is from 0 to 7 in semiconductor equipment and from 1 to 6 in apparel.

In terms of information provided, semiconductor equipment focus on market information with the press (72 percent), followed by technological information (28 percent; Table 5.3). By contrast, apparel firms give about equal weight to technology and market information (48 and 47 percent), with the remainder of ties dedicated to a smidgeon of politics and "other" matters. Since much of technology in the apparel industry centers around fashion and design, the stronger emphasis on technology is consistent with the idea that consumer goods firms need to provide more information to the end user.

In terms of importance, apparel manufacturers rated press contacts far more important than did semiconductor equipment makers: While the former ascribed to their press contacts an importance of *important* (3.23), the latter rated their ties merely *somewhat important plus* (2.38) (Table 5.5).

Apparel firms also reported somewhat more frequent contact with the press than semiconductor equipment makers. The former talk with the press on average once every 8 weeks (2.55), while the latter average about 9 weeks between contacts (2.38) (Table 5.6). This difference is somewhat smaller than one might expect given the large gap in terms of importance. A plausible reason for this discrepancy is that while apparel firms might want to talk with the press more often, journalists may be too busy to do so. Many journalists, in particular those working for larger papers, cover several industries. This limits the time they can devote to each, possibly resulting in a lower contact frequency with firms in consumer goods than firms might prefer.

Discussion

The evidence from the three case industries is consistent with our expectation that networking activity changes with stage in the industrial life cycle. Because of vastly different industry sizes, we cannot base our comparison on the number of ties (degree) firms maintain. In a small industry like micromachines, firms may wish to network and coordinate more, but the small number of firms and other actors may prevent them from doing so.

What we can compare across industries are measures of perceived importance of ties and frequency of use. The overall pattern for both measures shows highest networking intensity in apparel, followed by micromachines and semiconductor equipment. In terms of connections to the various kinds of networking partners (associations, government, etc., but excluding relations with the press), six out of ten cases show the predicted U-shaped pattern, while four do not. Of these latter four, two show the predicted pattern in either importance or frequency and a small deviation from the expectation in the other measure. The only consistent exception from the expected U shape is university ties.

Table 5.7 shows the resultant probabilities that the observed differences would be zero if a fresh sample were used. Means-difference tests of networking data require a corrected standard error, as the data are not independent and identically distributed. For example, most respondents report multiple ties, which is likely a cause of a violation of the independence assumption. Similarly, there is some overlap in the targets (e.g., METI, main industry associations), which again is probably a source of nonindependence, as some targets may tend to attract ties judged to be important, while others do not. To correct for these and other potential violations of the assumptions, I stack all observations of the two industries involved in the respective test and run a regression with robust standard errors of a dummy variable on the importance/frequency values. The *t*-score of the coefficient of the dummy variable is a corrected estimate of the Z/t-score of the means difference.

All observed differences for the totality of firms' network ties are statistically significant at the 0.05 level except for the difference of mean frequency scores in the micromachines and semiconductor equipment industries. This is likely to be the result of the high contact frequencies reported by semiconductor equipment firms with universities and banks, which push up the industry average to similar levels as in micromachines. At the level of the network as a whole, we can thus be quite confident that the observed U-shaped pattern has not arisen by chance alone. When we divide the overall sample by target categories (associations, government, etc., but excluding relations with the press), statistical significance weakens. For frequency scores, eleven out of thirteen differences at the target category level are statistically significant at the 0.1 level. For importance scores, six of the observed differences at the target category level are statistically significant at the 0.1 level, while seven are not.

Table 5.7. Means – difference test for importance and frequency scores

		All Ties	Firms	Associations	Government	Universities	Banks	Press
Importance	MM-SE	0.02**	0.28	0.03**	0.10*	0.55	–	–
	MM-AP	0.05**	0.12	0.14	0.02**	0.04**	–	–
	SE-AP	0.00**	0.43	0.64	0.00**	0.16	0.00**	0.00**
Frequency	MM-SE	0.37	0.01**	0.01**	0.07*	0.00**	–	–
	MM-AP	0.00**	0.00**	0.04**	0.05**	0.01**	–	–
	SE-AP	0.00**	0.00**	0.62	0.01**	0.04**	0.95	0.40

Note: Values denote the probability that the two means would coincide if a new sample were tested. MM = micromachines, SE = semiconductor equipment, AP = apparel. * = statistically significant at the 0.1 level, ** = statistically significant at the 0.05 level

As mentioned earlier, the data in this chapter in principle allow for the rival hypothesis that networking patterns vary with industry characteristics other than life cycle stage. Networking in micro-machines or apparel may always play a bigger role than in semiconductor equipment. Industry characteristics almost certainly influence what one could term the "natural rate" of networking. However, an ex-post evaluation of the semiconductor equipment industry suggests that if anything, this natural rate should be higher in semiconductor equipment than in the other industries. Semiconductor equipment makers need to ensure that products of different makers can work together in the same semiconductor production lines. Neither micromachines nor apparel are deployed as components of such larger systems. The rate of networking observed in semiconductor equipment is thus likely to be higher than it would have been in micromachines or apparel at a comparable industry stage. The system characteristic evident in the semiconductor equipment industry may thus represent another contingency mediating loop networking characteristics. In addition, the industry shows a high level of collaborative research initiatives, as evident in the proliferation of consortium-style structures such as ASET, SELETE, and SIRIJ. These confounding factors elevate networking levels in the industry and thus make it more difficult to find the expected U-shaped relationship between loop networking and life cycle stage. That the expected effect is still evident in the data is an encouraging sign.

The data further seem to rule out that the observed U-shaped pattern is the result of variations in firm size. Firm size may increase the propensity of firms to network with other firms by making available more resources for networking activities. Larger firms may be more able to afford to dedicate employees to networking, and they may generate more information that may be of interest to others and can be used to establish reciprocal exchange relations. On the other hand, smaller firms may be more dependent on networks to obtain outside resources, such as technological knowledge, that large firms may produce in-house. For instance, family-owned firms in such disparate places as South-East Asia and northern Italy compensate for small size by using social networks to coordinate production processes that exceed the capabilities of the individual firm (cf. Redding 1990; Whitley 1999). To the extent that the two effects do not cancel each other out, if firm size mattered in explaining intra-industry loop networking, we should see networking patterns vary with firm sizes in the case industries.

The data suggest that firm size is unlikely to explain the observed U-shaped pattern. Average (median) number of employees in micromachines is 20,479 (10,059), as opposed to 5,957 (1,190) in semiconductor equipment and 1,528 (705) in apparel. The same picture emerges in terms of total corporate sales. Average (median) corporate sales for firms in the micromachine industry are ¥1,192 billion (¥749 billion), as opposed to ¥322 billion (¥31 billion) in semiconductor equipment and ¥63 billion (¥25 billion) in apparel. If firm size mattered, this would suggest that networking should either be highest in apparel and lowest in micromachines, or vice versa. This is inconsistent with the U-shaped pattern we observed in the data.

The observed U-shape is similarly inconsistent with another possible confounding factor, business age. One might conjecture that firms with longer engagement in an industry may exhibit stronger networks merely by dint of having had longer time to develop them. Since business age is on average related to industry age and thus with life cycle stage, one would expect networking to be strongest in apparel and weakest in micromachines. This is evidently not the case.

Conclusion

In addition to providing an explorative description of loop networking characteristics in three case industries, the findings of this chapter suggest that Japanese firms may network, and thus coordinate, more toward the beginning and the end of the industrial life cycle, subject to the usual caveat about generalizability to other industries. To the extent that the pattern holds elsewhere, this implies that Japanese firms may coordinate most within their industries when uncertainty is highest and variety in solutions and supporting institutions would be most beneficial to the Japanese economy as a whole.

The causes of this safety in numbers approach to navigating uncertainty are at least two-fold. First, as we have seen in Chapter 2, Japanese firms have an incentive to respond to uncertainty with coordination in order to reduce their risk of distress and failure. Second, as proposed earlier in this chapter, industrial policy has conditioned firms in rising and declining industries to coordinate with one another and government.

The irony is that in rising industries, coordination probably works best under conditions of certainty. When Japan was still playing catch-up with the West, policy-makers and businessmen just had to observe developments elsewhere to know with reasonable certainty which industries to target next. The less successful examples of Japanese industrial policy, such as fifth-generation supercomputing, tended to occur under conditions of uncertainty about the future path of development. As we have seen in Chapter 3, there are numerous obstacles to reaching the right decision in a coordinated manner, and even where none of the decision-making pathologies we discussed come to bear, unanticipated developments may lead technological and industrial developments to take a different turn. From the perspective of the nation, a coordination strategy with its emphasis on unitary solutions implies considerable risk of choosing the wrong technological and institutional path.

The micromachine industry is a case in point. The Industrial Technology Council initiating the micromachine R&D consortium envisioned that micromachines would follow a path analogous to that taken by semiconductors: use existing manufacturing techniques and improve them to make smaller and smaller size possible. In the event, it has turned out since that the most promising approach to micromachine technology is to blend conventional machine tool techniques with semiconductor manufacturing processes. The industry has responded. For instance, Hitachi now offers a foundry service through the Micromachine Center in which produce micromachines on its semiconductor equipment according to blueprints submitted by other firms. Still, the micromachine project spent US$250m in research funds to occupy firms with 10 years of research into what in hindsight seems like an inferior production technology.

Coordination has also tended not to work well in declining industries. A well-known problem is that coordination may produce consensus on permanent life support for the industry rather than graceful exit (cf. Uriu 1996). In a nutshell, few of the actors involved in coordinated process have an interest in the industry's demise. First, neither firms nor industry association want to see the industry wound down. Since coordination implies some degree of consensus, it is difficult to act against these interests. Second, the government bureaucracy also has a vested interest in the survival of industries, as the death of an industry would deprive the ministry in charge of part of its bureaucratic empire. The administration and coordination of a declining industry means fruitful employment for bureaucrats. Their positions, and the resources attached to them, could be lost if an industry were successfully wound up. Third, politicians may intervene on behalf of industry survival if votes or funding are at stake. And fourth, academics and other actors involved in the industry similarly have an interest in its survival. The upshot is that most parties to coordinated processes in declining industries are in favor of industry survival because they have a direct stake in it. Only in rare cases – when the cost of support imposed on other actors becomes larger than the cost of action for these same actors (cf. Olson 1965) – will proponents of decommissioning the industry weigh in.

A second, and possibly more important, issue is that coordination in declining industries reduces incentive and ability to search for alternative means of competing that may lead at least some firms back into the green zone. For one, politically coordinated life support for the industry removes some of the economic urgency for firms to look for different ways to survive. Furthermore, the general propensity to keep coordinating with the same set of actors reduces the likelihood of finding innovative approaches to regaining viability. Network research has shown that individuals obtain new ideas and access to new opportunities not through their close circle of friends, but often through people with whom they maintain relatively weak contact (Granovetter 1973). The reason is that strong ties lead all individuals to possess, by and large, the same information. New information enters the network from outside. In terms of navigating the uncertainty about identifying novel approaches to business, increased coordination within the industry is thus the wrong response.

6 | R&D consortia and intra-industry loops in new industries

THE EXAMPLE of the micromachine industry in the last chapter suggests that even the youngest of Japanese industries tend to be fully coordinated through intra-industry loops. The likely reasons for the rapid spread of coordination to and through these new-born industries are several. One is the transfer of institutional templates (cf. Nelson and Winter 1982) from other industries. Most Japanese firms in infant industries are not start-up ventures but well-established large diversified enterprises embedded in the coordination structure of the other industries in which they are active. Having developed routines and formed expectations around coordination as a common practice, they are unlikely to deviate from coordination practices when entering new industries.

Second, the government helps erect the support structure for networking and thus aids the development of coordination. One main avenue is the creation of an industry association once an industry comes into being. This pattern is clearly evident in both the semiconductor equipment and micromachine industries, in which the government was instrumental in setting up the Semiconductor Equipment Association of Japan and the Micromachine Center. The fact that the semiconductor equipment industry petitioned METI for the creation of an association underlines that this practice is generally welcomed by firms. That these associations then aid in intra-industry coordination is clearly evident from the evidence in Chapter 5 as well as prior work on industry associations (e.g., Schaede 2000; Tilton 1996).

Third, especially in industries targeted by industrial policy, the government may actively facilitate the development of intra-industry loops and thus the ability of the industry to coordinate. As discussed in Chapter 4, the creation and funding of a public R&D consortium represents a common industrial policy tool for fostering infant industries. Networking in this context may develop in at least two ways. For one, firms are obliged for the duration of the project to coordinate research and development activities with one another as well as with the government, the respective industry association, and public and university research facilities. As the industry becomes established and the consortium ends, one would expect at least some of this coordination to disappear, as discussed in the previous chapter in the context of the life cycle hypothesis. Second, however, in forcing coordination during the consortium phase, the government may enable the building of trust among the participants. This would increase their ability and propensity to network, and thus informally coordinate, with one another even after the consortium has expired.

Using the example of the micromachine industry, this chapter presents an exploratory study of the role of R&D consortia in facilitating the growth of coordination in new industries. To this end, I complemented the first wave of data collection in the micromachine industry in 1997, as analyzed in the previous chapter, with a second wave in 2004, about three years after expiration of the government-sponsored micromachine R&D consortium. The evidence suggests that networking activity in the industry falls as the formal R&D consortium expires. However, even after the end of the consortium, firms that participated in the consortium seem to continue to network at higher levels of intensity with one another as compared with firms that did not participate in the consortium.

Cooperation in R&D consortia and social capital

Prior research on private-sector R&D consortia and similar organizational phenomena suggests that these structures may be conducive to the building of social capital and thus the creation of potential for coordination. For example, Browning, Beyer, and Shetler (1995) have illustrated the emergence of cooperation and coordination in the context of SEMATECH, a US-based private R&D consortium focusing on semiconductor technology. Rosenkopf, Metiu, and George (2001) have linked cooperation in technical committees to subsequent formalization of cooperation in alliances. A number of authors (e.g., Putnam 1993a; Rosenkopf, Metiu, and George 2001; Schaede 2000) point to enhancement of cooperation and social capital through joint membership in industry and other associations. Given the private-sector nature of these phenomena, social capital in these contexts is likely to be mostly volitional in origin.

In public R&D consortia, such as the one that started up the micromachine industry, additional dynamics are likely to develop through the presence of the state. As discussed in the context of the lifecycle hypothesis introduced in Chapter 5, the state plays a formal role in designing, funding, coordinating, and policing technological cooperation in public R&D consortia in Japan. The formation of at least part of the social capital present in these consortia is thus likely to be the result of state compulsion rather than participant volition: firms are forced to coordinate and share information even with direct rivals. This dynamic is consistent with the notion of enforceable trust in the social capital literature (Portes 1998), with enforcement in this case predominantly achieved through the threat of third-party enforcement of the rules of the game by the state.

Within this context of compulsory networking, however, at least two other sources of social capital may come into play to support the creation of volitional social capital. Portes (1998) has proposed that in addition to enforceable trust, there exist three sources of social capital: value introjection, bounded solidarity, and reciprocity exchanges. Value introjection occurs in the context of internalized norms that are available to others as resource. Bounded solidarity denotes the making available of resources motivated by solidarity with one's own group. In reciprocal exchange, resources are provided in expectation of repayment in the future, though timing and form of repayment are left unspecified.

While it is unclear how public R&D consortia could lead to value introjection beyond making the concept of cooperation among competitors acceptable to firms, consortia may be linked to the establishment of reciprocity exchanges and bounded solidarity. Compulsory cooperation under conditions of enforceable trust may give firms and organizations the opportunity to establish reciprocal exchange relationships. The compulsory relationships in the context of the consortium give participant firms and organizations the opportunity to interact and learn about one other, their mutual interests and goals, and their willingness to engage in cooperation (Rosenkopf, Metiu, and George 2001). Firms and organizations may also use the consortium to establish themselves as good "citizens" in order to signal their trustworthiness to others by contributing more than is required (cf. Bolino, Turnley, and Bloodgood 2002). Over time, actors may thus begin to engage in unforced exchanges on the side, possibly at first at a level of relatively low risk that escalates over time. Bouty (2000) lays out a similar process in the context of researchers of rival firms building cooperative relationships with one another. Through repeated reciprocal interaction, actors may thus be able to build up mutual trust (Brehm and Rahn 1997; Putnam 1993b).

Furthermore, joint R&D work in a public consortium may facilitate the emergence of bounded solidarity. For instance, firms and organizations may develop a collective commitment to the defense and advancement of the industry that leads them to suspend the usual modalities of competitive behavior (Browning, Beyer, and Shetler 1995). This effect may be particularly strong if cooperation is required in order to overcome a common external obstacle or to attain a common goal (cf. Sherif 1961). For instance, if the budding industry finds itself under external attack in the form of persistent questions about the commercial viability of the technology under development, actors involved in the industry may redouble their efforts to prove the worth of the project in order to avoid association with failure. Since questions persist whether the micromachine industry will live up to the great expectations prevailing at the time of the initiation of the micromachine consortium, this mechanism is likely to be at work in this concrete case.

The strength of social capital formed is likely to be expressed particularly in terms of the kinds of resources firms may mobilize through their relations. As actors engage in repeated interaction, ties become socially embedded, trust increases, and information exchange becomes more fine-grained (Uzzi 1997b). Bouty (2000) has documented this process in a non-Japanese context of researchers working for rival companies, noting that deepening of acquaintance and trust are accompanied by an extension of the range of resources available for exchange from common to more strategic and thus riskier resources. The formation of high levels of social capital during the consortium period may thus find its expression in particular in the ability of firms to exchange with one another strategic resources such as technological information.

The overall expectation arising from this discussion and the lifecycle hypothesis introduced in Chapter 5 is two-fold. First, the termination of the formal research consortium is likely to lead to a reduction of networking activity within the industry. The end of the project marks a transition from the very early stages of an industry, operating under conditions of enforceable trust with considerable government protection and support, to a producing – though still young and rising – industry. Second, one should observe elevated levels of social capital in firms that participated in the micromachine consortium when compared with non-participant firms. This should be evident in the patterns of intra-industry loop networking of firms.

Data and method

Data collection for the second wave of data from the micromachine industry occurred in 2004, about 3 years after the expiry of the micromachine R&D consortium. By this time, the number of known firms in the micromachine industry had increased to 32 (Table 6.1).

As in 1997, I employed both questionnaires and interviews. Analysis of the questionnaire data involves the same techniques as in the previous chapter as well as structural network analysis, the latter made possible by the relatively high response rates in the micromachine industry. The interview data underwent exploratory content analysis with the objective of identifying the processes leading to the outcomes evident in the questionnaire data. More information on data collection and method can be found in the Appendix.

Changes from 1997 to 2004: Overall pattern

The data suggest that following the termination of the government-sponsored R&D consortium on micromachines in 2000, networking activity in the industry underwent significant changes in strength and orientation. The median number of ties firms report to have with other actors in the intra-industry loop (outdegree) fell from 12 in 1997 to 7.5 in 2004 (Table 6.2). The range of the total number of networking partners falls between 1 and 25 in 1997 and 0 and 27 in 2004.

The kinds of information exchanged exhibit a shift in focus from technology to market developments. The proportion of ties dedicated to technology almost halved, from 74 percent in 1997 to 38 percent in 2004 (Table 6.3). At the same time, the share of market information

Table 6.1. Firms active in the Japanese micromachine industry, 2004

Aisin Cosmos R&D Co.	Oki Electric Industry
Denso	Oki Sensor Device
Fanuc	Olympus .
Fuji Electric	Omron
Fujikura	Sanyo Electric
Hitachi	Seiko Epson
JUKI	Seiko Instruments
Matsushita Electric Industrial	Sony
Matsushita Electric Works	Sumitomo Electric Industries
Mitsubishi Electric	Toshiba
Mitsubishi Heavy Industries	Toyota Central R&D Labs.
Mitsubishi Materials	Ulvac
Moritex	Yamatake
Murata Manufacturing	Yaskawa Electric
Nagona Keiki	YKK
Nikon	Yokogawa Electric

tripled, from 17 percent in 1997 to 52 percent in 2004. The new emphasis on market information is in line with patterns seen in the other industries explored in Chapter 5, semiconductor equipment and apparel (cf. Table 5.3), and may thus be the normal state of affairs in all but the very youngest of industries. As in 1997, political content was not reported by the respondents and thus is not included as a category in the table. "Other" information exchanged concerns mostly preparation for meetings at the Micromachine Center, as was already the case in 1997.

The information trade balance of firms improved markedly from 1997 to 2004. Firms in 1997 reported giving out as much information as they received with a balance value of 0.02 (Table 6.4), which is consistent with the expectation that participants in a public R&D consortium cooperate and share their insights. By contract, firms in 2004 seemed to reap considerable informational gains as indicated by a balance value of 0.50. This value is high even when compared with the other industries studied in the previous chapter (cf. Table 5.4), the causes are not known. The difference is statistically significant ($p = 0.000$).

Table 6.2. *Median, minimum and maximum number of ties (outdegree) of firms in the micromachine industry, 1997 and 2004*

	All Ties	Firms	Associations	Government	Universities	Banks	Press
1997	12 (1, 25)	7 (0, 18)	1 (1, 3)	2 (0, 5)	2 (0, 5)	0 (0, 0)	0 (0, 0)
2004	7.5 (0, 27)	4 (0, 13)	1 (0, 2)	1.5 (0, 4)	1 (0, 7)	0 (0, 0)	0 (0, 2)

Note: Numbers in parentheses denote minimum–maximum range

Table 6.3. *Distribution of kinds of information firms exchange (percentage), 1997 vs. 2004*

		All Ties	Firms	Associations	Government	Universities
1997	Technology	74	78	63	76	70
	Market	17	14	20	14	26
	Other	10	9	18	10	4
2004	Technology	38	34	37	40	45
	Market	52	53	43	53	48
	Other	11	13	20	7	7

Note: Categories marked in italics denote modal kind of information exchanged

Average importance and frequency scores both declined. In terms of importance, firms rated networking as *important minus* (2.74) in 1997, but only *somewhat important plus* (2.40) in 2004 (Table 6.4). Similarly, overall contact frequency declined from about once every 8 weeks in 1997 (2.49) to a little more than once a quarter (2.13) in 2004 (Table 6.4). Both differences are statistically significant (p = 0.001 and p = 0.000).

The overall pattern is thus one of a reduction in networking strength and a reorientation from a preoccupation with technology to a concern with marketability of micromachine technology. This is consistent with expectations. First, the life cycle hypothesis laid out in the previous chapter suggests that networking levels in the industry should decline as it transitions from the very early stages with government protection and support to a producing, albeit still young and rising, industry. Second, the expiration of the government-sponsored R&D consortium and the completion of basic research removed the requirement for firms and other actors in the industry to coordinate, which in turn reduced the need for networking. Third, with the technological foundations for micromachine production laid, firms have shifted their focus to finding applications for their technology. The resultant pattern in the kinds of information exchanged represents an arrival at relative normalcy, as a comparison with semiconductor equipment and apparel indicates (cf. Chapter 5).

Changes from 1997 to 2004: Firms networking with firms

Subsequent to the expiry of the micromachine R&D consortium, networking among firms declined more than networking with any other actors in the loop. Even though the number of firms in the industry increased from 25 to 32, the outdegree for firm-to-firm networking almost halved from 7 in 1997 to 4 in 2004, with a concomitant decline in the observed range (Table 6.2).

Networking contents show the same shift away from technology and toward market information already evident in the overall picture, only more so. Firm-to-firm information exchange in 1997 involved technology in 78 percent of ties and market information in 14 percent of all ties (Table 6.3). In 2004, the pattern reversed, with technology occupying 34 percent of exchange and market information, 53 percent. While firms in 1997 were more (less) likely to exchange

Table 6.4. Average information trade balance, importance, and frequency for firms, 1997 vs. 2004

		All Ties	Firms	Associations	Government	Universities
Average Information	1997	0.02	−0.04	0.38	−0.10	0.16
Trade Balance	2004	0.50	0.54	0.74	0.25	0.49
Average importance	1997	2.74	2.67	3.12	2.74	2.69
	2004	2.40	1.94	2.68	3.00	2.74
Average Frequency	1997	2.49	2.70	3.09	1.74	2.06
	2004	2.13	1.88	2.42	2.18	2.51

Note: For explanations, cf. Tables 5.4 through 5.6

technical (market) information with one another than with any other actor in the loop, by 2004 the inverse held true.

The information trade balance improved drastically from -0.04 in 1997 to 0.54 in 2004 (Table 6.4). Since one's firm's information outflow must be another firm's information inflow, the expected value for the overall balance in a closed network is 0. Close evaluation of the data show that in cases of ties where an actor reported receiving more information than giving out, the respective networking partners rarely report an information exchange deficit. The most likely explanation is that the receipt of useful data may well cause actors to perceive being in balance or running a surplus when in fact they are not. The difference is statistically significant (p = 0.000).

Importance and frequency scores likewise dropped more for firms than for any other actor category in the loop. Average importance fell from 2.67 in 1997, or *important minus*, to 1.94, or *somewhat important* in 2004 (Table 6.4). Average contact frequency declined from about once every 6 weeks (2.70) to less than quarterly (1.88) over the same period (Table 6.4). Both differences are statistically significant (p = 0.048 and p = 0.000).

Structural network analysis of firm-to-firm ties similarly suggests a considerable weakening of networking activity. The average Freeman degree, which indicates the mean number of ties of each actor, decreased from 8.2 in 1997 to 4.4 in 2004, a difference that is statistically significant (p = 0.000). The average normalized Freeman

Figure 6.1. Firm-to-Firm Networking in the Micromachine Industry, 1997
Note: The unconnected dot in the upper left corner is an isolate, that is, a firm that is not connected with any other firm in the industry.

degree, which indicates the mean number of ties standardized for network size, shows a decline from 32.6 in 1997 to 14.3 in 2004, again statistically significant (p = 0.000). This suggests that, the 2004 network is considerably less dense than that in 1997, as is also readily apparent when I graph the two networks (Figures 6.1 and 6.2). While the structural analysis estimates for 2004 may be slightly too low because of missing data from about one-third of the network members, the overall conclusion of a drop in networking activity is the same as for the other measures employed.

Changes from 1997 to 2004: Firms networking with other actors

Firm networking with nonfirms appears to have held up relatively well after termination of the micromachine R&D consortium. The

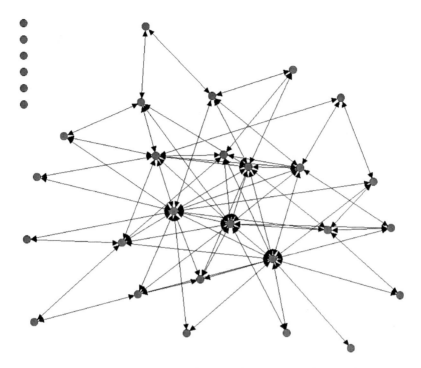

Figure 6.2. Firm-to-Firm Networking in the Micromachine Industry, 2004
Note: Dots in the upper left corner are isolates.

median number of connections with associations has not changed, while the range of ties has fallen somewhat (Table 6.2). Noteworthy is that even though the sample was selected by drawing from the roster of supporting members of the Micromachine Center, not all firms report networking with the Center. Their memberships thus seem to have become passive in nature. The median number of ties with government fell from 2 to 1.5, with an attendant decrease in the maximum number of ties from 5 to 4.

The median number of ties with universities halved from 1997 to 2004 and by the skin of a tooth reached a value of 1 for 2004. 45 percent of the firms surveyed in 2004 do not have any connections with universities, as opposed to 28.6 percent of firms in 1997. Those that do network with universities, however, have an average of 3.2 connections in 2004, compared with 2.7 connections in 1997.

Networking with universities in 2004 has thus become polarized: almost half of firms do not interface with them at all, while those networking with universities typically maintain multiple ties.

As in 1997, firms did not exchange any information about the micromachine industry with banks. Three of the twenty firms did report networking with the press in 2004, with an average number of 1.3 ties per firm reporting such ties. It does not appear prudent to draw conclusions from a total of 4 reported ties, so I will bracket this type of networking from further discussion.

The kinds of information exchanged with nonfirm actors show the same shift as evident for firms. The emphasis on technology in 1997 has given way to a focus on market information in 2004 (Table 6.3). Remarkable is that associations do not seem to be seen as a particularly outstanding source of market intelligence. This is surprising, as one of the key roles of industry associations in Japan is typically to collate and disseminate information about market developments and trends. Relations with the Micromachine Center also seem to be relatively high in transaction costs, as indicated by the 20 percent of ties devoted to "other" kinds of information exchange, which typically involves issues around preparing meetings at the association.

The balance of information flow with nonfirms improved markedly in firms' favor. The balance of information flow for associations almost doubled from 0.38 in 1997 to 0.74 in 2004 (Table 6.4). A large shift is also evident in the balance with government agencies, which shows a net outflow at -0.10 in 1997 turning into a net inflow at 0.25 in 2004. Universities likewise register an increase, from 0.16 in 1997 to 0.49 in 2004. The likely background of these moves is that the end of the R&D consortium in 2000 also marked the end of the need for firms to report on their research progress to their nonfirm partners in the consortium. The new values are roughly in line with those observed in other industries (cf. Chapter 5). The differences for government and universities are statistically significant at the 0.1 level ($p = 0.063$ and $p = 0.058$), that for associations is approaching it ($p = 0.124$).

Importance scores changed most for associations. The average association importance score declined from 3.12, or roughly *important*, to 2.68, or about *important minus* (Table 6.4). This would be consistent with the reduced role of the Micromachine Center in the industry, as part of its coordinating activities was closely linked with the running of the micromachine R&D consortium. The present importance score is in line with those seen in other industries. Government importance increased somewhat from *important minus* (2.74) in 1997 to *important* (3.00) in 2004, which falls within the range observed in the other case industries in Chapter 5. The university score remains almost unchanged at *important minus* (2.69 in 1997, 2.74 in 2004), in line with scores seen elsewhere. None of these differences are statistically significant, though the value for associations approaches significance at the 0.1 level (p = 0.144).

Contact frequencies exhibit some movement. Firms in 1997 contacted associations about once a month (3.09; Table 6.4). By 2004, this frequency had declined to about once every 9 weeks (2.42). This is consistent with the reduced role of the Micromachine Center in the industry as discussed earlier. By contrast, contact frequencies for government and universities increased. Government in 1997 used to be contacted about once every 4 months (1.74). In 2004, firms contacted government agencies about once every 11 weeks (2.18), almost as often as firms in the dying apparel industry. Similarly, contact frequency for universities rose from once every quarter (2.06) in 1997 to about once every 8 weeks (2.51) in 2004. This would suggest that while connectivity in terms of number of ties with government and universities was reduced in 2004, the ties that did exist were put to use more often. All of these differences in contact frequencies are statistically significant (p = 0.021, p = 0.048, and p = 0.019).

In sum, changes in network characteristics with nonfirm actors are less pronounced than for firm-to-firm networking. Networking with associations seems to have weakened as a consequence of the reduced role of the Micromachine Center following the termination of the government-sponsored consortium. Connectivity with government and universities has declined, but existing ties seem to be somewhat more active. The kinds of information exchanged show the same shift as seen for firm-to-firm networking from technology toward market data.

Changes from 1997 to 2004: Qualitative assessment

My interviews with the *madoguchi* confirmed an overall decline in the level of activity in the micromachine intra-industry loop. The termination of the government-sponsored project in 2000 did indeed seems to have marked a turning point in networking activity, both in terms of demand for networking and the supply of networking opportunities.

In terms of demand for networking, the most immediate context is that some networking only occurred because it was necessary for the project:

At that time [1997], because we closely cooperated doing cooperative research in the state project as I mentioned earlier, it was necessary to talk with one another. But now there is no project, so there is also no need to talk with one another.

Information exchange in the context of the project was an obligation incurred by taking on the research funds provided by the state. The end of the project gave firms the opportunity to terminate ties maintained only out of duty:

When the project was ongoing, well, how shall I put it, we were forced to contact each other, but this has ended.

Some firms took a clearly instrumental view of ties built up during the project, keeping those deemed useful and cutting off those not needed:

With the end of the project, there was no need [for networking with everyone], and we maintain the network in places necessary at times of later doing business. The network that is not needed for business is unnecessary. Well, we cut that network off.

One element in this decision was the closeness of the competitive rivalry between firms. Information exchange with direct competitors ceased in order to keep the competition in the dark about the direction of one's own R&D activities and to protect the secrecy of their outcomes. In addition, there also seem to be rivalry spillovers from other product markets:

What has become an obstacle to networking, I believe, is that not only in the field of micromachines, but in other areas of firm activity, there is a good deal of firms that are competitors. It is not necessarily the case that they are trying to develop the same micromachine devices, but where firms collide in their main areas of activity, there is little networking activity.

The likelihood that cooperation survives beyond the termination point of a public R&D consortium thus seems to be inversely related with the extent of competitive rivalry among the respective firms.

On a different level, the demand of firms themselves to network in order to obtain information from others in the industry apparently declined. There was wide acceptance that some coordination and cooperation was needed to establish the technological basis of the micromachine industry. By the end of the consortium, however, this technological basis was in place for at least some firms, and competitive rivalry began to set in:

At the basic research stage, one firm cannot do it, so two firms work together, or one works with the state. When it comes to thinking about making own products, secrecy increases.

This secrecy involves not only technical know-how, but also the kinds of projects firms are working on:

We have to a certain extent developed technology, if one goes out and ask about it, the other will end up knowing what one is doing.

At the same time, the need to obtain information directly from the source has decreased as more public information about micromachine technology has become available:

Before one could certainly not produce various things without engaging in information exchange, but now, even without information exchange, even in books one can find some information.

On the supply side, the end of the R&D consortium seems to have resulted in fewer opportunities to network. As laid out earlier in this book, meetings at associations provide a good basis for building connections. With the end of the project, the number of meetings declined, reducing networking opportunities:

At the time when we were doing the project, there were quite a lot of closely knit meetings concerning the project within the Micromachine Center.

Obviously people from various companies are in those project teams, so if one goes to those meetings, quite a bit of talk about how to advance the project and about other topics came up. So you got connections. [...] I think the fact that the project ended is [a] pretty big [factor for explaining the decline in networking activity].

The decline in ties with universities may similarly in part be due to reduced contact opportunities at the Micromachine Center:

We got advice [from universities] in order to advance the project ... In that course, my company also solved various problems. The reason why this was easy to do was because within the Micromachine Center, there were various research meetings and survey research was done. In many cases, the head [of these meetings] was a university professor. It is not that such meetings now no longer exist, but they have become rarer. For that reason, networking has become rarer.

Along with this reduction in research activity within the Center, the incentive to network with the Center itself also seems to have weakened:

When we were doing the project, we did research meetings within the organization of the Micromachine Center. However, since the project has ended, those research meetings have also become unnecessary. With that quite a few companies have also ended their connection with the Micromachine Center.

While no firm active in the industry seems to have terminated its relationship with the Micromachine Center by quitting, a good number of firms are disengaged in the sense of reporting very low levels of involvement with the Micromachine Center. Interviewees in general voiced dissatisfaction with the role of the Center as an information source, with several references to meetings now being useless or even a "waste of transportation expense."

The shift in networking content from technology toward market trends seems to be the consequence of several related developments. One is the commercial rivalry emerging among the collaborators as firms move beyond the basic research phase. Second, with the development of a market in products based on micromachine technology, there is now an increased need for firms to watch market developments in order to be able to read the trends:

Since you cannot do business without reading the trend, everyone is now focusing on this [market information].

A third and surprisingly common reason is that some firms are still looking for ways to put their newly development technological know-how to practical use:

We know that we have to design things this way. So now we have the technological base, but the application for it [is the problem]. Now the issue is how to make it a commodity.

A good number of firms apparently participated in the micromachine R&D consortium without a clear vision of how to put micromachine technology to practical use.

Consortium participants versus non-participants in 2004: Overall pattern

Earlier in this chapter, I have raised the question whether the experience of joint research in the government-sponsored R&D consortium may have the effect of increasing networking and thus coordination capacity even after the consortium has expired. What is the evidence in the data on this question?

The following analysis was undertaken for the sake of exploration and presenting a first falsification attempt of the considerations introduced in the beginning of this chapter. It involves comparing the 2004 networking patterns of consortium participants with those of non-participants, which requires splitting an already fairly small sample of 20 firms into two sub-samples of 13 and 7 firms, respectively. However, the present data are the best we are likely to have for the foreseeable future. Informal network data are difficult to collect, and industries that are at the same time larger than the micromachine industry–thus increasing the odds for a larger sample–and have only recently emerged from an R&D consortium are rare even in Japan. Under these conditions, statistical significance is almost impossible to come by. It is thus highly remarkable that several of the comparisons between the two groups do reveal differences that are statistically significant or approaching significant levels.

The overall pattern in 2004 suggests that participants in the consortium have more network ties than those firms that did not participate in the consortium. The median total number of ties for participants is 9, as opposed to 6 for non-participants (Table 6.5). The range for participants extends from 1 to 27 connections, while that for non-participants extends only from 0 through 13. This suggests that participants enjoy better connectivity in the 2004 intra-industry loop in the micromachine industry than non-participants.

The contrast is not as stark in terms of kinds of information exchanged. At 51 percent, respectively, both participants and non-participants use the same proportion of their ties to obtain market information (Table 6.6). However, participants network relatively less about technology and relatively more about other matters such as association meetings. Having spent 10 years in joint R&D projects to develop their own know-how, participant firms are likely to have lower demand for obtaining outside technological resources than non-participant firms. The causes of the relatively high incidence of "other" information for participants are unclear. Association matters seem to be more commonly discussed among participants than non-participants, but the data about relations with associations–discussed below–shows little evidence that participants may be more involved in association matters.

In all other measured respects, the networking patterns of both groups are very similar. Participants register a positive information balance of 0.47, while non-participants score a balance of 0.57 (Table 6.5). Importance scores for the two groups are 2.41 and 2.39, which translates to *somewhat important plus*. Contact frequencies are similar at 2.15 for participants and 2.07 for non-participants, or roughly every 11 weeks on average.

Overall, the most conspicuous divergence between the two groups seems to be in their connectivity. The median number of ties participants can draw upon to coordinate and exchange information is 50 percent higher than that of non-participants. However, to the extent that they possess ties, both groups seem to make use of them in a similar fashion.

Consortium participants versus non-participants in 2004: Firms networking with firms

Consortium participants maintain more ties with other firms in 2004 than non-participants do. The median number of ties for participants is 4, as opposed to 3 for non-participants (Table 6.5). The range of

Table 6.5. *Median, minimum, and maximum number of ties (outdegree), average information trade balance, importance, and frequency for firms, consortium participants vs. non-participants*

		All Ties	Firms	Associations	Government	Universities
Number of Ties	Participant	9 (1, 27)	4 (0, 13)	1 (0, 2)	3 (0, 4)	1 (0, 7)
	Non-Participant	6 (0, 13)	3 (0, 9)	1 (0, 2)	0 (0, 3)	1 (0, 6)
Average Information	Participant	0.47	0.45	0.69	0.35	0.54
Trade Balance	Non-Participant	0.57	0.78	0.83	-0.17	0.36
Average Importance	Participant	2.41	1.89	2.62	3.00	2.83
	Non-Participant	2.39	2.04	2.83	3.00	2.55
Average Frequency	Participant	2.15	1.90	2.38	2.22	2.58
	Non-Participant	2.07	1.83	2.50	2.00	2.36

Note: In keeping with Table 6.2, number of "all ties" includes press contacts. For further explanations, cf. Tables 5.4 through 5.6

Table 6.6. Distribution of kinds of information firms exchange (percentage), consortium participants vs. non-participants

		All Ties	Firms	Associations	Government	Universities
Participant	Technology	36	36	30	35	39
	Market	*51*	48	48	57	52
	Other	13	16	22	8	9
Non-Participant	Technology	47	26	57	71	67
	Market	*51*	74	29	29	33
	Other	2	0	14	0	0

Note: Categories marked in italics denote modal kind of information exchanged

number of ties is likewise wider for participants than for non-participants, extending from 0 through 13 for the former and 0 through 9 for the latter.

Striking is the variation in the kinds of information exchanged. While the modal kind of information exchanged is market data for both groups, this type of information exchange is about 1.5 times as prevalent among the non-participants (74 percent) as among the participants (48 percent) (Table 6.6). Participants instead show relatively more information exchange on technology, with 36 percent of ties involved as opposed to 26 percent for non-participants. Since considerably more trust is required to discuss technology with a potential or actual competitor than to discuss market information, this seems to suggest somewhat more trust and thus social capital among participants than non-participants.

As in the overall pattern, importance and frequency scores are quite similar across the groups (Table 6.5). A somewhat larger difference is evident in the information balance, with participants scoring lower at 0.45 as opposed to 0.78 for non-participants (Table 6.5). This difference is approaching statistical significance at $p = 0.14$. To the extent that the observed difference is real, one interpretation is that non-participants may be shrewder networkers. Another, more likely one is that non-participants may have relatively less information to share with others and a relatively greater need for acquiring information than participants. The pattern seen in the kinds of information exchanged may be the flipside of this need to hoover up information. With non-participants having less to offer and more to learn, they may find it more difficult to be trusted as partners in a reciprocal exchange of valuable technical information.

Structural network analysis reveals further evidence of the variation in connectivity and trust across the groups. The mean degree for the participant group is 5.3, which is about 61 percent higher than that for the non-participant group at 3.3 ($p = 0.18$). The difference is even greater for the median degrees, which come to 4.5 for the participant and 2.5 for the non-participant group – a difference of 80 percent. This suggests that participants enjoy considerably greater connectivity in terms of number of ties than non-participants.

This difference becomes even clearer if we analyze network structures separately within each group, participants and non-participants. Members of the participant group maintain on average 3.4 ties with other former participants, as opposed to an average of 0.9 ties non-participants maintain with one another. This difference is highly statistically significant ($p = 0.008$). The median values are 3.5 for participants and 0.5 for non-participants. This suggests two things. First, participant firms are more likely to network with one another than with non-participants. Second, non-participant firms network very little with one another. Instead, they seek to attach themselves to participants firms. Both make intuitive sense. Participant firms are generally more likely to have useful information about the industry than non-participant firms. It therefore makes sense to seek out participant firms as networking partners.

Participants are also more central to the network of micromachine firms than non-participants. The mean (median) betweenness score for participants is 14.8 (2.9), that for non-participants, 4.5 (0.46) ($p = 0.13$). In terms of betweenness, the position of participants in the network is consequently 3.3 times (6.3 times) more central than that of non-participants. Participants on average seem to occupy more central and thus more privileged positions in the micromachine industry loop than non-participants.

These differences in degree and centrality are also visible in the graphical representation of the network. The grey nodes in Figure 6.3 represent participants in the consortium, while the white nodes are the non-participants. Five participants are shown as isolates, which is a consequence of their not participating in the survey and no other firm reporting ties to them. To the extent that participants did report ties, however, the figure clearly shows that they tend to have considerably more ties than the non-participants, and that they tend to prefer to network with other participants. In addition, their spatial positioning in the figure tends to be more toward the center of the network than that of the non-participants. Indeed, while most participants are quite well connected with one another, many non-participants are connected to the network only through their ties with participants.

The divergence between participants and non-participants becomes even clearer when we focus on those ties with technological content and thus implied high trust. In this case, the mean (median) degree of participants is 2.7 (1.5), that for non-participants, 1.1 (1), implying a factor of 2.5 (1.5). Unusual for this small a sample size, this observed difference is statistically significant at the 0.10 level (p = 0.077). Examining participants and non-participants separately, the analysis yields a mean (median) degree among participants of 2 (1.5), as compared with 0.14 (0) for non-participants. This difference is statistically significant (p = 0.000). It underlines the tendency of participants to network with one another and of non-participants, not to work with other non-participants. Mean betweenness centrality score for the participants is 13.9, as opposed to 4.2 for non-participants, a factor of 3.3 (p = 0.23). The medians are 0 for both groups. Participants thus have considerably more ties dedicated to high-trust networking on technology and are considerably more centrally positioned in the network than non-participants.

This pattern is again clearly visible in the graph (Figure 6.4). As in Figure 6.3, the grey nodes representing participants tend to have more ties and to be more centrally located than the white nodes representing non-participants. Especially noteworthy is that Figure 6.4 shows only one single tie about technology between non-participants. All other technology connections involve at least one participant node, and the vast majority of technology networking occurs within the participant group.

Non-participants seem at less of a disadvantage in low-trust networking concerning market and "other" information. The mean (median) degree of participants is 2.8 (1.5), that for non-participants, 2.2 (1.5), implying a factor of 1.3 (1) and thus no tangible difference in terms of degree. Mean (median) betweenness centrality score for

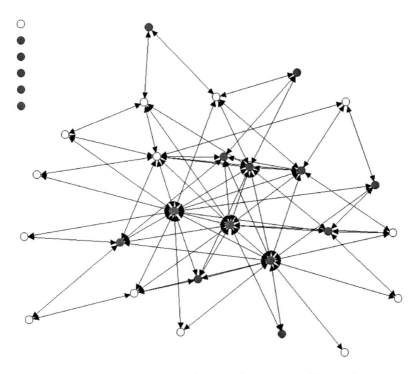

Figure 6.3. Firm-to-Firm Networking in the Micromachine Industry, 2004, Participants in R&D Consortium vs. Non-Participants
Note: Grey dots are participants in the consortium, white dots, non-participants. Dots in the upper left corner are isolates.

the participants is 15.5 (0.25), as opposed to 5.6 (0) for non-participants, a factor of 2.8 (n/a). In terms of low-trust networking, the playing field between the two groups seems more level.

Figure 6.5 shows the networking pattern for low-trust ties among micromachine firms. Though the central nodes continue to tend to be drawn from the participant group, there is more interaction between participants and non-participants as well as better connectivity among non-participants. Toward the upper left, we can identify one relatively centrally positioned non-participant forming a non-participant network of five nodes and five ties. The remainder of the non-participant group are either isolates or dependent on connections with members of the participant group. By contrast, only one participant firm (top

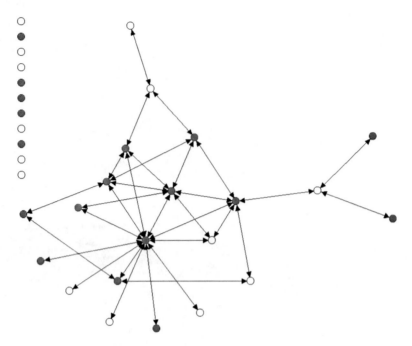

Figure 6.4. Firm-to-Firm Networking about Technology in the
Micromachine Industry, 2004, Participants in R&D Consortium vs.
Non-Participants
Note: Grey dots are participants in the consortium, white dots,
non-participants. Dots in the upper left corner are isolates.

left) would be an isolate if the non-participant nodes were removed
from the network.

One factor possibly confounding the kind of comparison undertaken above is the duration of time a firm has been active in the
micromachine industry. All participant firms are known to have
commenced their engagement in micromachines around the time of
the start of the micromachine R&D consortium in 1991. By contrast,
some of the non-participants discovered their interest in the industry
only later on. As discussed in Chapter 5, part of the observed difference
between participants and non-participants may thus be the result of the
former having had more time to establish contact with other firms.

To explore this possibility further, I focus on the eight non-
participant firms known to have been developing their micromachine

business since the early 1990s. For this subsample of the non-participant group, I compute the overall mean degree as well as the mean degree for ties related to technology and the mean degree related to nontechnological issues. The results suggest that this subgroup is somewhat better connected than the group of non-participants as a whole, but generally not as well connected as the participants. The mean degree for participants is 5.3, as compared with 4.5 for the sub-sample. The mean degree for networking related to technology comes to 2.7 for the participants, but only 1.6 for the sub sample. And the mean degree for nontechnological ties is 2.83 for the participants and 2.88 for the non-participant sub-sample.

Overall, this suggests two things. First, length of engagement in the industry does seem to matter to some extent, as evident in the somewhat higher level of connectivity of the eight firms in the sub-sample compared with the group of non-participant firms as a whole. Second, however, length of engagement in the industry does not seem to explain the entire difference. Even if one standardizes for duration of firms' engagement in the industry, the participant group still tends to be perceivably better connected in terms of high-trust ties conveying technological information. This would suggest that the experience of joint consortium participation may be especially effective for fostering the creation of trust.

Differences in firm sizes may similarly confound the results, as discussed in Chapter 5. I consequently compute and compare the means and medians of the number of employees and sales volume for the two groups. The mean (median) number of employees is 64,898[1] (27,144) for participants and 57,291 (16,925) for non-participants, while the mean (median) sales volume of the two groups is ¥1,953 billion (¥844 billion) and ¥1,762 billion (¥610 billion), respectively. This would suggest that the participant firms are somewhat larger than non-participant firms, which is consistent with the observation that most initial entries into new industries in Japan tend to involve divisions of large established firms while some small- and medium-sized enterprises may follow later. This is likely a function of both

---

[1] Unlike the much smaller numbers presented in Chapter 5, these numbers are taken from consolidated financial accounts, which should provide a more accurate picture of the availability of "in-house" resources than unconsolidated figures. Since consolidated financial accounting became common in Japan only in 2000, no consolidated figures are available for the comparison in Chapter 5.

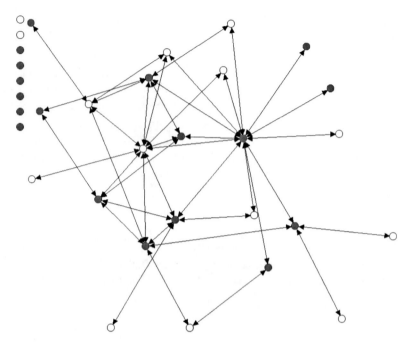

Figure 6.5. Firm-to-Firm Networking about Market and Other Information in the Micromachine Industry, 2004, Participants in R&D Consortium vs. Non-Participants
Note: Grey dots are participants in the consortium, white dots, non-participants. Dots in the upper left corner are isolates.

industrial policy, which tends to lend support to large firms rather than small ventures, and ability to pursue risky new technologies without jeopardizing the survival of the firm, which is greater in larger than in smaller firms. It is perhaps for the latter reason that the eight non-participant firms known to have been active in the micromachine industry since the early 1990s are on average larger than the participant firms: The group of eight has a mean (median) number of 83,452 (35,779) employees and mean (median) sales of ¥2,862 billion (¥1,335 billion). Size may have helped these firms compensate for the absence of government support in the context of the public R&D consortium and the attendant higher financial risk of pursuing micromachine technology without government subsidies. Firm size thus seems to be more related to time of entry rather than to network shape, though only further research will be able to provide a conclusive answer.

The overall conclusion of this discussion of firm-to-firm networking is that firms that participated in the consortium seem to enjoy an advantage over non-participants in terms of number of connections and centrality to the network. This advantage is particularly pronounced in the context of networking about technology, which requires relatively higher levels of trust. While participants network more about technology with other firms than non-participants, other measures such as perceived importance of ties and contact frequency are almost the same across groups.

Consortium participants versus non-participants in 2004: Firms networking with other actors

In terms of ties with nonfirms, the major difference between participant and non-participant firms is that the former enjoy more ties with government agencies. The median number of ties with government reported by participants is 3, that reported by non-participants, 0 (Table 6.5). The ranges for government ties for both groups are similar, with participants having between 0 and 4 ties, and non-participants drawing on 0 to 3 ties. There is no tangible difference between the groups in terms of number of ties with associations and universities, with median values uniformly at 1. Only the range of ties with universities is slightly larger for participants with a top value of 7 as compared with 6 for non-participants.

The kinds of information exchanged with nonfirms vary considerably across the two groups. Participants tend to concentrate on market information when networking with nonfirms, while non-participants focus on technology (Table 6.6). It seems that non-participants turn to the nonfirm actors to obtain the technology information that they can probably not obtain from other firms. Participant firms, by contrast, draw relatively more heavily on other firms for technological information, which may reduce their need to look for it in nonfirm actors.

Information trade balances are relatively close for associations and universities, though non-participants seem to gain relatively more from associations and relatively less from universities (Table 6.5). There is more variation across groups in the balance with government agencies, with participants receiving more information than they give out at a value of 0.35, but non-participants giving more out than they are receiving at a value of −0.17. The underlying reasons are not clear, as Japanese government agencies typically take great pains to be seen as showing equitable treatment. However, given the small sample size, even this large variation is not statistically significant.

Importance scores for associations show some variation across groups, with non-participants rating them at 2.83 (*important*) and participants, at 2.62 (*important minus*) (Table 6.5). The perceived importance of government ties is rated *important* by both groups, with both assigning a score of 3.00. The ratings for universities vary somewhat, with participants assigning a mean score of 2.83 (*important*) and non-participants reporting a score of 2.55 (*important minus*). None of these differences are statistically significant.

Contact frequencies also exhibit some variation. Participants seem to contact associations about once in 9 weeks (2.38), while non-participants contact them about every 8 weeks (2.50) (Table 6.5). Participants talk to governments about once every 10 weeks (2.22), while non-participants do so about quarterly (2.00). Participants seem to talk more to universities, with contacts perhaps every 7 weeks (2.58), as opposed to once every 9 weeks (2.36) for non-participants.

Interesting to note is that trade balance, importance scores, and contact frequencies follow the same basic pattern of variation across the groups. Each paired comparison suggests that non-participants may be networking somewhat more with associations than participants, while the inverse may be true for universities.

Overall, these data suggest that participant firms may be somewhat better connected with nonfirm actors than non-participant firms, a finding that is in line with what we have seen for networking with firms. Contents of these ties varies considerably across the groups, with participants focusing on market data and non-participants, on technology.

Consortium participants versus non-participants in 2004: Qualitative assessment

The main divergence in networking patterns between participants and non-participants thus lies in their connections with other firms. What is the origin of these differences in firm-to-firm networking? The interview data suggest that the persistence of some ties beyond the termination of the formal consortium was facilitated by three mechanisms that came to bear on joint participants in the consortium: the fostering of mutual understanding, the development of personal ties, and the building of a sense of community. By contrast, non-participant firms do not benefit from these dynamics. They are not seen as part of the community, and their ability to engage in reciprocal exchange relationships is limited by perceived lack of expertise and sincerity.

For noncompeting firms, consortium experience provided information for judging whether to keep or disband a tie. For one, firms were able to observe who was developing what kinds of technologies, which then allowed them to choose as networking partners those with a complementary technological portfolio. A firm interested in developing micro-optical devices using micromachine technology may thus decide to form an informal research group with a firm that is strong in actuators and another that excels in power transmission technology. At the same time, consortium experience was also useful for establishing the likelihood of being able to make these exchange relationships work in practice:

Because there is the project experience, you understand what the other is like. Without the project, you would not. Because you participated in the project, you know the kind of technology and the faces. What kind of person the other is. [The person from] company X is like this. His manager is like this, and the people working under him are like this. They think like this. Well, with these folks, given their culture, well, let's tie up.

Collaboration during the consortium is thus akin to a probationary period during which firms can sniff each other out and gain what one interviewee called "a holistic understanding." This understanding, in turn, gives rise to a "sense of security" (*anshinkan*), which is particularly important in Japanese social relations given high levels of discomfort with uncertainty (cf. Hofstede 1997).

Thick information about possible networking partners is established not only through the process of direct cooperation in consortium research, but also through mutual exposure in committee meetings:

At the time when we were doing the project, there were quite a lot of closely-knit meetings concerning the project within the Micromachine Center. Obviously people from various companies are in those project teams, so if one goes to those meetings, quite a bit of talk about how to advance the project and about other topics came up. So you got connections.

Further opportunities for members to get to know one another arise out of formal events associated with the project and the informal barhopping (*nijikai*) that often follows them, as already mentioned in Chapter 4.

Along with these processes went personalization of social capital among consortium members. While some connections were maintained after the expiration of the R&D consortium by conscious choice, others have persevered through friendship and acquaintance. As one interviewee put it, "we participated in the network [of the consortium] as a company, but after it had ended, it became a personal network." These friendships can create fairly strong ties across firms:

It is easy [to contact them.] Especially in the case of this project, because we have done quite a bit together, the connections become good, sometimes to the point that it is easier to talk with them than with people of one's own company.

These connections are further being reinforced through face-to-face meetings at the Micromachine Center, which have continued on a regular basis since the end of the consortium, though at lower levels of frequency and intensity.

Consistent with findings in other contexts (e.g., Bouty 2000), it is these personalized ties that seem to produce the most valuable information exchange. In most cases, networkers seem to wait for a suitable opportunity to present itself in order to bring up a certain topic with a friend or acquaintance. For instance, one interviewee had used the context of an association meeting the day before the interview to obtain information from an acquaintance about latest developments in the acquaintance's firm's actuator research. However, some firms are more proactive in leveraging personal connections, for instance, by calling up friends at other companies to ask for technical assistance or to request introductions to others who could be helpful. Either way, personalized ties tend to produce thicker information than would be available through more formal channels, as they may lead to sharing of proprietary, non-public information and the provision of relevant background information useful for interpreting and understanding these data.

There is also evidence that the consortium has resulted in the building of a community spirit (*nakama ishiki*) and thus bounded solidarity among the participants. This manifests itself in a delineation of an ingroup of firms that participated in the consortium against an outgroup of non-participants. Within this group, there is "a spirit of answering [information requests] with goodwill and without lying," it is perceived to be "easy to talk in a relaxed atmosphere," and when information cannot be shared, firms will remain silent on a query rather than tell lies.

The most salient outgroup in this context consists of firms that are active in the micromachine industry but did not participate in the micromachine consortium. These firms do not appear to be fully accepted as peers. In the words of a representative of a non-participant firm,

They worked together for close to 10 years on the project and have the same sense of community *(nakama ishiki)*, so those people feel they are part of the same web. I believe it is absolutely not the case that they, how shall I put it, feel that people who were not at that time in the same project are members.

This view is echoed in comments by members of the ingroup of participant firms:

I believe many people became new members [of the Micromachine Center after the consortium] with the feeling "I wonder what a micromachine is. Shall we try it out a bit?" And so, since they after all do not know the world of micromachines that so far has been small, even if they want to get into the community they cannot. [...] This is because there is a sense of community [among the participant firms].

This latter statement also offers an insight into the underlying causes of the delineation of ingroup vs. outgroup as well as a relatively lower ability of non-participant firms to form ties: perceived lack of expertise and sincerity.

All firms, participant or not, identified as their main criterion for selecting a new networking partner (as opposed to maintaining an existing one, which we have seen to be governed in part by personal affinity) the possibility of obtaining what one does not have, such as new pieces of technology or access to business opportunities. There is consensus that as a consequence of their joint research during the R&D consortium, participant firms possess much more advanced technology and facilities than non-participant firms. This makes participant firms an attractive target from the perspective of non-participant firms, but not vice versa: Nonparticipant firms are seen as having nothing of interest to offer:

As for non-participant firms, with what we said earlier, it is a give and take of information, and in the end, they do not have much to give.

This reduces the ability of non-participant firms to establish reciprocal exchange relationships, as especially participant firms show concern that information given to non-participant firms may not be reciprocated.

This issue is compounded by doubts among participant firms whether non-participant firms can be trusted. Nonparticipant firms are generally seen as opportunistic players that are scouting for profit opportunities without showing much commitment to the industry. At least in some cases, this interpretation is correct, as evident in the remarks of an interviewee from a non-participant firm:

There is the view that if there is something that could become one of our products, let's participate more earnestly. For now, we joined the Micromachine Center for information collection.

On the side of participant firms, these scanning activities have given rise to suspiciousness of the motives of non-participant firms. There is a sense that non-participant firms are trying to get at the fruits of the 10 years of joint research in the public R&D consortium without expending the requisite efforts and resources themselves:

They want to do this business but do not have the technology, so in order to get their hands on that technology, they came to have ties.

The ability or willingness of non-participant firms to engage in fruitful cooperation about technology is discounted:

For example, yesterday I went to the Micromachine Center to attend the X Committee meeting. The person sitting next to me was a person who did not do the project, a person who joined later. I believe that people like that probably do not really talk about technology in a forthright way.

This lack of trust in the sincerity of non-participants may be related to the absence of a track record in the industry. Unlike participant firms, non-participant firms were not able to use the project period to prove themselves to be sincere cooperation partners. At the same time, the notion that non-participant firms are opportunists without firm commitment to the industry is also likely to raise doubts whether a long-term reciprocal relationship is possible. If there is a perception that the exchange partner may quit the industry, and thus the exchange relationship, at any time, it becomes uncertain whether any favor granted today may ever be reciprocated. The "shadow of the future" thus disappears, and with it the incentive to start building an exchange relationship.

In sum, the persistence of some ties beyond consortium termination seems to have been facilitated by the exposure of consortium participants to three mechanisms: the fostering of mutual understanding, the development of personal ties, and the building of a sense of community. By contrast, non-participant firms seem to be hampered in their networking activities by lack of acceptance as part of the community and a relatively limited ability to engage in reciprocal exchange relationships.

Discussion and conclusion

The departure point of this chapter was the question of how patterns of coordination spread to new industries in the Japanese political economy. As this chapter illustrates using longitudinal data from the micromachine industry, government-sponsored R&D consortia may constitute part of the answer in at least two ways. First, for the duration of the consortium, coordination levels are elevated because participant firms are required to coordinate and cooperate. Evidence of a drop in networking after expiration of the consortium is consistent with this notion, which was already introduced in the context of the life cycle hypothesis of the previous chapter.

Second, and more importantly with respect to the longer term, the available evidence is consistent with the notion that consortium participation seems to help build trust, and thus coordination and cooperation, among the participants. The evidence suggests that micromachine firms that participated in the R&D consortium still enjoyed better network connectivity in 2004, especially for the kinds of information exchange requiring higher levels of trust, than firms that did not participate in the consortium. Indications of this effect are visible for networking among firms, but also for networking with nonfirm actors. Interview data are in line with these findings, suggesting that the consortium contributed to an increase in trust among the participant firms by enabling them to develop mutual understanding, strike up personalized ties, and build a sense of community.

Government policy may thus play an active role in facilitating the rise of coordination in infant industries. As argued before, this approach is probably suboptimal from the perspective of the economy as a whole. It is true that R&D consortia may increase research productivity and the number of patents within the perimeter of the project (Branstetter and Sakakibara 2002). The risk is that such research, while more efficient, may lead the entire industry down a technological path that ultimately turns out unviable. At the same time, by inducing early convergence of infant industries on institutional orthodoxy of coordination, government policy is likely to deprive the political economy of a potential source of institutional innovation and experimentation that may evolve new ways of organizing and conducting research and development and business activities. This constraint on institutional innovation may have an adverse impact on the viability of the new industry. In addition, viewed from the level of the economy as a whole, it represents a lost opportunity to accelerate the rate of institutional adjustment toward levels seen in the less coordinated economies.

7 | *Conclusion*

I BEGAN THIS BOOK by asking in Chapter 2 how much institutional change had actually occurred in the Japanese business system in the fifteen years of economic pain since the burst of the bubble economy in 1990. To answer the question empirically, I followed Redding's (2005) business systems framework and explored institutional change at three levels of determination: culture, business environment, and business system. At the cultural level, the framework calls for analysis of three categories: rationale of business, identity, and authority. The evidence suggests that in terms of rationale, society as well as the senior executives who are presently running big corporate Japan continue to place the interests of stakeholders over those of shareholders. For identity, the data are consistent with continued group-orientation and identification with the company. The data on authority suggest that it remains strongly linked to age and sex. Education levels probably represent a third element linked to authority in society, but no data on this question are available.

At the second level of determination, the business environment, the analysis involves exploring trends in the categories of financial capital, human capital, and social capital. The Japanese financial system continues to be bank-led, with about two-thirds of corporate funding still drawn from banks rather than the markets. In terms of human capital, the Japanese school system has undergone a series of structural reform whose impact on the system is not yet clear. On-the-job training seems to have remained widespread. Industrial relations have mirrored world-wide trends toward weaker unionization, with Japanese unions continuing to be company-centered and little prone to strikes. Lifetime employment has survived its many obituaries in the financial press, employment protection is still high, and unemployment protection, still low. Social capital on balance seems to show a deepening, with higher association density and higher expressions of institutional trust. Interpersonal trust seems to have weakened since 1993, but has strengthened relative to 1983.

At the third level of determination, the business system itself, I finally find evidence of a system component that, in part, deviates considerably from the status in 1990: ownership. Virtually all of the stocks sold off by distressed Japanese financial institutions over the 1990s and early 2000s seem to have found their way into the hands of foreign shareholders. About one-fifth of corporate Japan is now foreign-owned, which is likely to represent a source of pressure for institutional change, especially on the corporate government front. However, there seems to have been limited implementation of corporate governance changes, and there continues to be no market for corporate governance, as indicated by the virtual absence of hostile takeovers. The evidence further suggests that on balance, the unwinding of cross-shareholdings in the market as a whole largely bypassed the six major business groups. In the networking box, the data show no clear evidence of an unraveling of business groups. No recent evidence seems available of trends in vertical *keiretsu*. In management, finally, we find strengthened employer-employee inter-dependence and evidence for the survival of the seniority principle.

The picture emerging from these findings is hardly one of radical or transformational change. The one major development, and with it source of pressure for institutional change, is the vastly increased role of foreign ownership in corporate Japan. Counterpressures emerge from three sources: First, the evaluation of rationale suggests a preference in favor of maintaining the existing institutional structure including and especially at the level of the corporate elite. Second, there is reason to believe that part of Japan's competitive advantage is embedded in complementary institutional structures (cf. Hall and Soskice 2001). Institutional change affecting these complementarities may thus prove costly. Third, the system shows a clear proclivity for societal coordination as a consequence of risk aversion, which grows out of various elements such as long-term employment, indirect finance, and the stakeholder value view of the firm. Various forms of firm-to-firm networking, facilitated by high levels of trust, are built into the business system and play an important role in enabling the flow of information, norms, and values necessary for coordination.

While societal coordination may be desirable for the individual firm in the context of mitigating risk, it can have an adverse impact on the economic performance of the system as a whole by slowing the rate of institutional adjustment. As discussed in Chapter 3, adjustment in coordinated processes typically occurs through bargaining within and among organizational actors such as employer associations, labor unions, interest groups, and government. The outcome is usually institutional innovation that is uniform across the business system, relatively riskier to undertake, and more time-intensive. This contrasts with autonomous processes, in which actors initiate and implement institutional change without the need for active coordination or bargaining with one or several external actors. This mode produces considerable initial variety, which represents a hedge against decision-making risk, and the process is relatively time-efficient in terms of initial response because decisions lie in the hands of the proverbial "man on the spot." Societal coordination is thus likely to go hand-in-hand with relatively slower rates of adjustment. These rates were apparently sufficient in the relatively stable postwar years through the 1970s. Since then, however, they seem to have difficulty keeping pace with an increased need for adjustment in general and more radical adjustment in particular linked to heightened levels of dynamism in the environment. The empirical evidence is consistent with this notion, with economic indicators of institutional fit being negatively correlated with levels of societal coordination.

Micro-level actors such as individuals and firms are not powerless in the face of economic costs emanating from slow adjustment responses. One option for them is to exert political pressure through collective action, in which case they represent an additional party to the coordinated adjustment process that may tilt the table in favor of accelerated change or at least provide for compensation. The other option is for them to take autonomous and apolitical action that is not aimed at institutional change at the system level, but at providing relief from institutional misalignment at the micro-level. Three basic options of taking action exist, each in legal and illegal form: abatement, diminution, and exit. As these responses become widespread, they tend to threaten the legitimacy of the extant ruling structure and may thus help build pressure for institutional adjustment. Empirical evidence on the shadow economy and foreign direct investment outflows suggests that these kinds of responses tend to be positively correlated with degree of societal coordination. Autonomous micro-level action is thus likely to represent a mechanism that helps counteract the propensity of coordinated systems to show relatively slow rates of institutional change.

The Japanese economy, however, is not only highly coordinated, but also shows very low levels of micro-level action that could serve to speed up the coordinated adjustment process. This seems to be linked to at least three reasons: geographic location making exit strategies relatively difficult, continued legitimacy of the extant system, and illegitimacy of deviant micro-level action, with social networks as key mechanism for monitoring and preventing deviant behavior. As a consequence, the delaying influence of coordination comes fully to bear on the institutional adjustment process in Japan.

Social networks emerge as a key component in these deliberations. They enable coordination in three important ways. First, they allow the sharing of information among firms and other actors such as the state. Even if coordinated behavior is not the explicitly desired outcome of this kind of process, the social construction of information being shared may lead to a consensus emerging around one possible behavioral option. Second, they facilitate active coordination, for instance, in coordinated adjustment processes. Third, their role as conduits of information, norms, and values makes them monitoring devices and transmitters of isomorphic pressures.

Understanding coordination in the Japanese business system thus requires understanding the various forms of social networks within it. Key mechanisms already known from the literature include business groups and vertical *keiretsu*, but also R&D consortia and the state-associations-firms nexus. Chapter 4 briefly reviews the coordination aspects of these networks and then introduces an additional type that has previously been underexplored in the literature: intra-industry loops. Intra-industry loops link firms in a given industry with one another as well as with other actors and organizations involved in the industry, such as associations and academics. Their formation is aided by industry associations and, as illustrated in Chapter 6, R&D consortia, which allow firm representatives to meet and develop the informal ties characteristic of this form of networking. The importance of this form of networking to Japanese firms is underscored by the fact that larger firms tend to maintain dedicated personnel for collecting information through these networks. In many firms, these mid-level managers can be found in the planning department or the external affairs department.

A comparison in Chapter 5 of intra-industry loop networking across industries of different life cycle stages – micromachines, semiconductor equipment, and apparel – suggests that loop characteristics appear to change with lifecycle stage, which is consistent with the idea that industries of different ages tend to coordinate on different dimensions and use coordination as a buffer against uncertainty. For example, perceived network importance and frequency of use of network ties tend to be higher in sunrise and sunset industries than in mature industries, as the former face greater uncertainty about the future course of the industry. Similarly, networking contents – the kinds of information exchanged – seem to evolve over time in patterns that are consistent with the needs of firms at the respective life cycle stage.

Evidence from the micromachine industry presented in Chapter 6 illustrates how the Japanese government may help build intra-industry networks – and thus reinforce coordination in the Japanese business system – by sponsoring R&D consortia in the early stages of an industry. Questionnaire and interview data from the micromachine industry suggest that firms that participated in the consortium continue to network more extensively with one another after termination of the consortium than firms that did not participate in the consortium. This implies that by inducing competing firms to cooperate toward a common goal, the consortium may have contributed to laying the foundations for increased intra-industry networking and thus higher potential for coordination among the participant firms. While this may de facto serve to extend the life of the R&D consortium after its formal expiration date, with concomitant benefits for research productivity (cf. Branstetter and Sakakibara 2002), it is also likely to create a basis for higher levels of societal coordination in new industries and thus lower rates of institutional adjustment.

Predictions for the Japanese business system

The most straightforward prediction for the future of the Japanese business system growing out of these discussions is that on average and all else equal, Japan is likely to continue to see institutional change proceeding at relatively slower rates than those seen in many other advanced industrialized nations. Societal coordination is a structural constraint that acts as a moderator on the rate of institutional change. That does not mean that institutional change will always occur at very slow speed, nor that the speed of adjustment is constant across time. An illustrative, though admittedly imperfect, analogy may be to construe of institutional change in Japan as driving a car with the parking brake engaged. One can still get from one place to another, and stepping on the accelerator does increase the speed with which this occurs. But the minimum level of engine power needed to produce movement is higher, and the maximum attainable speed is lower, than without the brake engaged. While the role of political leadership is important in spurring on institutional change processes in Japan, even under a government with a strong reformist agenda, "fast" change is likely to be "fast" only relative to Japanese standards. Prime Minister Koizumi's much ballyhooed postal reforms provide a fitting illustration. Passed into law in 2005 after years of deliberation, reforms will begin only in 2007 and will not be completed until 2017, assuming no changes to the reform package once Mr. Koizumi retires from office.

This prediction is, of course, contingent on a continued role of societal coordination in institutional adjustment processes in the Japanese business system. In the political world, Mr. Koizumi appears to be working on weakening factions (cf. Curtis 1999) within the LDP and limiting the extent of backroom wheeling and dealing. The result may well be a more streamlined and less coordinated decision-making process within the LDP, though it remains to be seen whether these reforms will stick once Mr. Koizumi resigns his post as party president in 2006 as required by party rules. At the same time, Mr. Koizumi's zeal for reforms seems to be mostly limited to the LDP and government agencies. Neither Mr. Koizumi nor any of the major political parties seem intent on destroying the coordinated character of the Japanese *business system*. And even if a reformist government somehow enacted the requisite laws and regulations against all opposition such a move would likely provoke, much of the coordination structure would be likely to survive by continuing at an informal level.

Probably the surest way to eliminate coordination in the business system would be if firms themselves started to opt out. This is unlikely for at least two reaons. First, as discussed in Chapter 2, coordination helps reduce risk, which in turn enables them to maintain long-term employment and financial relations and thus pursue as the rationale of business stakeholder value with employees as the main beneficiaries. Second, as mentioned in Chapter 3, non-conformity with the norm of coordination imposes social and possibly economic costs on the deviant. The incentives to coordinate are thus immediate, which in the view of most firms seems to outweigh the indirectly incurred costs associated with slower rates of institutional change.

The odds for an acceleration of institutional adjustment in the business system thus seem to be long and, at least for the moment, lengthening. A major factor in this development is that macroeconomic recovery may finally, after three false starts, be taking hold. While recovery does not contribute to the abatement of institutional misalignments, improved economic conditions can help micro-level actors sustain and compensate the associated costs. As more and more firms, including Japan's banks, emerge from the red and employment as well as employment compensation packages pick up, some of the economic pressure for institutional change is released, and the perceived urgency of institutional change is diminished.

In the past, Japan could to some degree rely on external pressure, especially from the United States, to spur on institutional change processes in the business system. During the late 1980s and 1990s, the United States expressed concern with its ever-increasing bilateral trade deficit with Japan and the inability of many U.S. manufacturers to gain a foothold in Japan (e.g., Lincoln 1999). Coordination features such as business groups and vertical *keiretsu* were identified as structural impediments to trade and became a hotly debated bone of contention. Later, especially during the Asian financial crisis, Japan faced intense criticism for its inability to set its economy back on a sustainable growth path. While much of this pressure never bore any fruit, some of it did help break political deadlock and resulted in institutional change (Schoppa 1997).

Over recent years, however, economic relations between the two nations have become more harmonious, and there is little reason to believe that they could return to their earlier acerbic state. This appears to be the consequence of several factors. First, it seems that the lost decade has demonstrated to the United States that there is no threat of Japan challenging its preeminence in the Pacific. No one today considers it realistic that Japan's economy could surpass that of the United States in size. This stands in marked contrast with the atmosphere of fear in the United States in the 1980s and early 1990s that spawned now unthinkable discussions about impending military conflict (e.g., Friedman and LeBard 1991).

Second, Japan has considerable leverage over the U.S. government through its holding of large volumes of U.S. Treasury bonds. The possibility, no matter how remote, that Japan could sell of a sizeable proportion of them and thus trigger a dollar devaluation, with all its adverse knock-on effects on the United States and the world economy, is likely to discourage the United States from taking too controversial a posture vis-à-vis Japan.

Third, and possibly most important, the United States needs Japan as a regional ally against a China that is increasingly seen as an emerging economic and military rival. The United States showed high tolerance of nonliberal economic structures like Japan's during the Cold War, when it needed allies in the containment of the Soviet Union (cf. Ruggie 1982). While there is no official policy of Chinese containment, Japan is nonetheless a frontline ally in the apparently growing U.S. rivalry with China. This may reduce the propensity of the United States to put pressure for institutional change on Japan.

With the recovery alleviating some of the costs of institutional misalignment and trade frictions having dwindled to low levels, the most salient remaining source of pressure for change is the foreign shareholders that now own about one-fifth of corporate Japan and are pressing firms to give more weight to shareholder value. In this, their interests are diametrically opposed to the stakeholder rationale of business held by most Japanese people, but in particular also the corporate leadership (Chapter 2). How will the conflict pan out?

The recent developments in corporate governance in Japan may offer a clue. Many of the amendments to corporate governance rules have been optional in nature. One view is that this is a sign that the Japanese business system is becoming more pluralistic (Jackson and Miyajima 2004). An alternative interpretation, and I believe in light of our discussion of coordination the more likely one, is that the absence of coordination on corporate governance reform bears witness to its perceived insignificance for the Japanese business system *as a whole* (as opposed to individual firms). If corporate governance reform were considered vital for the future of Japanese business, we would probably have seen a massive movement toward reform, as no company would want to be left out. This has not occurred. On the contrary, METI is doing its level best to reduce the need for corporate governance reform by studying how to increase defenses against hostile takeovers.

The most likely short- to medium-term evolutionary path of the Japanese business system is thus incremental adaptive change from the status quo for most firms and selective adoption of shareholder-oriented elements by those firms with high proportions of international shareholders. It is these latter firms that are most exposed to pressure for corporate governance reform, and the new laws are designed to allow them to meet investors' demands. Some firms – mostly mavericks such as Sony – may embrace the reforms. Given the sources of rigidity in the system, though, most are likely to be less enthusiastic. I predict for these firms, in the time-honored custom of *honne* (actual intent) and *tatemae* (professed position), a considerable amount of "decoupling" (Westphal and Zajac 1994; Zajac and Westphal 2004) of announced or purportedly implemented reforms and actual practice.

In the long run, however, the question of a fundamental reordering of the Japanese business system is likely to resurface. The challenges posed by the transition to the information technology age, the advance of globalization, the coming on-stream of China and India, and societal ageing are unlikely to go away. The key question for Japan is whether the present period of high-velocity changes in the broader business context will eventually be followed by new period of relative stability, as was the case for most of the Cold War period. If the answer is yes, Japan's coordinated structure, with some adaptive changes, may find itself with another lease on life. The opportunity cost of waiting out the present dynamics until stabilization occurs is likely to be considerable, but Japanese society may be prepared to accept it.

The problem with this wait-and-see strategy is that nobody knows what the future holds in store. It is possible that the stability under which coordinated market economies seem to thrive may never return. The preference for coordination, which is partly based on risk aversion, thus leads Japan to place a highly risky bet about the future of the Japanese business system on an uncertain expectation of renewed tranquility. It seems unlikely that future generations of Japanese will appreciate the inherent irony if the bet goes sour and stability fails to return. But societal coordination is not a binary choice. There are many gradations, as evident in Hall and Gingerich's

(2004) coordination index. The least risky approach for Japan may thus be to hedge the bet by creating somewhat more room for autonomous changes in the Japanese business system – not to destroy societal coordination, but to save it by increasing its adaptive responsiveness. However, since such a step in itself would constitute institutional change and thus involve high levels of societal coordination, the path to its adoption is likely to be a lengthy and arduous one.

Appendix

Chapter 2: List of interviewed executives

- Yoshikazu Hanawa, Chairman, Nissan
- Toru Hashimoto, former Chairman, Fuji Bank
- Terukazu Inoue, Special Auditor, Toyota
- Takeo Inokuchi, Chairman and President, Mitsui Sumitomo Insurance
- Masami Ito, President, Ito Ham
- Tetsuro Kawakami, former Chairman, Sumitomo Electric
- Yorihiko Kojima, Senior Executive Vice President, Mitsubishi Corp.
- Akira Uehara, President, Taisho Seiyaku
- Kaneichi Maebara, former board member, Sumitomo Life Insurance, Chairman, Sumitomo Life Research Institute
- Minoru Makihara, Chairman, Mitsubishi Corp.
- Hiroshi Nagata, Executive Vice President & Board Member, Mitsui & Co.
- Taizo Nishimuro, Chairman, Toshiba
- Akira Nishikawa, President & CEO, Mitsubishi Materials
- Koichi Ohmuro, Senior Managing Director & Senior Executive Officer, Mitsui Fudosan
- Masahiro Sakane, President, Komatsu Machinery
- Teruo Shimamura, President & COO, Nikon
- Yasuhiko Watanabe, former board member, Bank of Tokyo Mitsubishi, Senior Managing Director, Mitsubishi Estate

Note: Titles as of the time of the interviews (2002–2003)

Chapter 5: Notes on data collection

I obtained information about loop networking in the case industries through a total of 101 interviews and 78 questionnaire replies, mostly

191

from firms, but also from other actors involved in each industry's loop.

Any firm or nonfirm with regular and substantial involvement in a case industry was defined as being part of that industry's loop. "Substantial" means that the firm or nonfirm in question has dedicated at least part of its assets to activities directly related to the industry such as manufacturing of products (but not parts), research, or regulatory oversight. "Firm" in this context denotes companies producing, or preparing to produce, micromachines, semiconductor equipment, or apparel. Banks and the press are companies as well, but for the present purpose, I include them in categories of their own.

Data collection from firms followed a two-pronged approach: Collection of interview and questionnaire data from a manageable group of firms, and supplementary collection of questionnaire data only from a larger group of firms. All data were collected in 1997 and 1998. A second wave of data collection in the micromachine industry in 2004 – analyzed in Chapter 6 – has yielded data suggesting that the fundamental characteristics of loop networking have not changed since. This is also consistent with the finding in Chapter 2 of high structural inertia preventing quick change in the Japanese business system.

In the micromachine industry, I approached all 22 firms participating in the public R&D consortium on micromachine technology for interviews and questionnaires. In addition, four companies (Ford, JUKI, Komatsu, Sony) that were members of the MMC but did not participate in the consortium received questionnaire requests. In the semiconductor equipment industry, sampling for both interviews and supplementary questionnaires was random from the SEMI Japan catalogue. In the apparel industry, no comprehensive roster of all firms exists. Data collection thus focused on the then 165 JAIC members, with a random sample of firms selected for interviews and the remainder of firms receiving supplementary questionnaire request.

To complement the information provided by firms in all three industries, I further interviewed government agencies, associations, universities, reporters, financial organizations, and politicians in each industry's loop. Several of these actors also provided questionnaire responses.

Questionnaire respondents reported on networking activities of their business or organization. For each firm or organization in the same industry, respondents indicated the frequency of information exchange (5-point Likert scale), the perceived importance of information exchange with that particular partner to their firm or organization (4-point Likert scale), the direction of information flow (5-point Likert scale), and the kinds of information exchanged (technology, market and trends, politics, other). All respondents received instructions to report only direct ties, that is, networking that does not occur through or within the context of the work of another organization such as an industry association.

The total number of interviews conducted is 101. Of these, 28 relate to micromachines, 40, to semiconductor equipment, 23, to apparel, and 10, to all three or general issues. Total response rates for interviews are 77.8 percent for micromachines, 58.8 percent for semiconductor equipment, and 48.9 percent for apparel.

The total number of questionnaire responses is 78. Of these, 31 relate to micromachines, 28, to semiconductor equipment, and 19, to apparel. Response rates for questionnaires requested after interviews are 91.3, 85.7, and 72.2 percent, respectively. As one would expect, response rates for mailed questionnaires came in at much lower levels, namely 41.7, 2.4, and 4.7 percent, respectively. The micromachine response rate is still relatively high because I was able to approach a number of respondents with introductions from METI or both, METI and MMC.

As is typical of this kind of research, I cannot fully rule out response bias. However, it seems unlikely to be a major issue for the resultant data pool. The major cause of rejection of interview requests was lack of time, which is unrelated to networking characteristics. In my interviews, I observed no major differences in terms of reported networking characteristics between firms that did submit question-naires subsequent to an interview and those that did not. For the mailed questionnaires, my experience with interview requests as well as follow-up phone calls suggest that lack of time and especially lack of trust is likely to have been the major cause of nonparticipation. Both of these are unrelated to loop networking and thus unlikely to be the source of response bias.

Chapter 6: Notes on data collection and method

Data collection for the second wave of data from the micromachine industry occurred in 2004, about 3 years after the expiry of the micromachine R&D consortium. As in 1997, I employed both questionnaires and interviews.

To ensure comparability, the questionnaire followed the same format as in 1997. The only alteration was that the list of possible networking contacts was updated to reflect changes in the Micromachine Center membership roster and structural reforms in the government bureaucracy. Since I was already a known quantity in the industry by the time of the second wave, I received active support from the Micromachine Center, which arranged for me to give a lecture to its members to (re)establish my credentials and actively handled the distribution and collection of the questionnaires.

I followed up with interviews in which the respondents were interviewed in the context of a debrief of the preliminary findings. With my track record established in the first wave, it was no longer necessary to rely on the interviews as a means to demonstrate my trustworthiness in order to obtain questionnaire data. Instead, I could use the interviews to generate deeper insights into the meaning and mechanisms underlying the phenomena evident in the questionnaire data. In particular, I sought to generate deeper insights into the questions of how networking patterns changed with the expiration of the public R&D consortium, why ties were being maintained and how new ties were initiated, and how R&D consortium participants differed in their networking patterns and attendant characteristics from firms that had not participated in the consortium. The interviews were semi-structured in format (cf. Redding 1990), that is, they combined a fixed interview schedule with flexible order and leeway for interviewees to introduce, and myself to pursue further, aspects not included in the interview schedule. This format is particularly useful for the kinds of exploratory research undertaken here because it allows for the discovery and pursuit of issues not previously known and thus not included in the interview schedule.

As in the previous wave, questionnaires and interviews were handled by the *madoguchi* of the respective firm. In some cases, a colleague with experience in the industry joined the *madoguchi* for the interview. To ensure the integrity of the data, all respondents as well as the representatives of the Micromachine Center were only told that the objective of the study was to generate insights into the evolution of networking in their industry. They were kept blind of the specific objective of the project.

Targets of the survey and interviews were all firms with regular and substantial involvement in the micromachine industry. "Substantial" means that the firm in question has dedicated at least part of its assets to activities directly related to the industry such as manufacturing of products (but not parts) or research. Of the 41 supporting members of the Micromachine Center at the time of the field research, 32 met these requirements (Table). Of the remaining 9 members, 3 were struck from the list for not being firms, 1 because it reported just having ceased activities in the micromachine industry, 2 for being suppliers to micromachine producers without activity in the industry as such, and 3 for belonging to other industries (1 bank, 1 natural resources exploration firm, 1 firm organizing industrial exhibitions).

From these 32 firms, I obtained 20 questionnaire responses, yielding a response rate of 63%. Of these firms, 13 had participated in the government-sponsored micromachine R&D consortium, while 7 had not. Of the 20 firms providing questionnaire data, 16 were interviewed in person, and 1 provided a written response to the interview questions. Response rate for the interviews was thus 53% relative to the full population, and 85% relative to those firms providing a questionnaire response. 2 of the 3 firms not providing an interview had participated in the consortium, 1 had not. Interviews lasted on average about one hour and were recorded with the consent of the interviewees on condition of confidentiality. All interviews were conducted in Japanese.

Analysis of the questionnaire data follows the approach taken in the last chapter for the ties firms report having with the different kinds of actors, complemented by structural network analysis for network-ing among firms using UCINET 6 (Borgatti, Everett, and Freeman 2002). As in the last chapter, I compare medians of the number of ties reported (outdegree) and of means of the characteristics of the reported ties such as information content, balance, importance, and frequency. In addition, the relatively high response rates for both waves allow for structural network analysis of firm ties with one another in terms of degree and centrality. The network matrices for firm ties are 80.6% symmetric for the first wave and 86.7% symmetric for the second wave, meaning that in the vast majority of cases in which one actor reported the presence or absence of a tie with another actor, the other actor reported the same. This high level of symmetry is an indication of the reliability of the questionnaire responses. Given the reciprocal nature of loop networking, I symmetrize the network matrix for the structural analysis, which also allows us to generate some insights into the network parameters of those firms that did not provide a questionnaire response but with which other firms reported maintaining ties. Statistical significance was tested for differences in information balance, importance, and frequency values as laid out earlier, plus for the differences observed in structural analysis measures.

Interpretative content analysis of the interview data was used to generate insights into the mechanisms and processes of social capital formation evident in the interview data. To avoid loss of meaning in translation, all analysis was performed on the original Japanese-language transcriptions of my interviews. I extracted all propositions about social capital contained in these transcriptions and grouped them by thematic content. Given the exploratory nature of this study, I did not a priori impose categories, but allowed them to emerge (cf. Redding 1990). The extracted propositions were then reviewed repeatedly with the aim of refining and rationalizing the coding categories. For instance, a proposition initially coded in the category of "influence of the project on present-day relationships/ties, information exchange, trust" might subsequently be assigned to the subcategory "project helped create personal ties." Coding reliability was verified by having a Japanese research assistant with no prior exposure to the project extract and code propositions. The research assistant received about 30 minutes of explanations of the project and the coding process before coding a random sample of the interview transcriptions amounting to 6.7% of the combined total length of all transcriptions. The percentage of intercoder agreement was 92.3%. This compares to an expected agreement of 20.1% by chance alone. Cohen's kappa (Cohen 1960) is 0.90, well above the commonly applied minimum threshold of 0.70.

Chapters 5 and 6: Supplementary analyses

This section supplements the analyses of two key measures used in Chapters 5 and 6, perceived importance and contact frequency. While Chapters 5 and 6 approach these measures from the perspective of the network as a whole, the following table presents the picture from the viewpoint of the average firm in the respective population. In other

Importance and Frequency by Average Firm

		All Ties	Firms	Associations	Government	Universities	Banks	Press
Importance	Micromachines	2.76	2.73	3.25	2.83	2.66	–	–
	Semiconductor Equipment	2.61	2.86	2.59	2.23	2.76	2.67	2.52
	Apparel	2.73	2.45	2.57	2.75	2.65	3.09	2.98
Frequency	Micromachines	2.49	2.43	3.32	1.33	1.55	–	–
	Semiconductor Equipment	2.35	2.13	2.52	0.96	2.20	1.11	1.24
	Apparel	2.67	1.90	2.58	1.00	0.94	2.59	1.83
Importance	1997	2.76	2.73	3.25	2.83	2.66	–	–
	2004	2.26	2.01	2.69	2.82	2.63	–	–
Frequency	1997	2.49	2.43	3.32	1.33	1.55	–	–
	2004	1.83	1.42	1.93	1.17	1.34	–	–
Importance	Participant	2.21	1.91	2.73	2.88	2.70	–	–
	Non-Participant	2.38	2.22	2.60	2.67	2.50	–	–
Frequency	Participant	2.03	1.43	2.08	1.35	1.32	–	–
	Non-Participant	1.44	1.40	1.64	0.83	1.38	–	–

words, Chapter 5 and 6 ask, what are the average importance and frequency scores for the reported network in a given industry (or, in parts of Chapter 6, sub-group of an industry)? By contrast, these analyses ask, what average importance does the average firm in a given industry (or sub-group) ascribe to its network ties, and what is the average contact frequency with which the average firm puts its ties to use?

In computing these numbers, firms reporting no networking with a given target category were assigned a score of "0" for contact frequency for that category. Under the same condition, no score was assigned for importance, as the absence of ties could equally signify that the firm in question considered networking with the given target category unimportant or that the firm for whatever reason was not able to network with any actor in the given target category.

As one would expect given the different analytical approach, the numerical results in the below table are distinct from those presented in Chapters 5 and 6. At the same time, the results tend to show patterns that are generally consistent with those hypothesized and identified in Chapters 5 and 6, namely, U-shaped variation in importance and frequency for firms in industries at different stages of the industrial life cycle, a decrease in importance and frequency in the micromachine industry from 1997 to 2004, and elevated levels of networking among former participants in the micromachine R&D consortium compared with non-participants.

References

Abernathy, Frederick H., Dunlop, John T., Hammond, Janice H., and Weil, David 1999. *A stitch in time: Lean retailing and the transformation of manufacturing – Lessons from the apparel and textile industries*. Oxford, UK: Oxford University Press.

Abernathy, W. J., and Utterback, James M. 1978. "Patterns of industrial innovation," *Technology Review* 80: 40–7.

Abrahamson, Eric 1996. "Management fashion," *Academy of Management Review* 21: 254–85.

Abrahamson, Eric, and Fairchild, Gregory 1999. "Management fashion: lifecycles, triggers, and collective learning processes," *Administrative Science Quarterly* 44: 708–40.

Adler, Paul S., and Kwon, Seok-Woo 2002. "Social capital: Prospects for a new concept," *Academy of Management Review* 27: 17–40.

Ahmadjian, Christina L., and Lincoln, James R. 2001. "Keiretsu, governance, and learning: Case studies in change from the Japanese automotive industry," *Organization Science* 12: 683–701.

Albert, Michel 1993. *Capitalism vs. capitalism: How America's obsession with individual achievement and short-term profit has led it to the brink of collapse*. Translated by Haviland, Paul. New York: Four Wall Eight Windows.

Aldrich, Howard E., and Sasaki, Toshihiro 1995. "R&D consortia in the United States and Japan," *Research Policy* 24: 301–16.

Allinson, Gary D. 1993. "Citizenship, fragmentation, and the negotiated polity," in Allinson, Gary D. and Sone, Yasunori (eds.), *Political dynamics in contemporary Japan*, pp. 17–49. Ithaca, NY: Cornell University Press.

Amable, Bruno 2003. *The diversity of modern capitalism*. Oxford, UK: Oxford University Press.

Amsden, Alice H. 1989. *Asia's next giant: South Korea and late industrialization*. Oxford, UK: Oxford University Press.

Amsden, Alice H., and Hikino, Takashi 1994. "Project execution capability, organizational know-how, and conglomerate corporate growth in late industrialization," *Industrial and Corporate Change* 3: 111–48.

Amyx, Jennifer 2004. *Japan's financial crisis: Institutional rigidity and reluctant change*. Princeton, NJ: Princeton University Press.

Anderson, Philip 1999. "Complexity theory and organization science," *Organization Science* 10: 216–32.

Aoki, Masahiko 1988. *Information, incentives, and bargaining in the Japanese economy*. Cambridge, UK: Cambridge University Press.

2003. *Toward a comparative institutional analysis*. Cambridge, MA: MIT Press.

Arthur, W. Brian 1994a. *Increasing returns and path dependence in the economy*. Ann Arbor, MI: University of Michigan Press.

Arthur, W. Brian 1994b. "On the evolution of complexity," in Cowen, G. A., Pines, D. and Meltzer, D. (eds.), *Complexity: Metaphors, models, and reality*, pp. New York: Addison-Wesley.

Asanuma, Banri 1994. "Co-ordination between production and distribution in a globalizing network of firms: Assessing flexibility achieved in the Japanese automobile industry," in Aoki, Masahiko and Dore, Ronald Philip (eds.), *The Japanese firm: Sources of competitive strength*, pp. 117–53. Oxford, UK: Oxford University Press.

Axelrod, Robert M. 1984. *The evolution of cooperation*. New York: Basic Books.

Baker, Wayne E. 1992. "The network organization in theory and practice," in Nohria, Nitin and Eccles, Robert G. (eds.), *Networks and organizations: Structure, form, and action*, pp. Boston: Harvard Business School Press.

Bandura, Albert 1977. *Social learning theory*. Englewood Cliffs, NJ: Prentice Hall.

Barley, Stephen R., and Tolbert, Pamela S. 1997. "Institutionalization and structuration: Studying the links between action and institution," *Organization Studies* 18: 93–117.

Barr, Pamela S., and Huff, Anne S. 1997. "Seeing isn't believing: Understanding diversity in the timing of strategic response," *Journal of Management Studies* 34: 337–70.

Baum, J. A., and Oliver, Christine 1992. "Institutional embeddedness and the dynamics of organizational populations," *American Sociological Review* 57: 540–59.

Baumgartner, Frank R., and Jones, Bryan D. 2002. "Positive and negative feedback in politics," in Baumgartner, Frank R. and Jones, Bryan D. (eds.), *Policy dynamics*, pp. 3–28. Chicago: Chicago University Press.

Beason, Richard, and Weinstein, David E. 1996. "Growth, economies of scale, and targeting in Japan (1955–1990)," *Review of Economics and Statistics* 78: 286–95.

Beckert, Jens 1999. "Agency, entrepreneurs, and institutional change. The role of strategic choice and institutionalized practices in organizations," *Organization Studies* 20: 777–99.

Berg, David M., and Guisinger, Stephen E. 2001. "Capital flows, capital controls, and international business risk," in Rugman, Alan M. and Brewer, Thomas L. (eds.), *The Oxford handbook of international business*, pp. 259–81. Oxford, UK: Oxford University Press.

Berger, Suzanne (ed.) 1981. *Organizing interests in Western Europe.* Cambridge, UK: Cambridge University Press.

Bhide, A. 1999. *The origin and evolution of new businesses.* Oxford, UK: Oxford University Press.

Blanchard, Olivier, and Wolfers, Justin 2000. "The role of shocks and institutions in the rise of European unemployment: The aggregate evidence," *The Economic Journal* 110: C1–C33.

Bolino, Mark C., Turnley, William H., and Bloodgood, James H. 2002. "Citizenship behavior and the creation of social capital in organizations," *Academy of Management Review* 27: 505–22.

Borgatti, Stephen P., Everett, M. G., and Freeman, L. C. 2002. *UCINET for Windows: Software for Social Network Analysis.* Cambridge, MA: Analytic Technologies.

Bouty, Isabelle 2000. "Interpersonal and interaction influences on informal resource exchanges between R&D researchers across organizational boundaries," *Academy of Management Journal* 43: 50–65.

Boyer, Robert 1997. "French statism at the crossroads," in Crouch, Colin and Streeck, Wolfgang (eds.), *Political economy of modern capitalism: Mapping convergence and diversity*, pp. 71–101. London: Sage Publications.

Branscomb, Lewis M., Kodama, Fumio, and Florida, Richard (eds.) 1999. *Industrializing knowledge: University-industry linkages in Japan and the United States.* Cambridge, MA: MIT Press.

Branstetter, Lee G., and Sakakibara, Mariko 1998. "Japanese research consortia: A microeconometric analysis of industrial policy," *Journal of Industrial Economics* 46: 207–33.

  2002. "When do research consortia work well and why? Evidence from Japanese panel data," *American Economic Review* 92: 143–59.

Brehm, John, and Rahn, Wendy 1997. "Individual-level evidence for the causes and consequences of social capital," *American Journal of Political Science* 41: 999–1023.

Browning, Larry D., Beyer, Janice M., and Shetler, Judy C. 1995. "Building cooperation in a competitive industry: SEMATECH and the semiconductor industry," *Academy of Management Journal* 38: 113–51.

Buchanan, James M., and Tullock, Gordon 1962. *The calculus of consent.* Ann Arbor, MI: University of Michigan Press.

Burt, Ronald S. 1992. *Structural holes: The social structure of competition.* Cambridge, MA: Harvard University Press.

Calder, Kent E. 1993. *Strategic capitalism: Private business and public response in Japanese industrial finance.* Princeton, NJ: Princeton University Press.

Callon, Scott 1995. *Divided sun: MITI and the breakdown of Japanese high-tech industrial policy, 1975–1993.* Stanford, CA: Stanford University Press.

Caves, Richard E., and Uekusa, Masu 1976. *Industrial organization in Japan.* Washington, DC: Brookings Institution Press.

Churchill, N. C., and Lewis, V. L. 1983. "The five stages of small business growth," *Harvard Business Review* 61: 30–50.

Cohen, J. 1960. "A coefficient of agreement for nominal scales," *Educational and Psychological Measurement* 20: 37–46.

Cohen, Michael D., March, James G., and Olsen, Johan P. 1972. "A garbage can model of organizational choice," *Administrative Science Quarterly* 17: 1–25.

Commons, John Rogers 1950. *The economics of collective action.* New York: Macmillan.

Contractor, Farok J., and Lorange, Peter 1988. "Why should firms cooperate? The strategy and economic basis for cooperative ventures," in Contractor, Farok J. and Lorange, Peter (eds.), *Cooperative strategies in international business,* pp. 3–30. Lexington, MA: D.C. Heath and Company.

Conway, Paul, Janod, Véronique, and Nicoletti, Giuseppe. 2005. *Product market regulation in OECD countries: 1998 to 2003.* Paris: OECD.

Curtis, Gerald L. 1988. *The Japanese way of politics.* New York: Columbia University Press.

1999. *The logic of Japanese politics: Leaders, institutions, and the limits of change.* New York: Columbia University Press.

Cyert, Richard M., and March, James G. 1963. *A behavioral theory of the firm.* Englewood Cliffs, NJ: Prentice-Hall.

d'Aspremont, Claude, and Jacquemin, Alexis 1988. "Cooperative and noncooperative R&D in duopoly with spillovers," *American Economic Review* 78: 1133–1137.

David, Paul 1985. "Clio and the economics of QWERTY," *American Economic Review* 75: 332–7.

Deutsches Verbändeforum 2005. Statistische Hintergrundinformationen [Statistical background information]. http://www.lobbyist.de/files/

ueber_verbaende/897F29ECB68C4C1FA99E0E6C6FD00D6E.htm, accessed on 30 April 2005.

DeWit, Andrew. 1999. *Saying no to "socialism:" The new politics of the income tax in Japan*. Washington, DC: Japan Policy Research Institute.

DiMaggio, Paul J. 1988. "Interest and agency in institutional theory," in Zucker, Lynn G. (ed.) *Institutional patterns and organizations: Culture and environment*, pp. 3–21. Cambridge, MA: Ballinger.

DiMaggio, Paul J., and Powell, Walter W. 1983. "The iron cage revisited: Institutional isomorphism and collective rationality in organizational fields," *American Sociological Review* 48: 147–60.

Doner, Richard F. 1997. "Japan in East Asia: Institutions and regional leadership," in Katzenstein, Peter J. and Shiraishi, Takashi (eds.), *Network power: Japan and Asia*, pp. Ithaca, NY: Cornell University Press.

Dooley, Kevin J., and Van de Ven, Andrew H. 1999. "Explaining complex organizational dynamics," *Organization Science* 10: 358–72.

Dore, Ronald Philip 1983. "Goodwill and the spirit of market capitalism," *The British Journal of Sociology* 34: 459–82.

1986. *Flexible rigidities: Industrial policy and structural adjustment in the Japanese economy, 1970–1980*. Stanford, CA: Stanford University Press.

2000. *Stock market capitalism: welfare capitalism: Japan and Germany versus the Anglo-Saxons*. Oxford, UK: Oxford University Press.

Dore, Ronald Philip, and Sako, Mari 1989. *How the Japanese learn to work*. London: Routledge.

Dowding, Keith, John, Peter, Mergoupis, Thanos, and van Vugt, Mark 2000. "Exit, voice and loyalty: Analytic and empirical developments," *European Journal of Political Research*, 37: 469–495.

Eccles, Robert G., and Crane, Dwight D. 1987. "Managing through networks in investment banking," *California Management Review* 30.

Economist 2000. "A new golden age," *Economist*, 9 March 2000.

2001. "Japanese corporate raiders: Ever so polite," *Economist*, 15 February 2001.

2004. "Tiger, tiger, burning bright," *Economist*, 14 October 2004.

2005. "From t-shirts to T-bonds," *Economist*, 28 July 2005.

Enste, Dominik H. 2003. "Ursachen der Schattenwirtschaft in den OECD-Staaten [Causes of the shadow economy in the OECD countries]," *IW-Trends* 31: 1–19.

Estevez-Abe, Margarita, Iversen, Torben, and Soskice, David 2001. "Social protection and the formation of skills: A reinterpretatio of the welfare state," in Hall, Peter A. and Soskice, David (eds.), *Varieties of capitalism: The institutional foundations of comparative advantage*, pp. Oxford, UK: Oxford University Press.

Evans, Peter B. 1995. *Embedded autonomy: States and industrial transformation*. Princeton, NJ: Princeton University Press.

Fiss, Peer C., and Zajac, Edward J. 2004. "The diffusion of ideas over contested terrain: The (non)adoption of a shareholder value orientation among German firms," *Administrative Science Quarterly* 49: 501–34.

Flamm, Kenneth 1996. *Mismanaged trade? Strategic policy and the semiconductor industry*. Washington, DC: Brookings Institution Press.

Fountain, Jane E. 1998. "Social capital: A key enabler of innovation in science and technology," in Branscomb, Lewis M. and Keller, James H. (eds.), *Investing in innovation: Toward a consensus strategy for federal technology policy*, pp. 85–111. Cambridge, MA: MIT Press.

Friedland, Roger, and Robertson, A. F. 1990. "Beyond the marketplace," in Roger, Friedland and Robertson, A. F. (eds.), *Beyond the marketplace: Rethinking economy and society*, pp. 3–49. New York: Aldine de Gruyter.

Friedman, David 1988. *The misunderstood miracle: Industrial development and political change in Japan*. Ithaca, NY: Cornell University Press.

Friedman, George, and LeBard, Meredith 1991. *The coming war with Japan*. New York: St. Martin's Press.

Fruin, W. Mark 1992. *The Japanese enterprise system: Competitive strategies and cooperative structures*. Oxford, UK: Clarendon Press.

Fukuyama, Francis 1995. *Trust: The social virtues & the creation of prosperity*. New York: Free Press.

Fulk, Janet, and DeSanctis, Gerardine 1995. "Electronic communication and changing organizational forms," *Organization Science* 6: 1–13.

Galaskiewicz, Joseph, and Wasserman, Stanley 1989. "Leadership and networking among neighborhood human service organizations," *Administrative Science Quarterly* 26: 434–48.

Gargiulo, Martin, and Benassi, Mario 2000. "Trapped in your own net? Network cohesion, structural holes, and the adaptation of social capital," *Organization Science* 11: 183–96.

Gargiulo, Martin, and Ertug, Gokhan 2006. "The dark side of trust," in Bachmann, Reinhard and Zaheer, Akbar (eds.), Cheltenham: Edward Elgar.

Gell-Mann, M. 1994. *The quark and the jaguar*. New York: Freeman & Co.

Gerlach, Michael L. 1992. *Alliance capitalism: The social organization of Japanese business*. Berkeley, CA: University of California Press.

Goldstone, Jack A., Gurr, Ted Robert, and Moshiri, Farrokh (eds.) 1991. *Revolutions of the late twentieth century*. Boulder, CO: Westview Press.

Goodman, Roger 2005. "W(h)ither the Japanese university? An introduction to the 2004 higher education reforms in Japan," in Eades, J. S., Goodman, Roger and Hada, Yumiko (eds.), *The "Big Bang" in Japanese higher education: The 2004 reforms and the dynamics of change*, pp. Victoria, Australia: Trans Pacific Press.

Granovetter, Mark S. 1973. "The strength of weak ties," *American Journal of Sociology* 78: 1360–80.

1985. "Economic action and social structure: The problem of embeddedness," *American Journal of Sociology* 91: 481–10.

1994. "Business groups," in Smelser, Neil J. and Swedberg, Richard (eds.), *The handbook of economic sociology*, pp. 453–76. New York: Russell Sage Foundation.

Grant, Wyn, Paterson, William, and Whitston, Colin 1987. "Government-industry relations in the chemical industry: An Anglo-German comparison," in Wilks, Stephen and Wright, Maurice (eds.), *Comparative government-industry relations: Western Europe, the United States, and Japan*, pp. 35–60. Oxford, UK: Oxford University Press.

Greenwood, Royston, and Hinings, C. R. 1996. "Understanding radical organizational change: Bringing together the old and the new institutionalism," *Academy of Management Review* 21: 1022–54.

Greenwood, Royston, Suddaby, Roy, and Hinings, C. R. 2002. "Theorizing change: The role of professional associations in the transformation of institutionalized fields," *Academy of Management Journal* 45: 58–80.

Greif, Avner 1993. "Contract enforceability and economic institutions in eary trade: The Maghribi traders' coalition," *American Economic Review* 83: 525–48.

1994. "Trading institutions and the commercial revolution in medieval Europe," in Abanbegyan, Abel, Bogomolov, Oleg and Kaser, Michael (eds.), *Economics in a changing world, vol. 1: System tranformation: Eastern and Western assessments*, pp. 115–25. New York: St. Martin's Press.

Gulati, Ranjay 1995. "Does familiarity breed trust? The implications of repeated ties for contractual choice in alliances," *Academy of Management Journal* 38: 85–112.

1998. "Alliances and networks," *Strategic Management Journal* 19: 293–317.

Gurr, Ted Robert 1973. "The revolution-social change nexus," *Comparative Politics* 5: 359–92.

Hage, Jerald, and Alter, Catherine 1997. "A typology of interorganizational relationships and networks," in Hollingsworth, J. Rogers and Boyer,

Robert (eds.), *Contemporary capitalism: The embeddedness of institutions*, pp. 94–126. Cambridge, UK: Cambridge University Press.

Hall, Peter A., and Gingerich, Daniel W. 2004. Varieties of capitalism and institutional complementarities in the macroeconomy: An empirical analysis. In *MPIfG Discussion Paper 04/5*. Cologne.

Hall, Peter A., and Soskice, David 2001. "An introduction to varieties of capitalism," in Hall, Peter A. and Soskice, David (eds.), *Varieties of capitalism: The institutional foundations of comparative advantage*, pp. 1–68. Oxford, UK: Oxford University Press.

Hall, Peter A., and Taylor, Rosemary C. R. 1996. "Political science and the three new institutionalisms," *Political Studies* 44: 936–57.

Hambrick, Donald C., and Lei, David 1985. "Toward an empirical prioritization of contingency variables for business strategy," *Academy of Management Journal* 28: 763–88.

Hamel, G. 1991. "Competition for competence and inter-partner learning within international strategic alliances," *Strategic Management Journal* 9: 361–74.

Harrison, Lawrence E. 1992. *Who prospers? How cultural values shape economic and political success*. New York: Basic Books.

1997. *The pan-American dream: Do Latin American cultural values discourage true partnership with the United States and Canada?* New York: Basic Books.

Hayek, Friedrich Anton 1945. "The use of knowledge in society," *American Economic Review* 35: 519–30.

Henisz, Witold J. 2002. *Politics and international investment: Measuring risks and protecting profits*. London: Edward Elgar.

Henisz, Witold J., and Zelner, Bennet A. 2005. "Legitimacy, interest group pressures, and change in emergent institutions: The case of foreign investors and host country governments," *Academy of Management Review* 30: 361–82.

Henry, E. Keith. 1992. *Shougai katsudou* (external relations) and the foreign firm, Institute of Comparative Culture, Sophia University, Tokyo.

Hicks, Diana 1993. "University-industry research links in Japan," *Policy Sciences* 26: 361–95.

Hirschman, Albert O. 1970. *Exit, voice, and loyalty: Responses to decline in firms, organizations, and states*. Cambridge, MA: Harvard University Press.

Hite, Julie M., and Hesterly, William S. 2001. "The evolution of firm networks: From emergence to early growth of the firm," *Strategic Management Journal* 22: 275–86.

Hofer, C. W. 1977. *Conceptual constructs for formulating corporate and business strategy*. Boston: Harvard Intercollegiate Case Clearing House.

Hofstede, Geert H. 1997. *Cultures and organizations: Software of the mind.* New York: McGraw-Hill.

Hoshi, Takeo 1994. "The economic role of corporate grouping and the main bank system," in Aoki, Masahiko and Dore, Ronald Philip (eds.), *The Japanese firm: Sources of competitive strength,* pp. 285–309. Oxford, UK: Oxford University Press.

Hoshi, Takeo, Kashyap, Anil, and Scharfstein, David 1991. "The role of banks in reducing the cost of financial distress in Japan," *Journal of Financial Economics* 27: 67–88.

House, Robert J., Hanges, Paul J., Javidan, Mansour, Dorfman, Peter W., and Gupta, Vipin (eds.) 2004. *Culture, leadership, and organizations: The GLOBE study of 62 societies.* London: Sage Publications.

Imai, Ken'ichi 1982. "Japan's industrial structure and United States-Japan industrial relations," in Yamamura, Kozo (ed.) *Policy and trade issues of the Japanese economy: American and Japanese perspectives,* pp. 47–75. Seattle, WA: University of Washington Press.

1988. "Industrial policy and technological innovation," in Komiya, Ryutaro, Okuno, Masahiro and Suzumura, Kotaru (eds.), *Industrial policy of Japan,* pp. 205–29. Tokyo: Academic Press Japan.

Imai, Ken'ichi 1992. "Japan's corporate networks," in Kumon, Shumpei and Rosovsky, Henry (eds.), *The political economy of Japan, volume 3: Cultural and social dynamics,* pp. 198–230. Stanford, CA: Stanford University Press.

1994. "Enterprise groups," in Imai, Ken'ichi and Komiya, Ryutaro (eds.), *Business enterprise in Japan: Views of leading Japanese economists,* pp. 117–40. Cambridge, MA: MIT Press.

Imai, Ken'ichi, Nonaka, Ikujiro, and Takeuchi, Hirotaka 1985. "Managing the new product development process: How Japanese companies learn and unlearn," in Clark, Kim B., Hayes, Robert H. and Lorenz, Christopher (eds.), *The uneasy alliance: Managing the productivity-technology dilemma,* pp. 337–76. Boston: Harvard Business School Press.

Inagami, Takeshi, and Whittaker, D. Hugh 2005. *The new community firm: Employment, governance and management reform in Japan.* Cambridge, UK: Cambridge University Press.

Inkpen, Andrew C., and Tsang, Eric W. K. 2005. "Social capital, networks, and knowledge transfer," *Academy of Management Review* 30: 146–65.

Institute of Statistical Mathematics. 2004. A study of the Japanese national character: The eleventh nationwide survey. Tokyo: Institute of Statistical Mathematics.

Ito, Takatoshi 1992. *The Japanese economy.* Cambridge, MA: MIT Press.

Jackman, Robert W., and Miller, Ross. A. 1998. "Social capital and politics," *Annual Review of Political Science* 1: 47–73.

Jackson, Gregory 2003a. "Corporate governance in Germany and Japan: Liberalization pressures and responses during the 1990s," in Yamamura, Kozo and Streeck, Wolfgang (eds.), *The end of diversity? Prospects for German and Japanese capitalism*, pp. 261–305. Ithaca, NY: Cornell University Press.

   2003b. "Corporate governance in Germany and JapanL Liberalization pressures and responses during the 1990s," in Yamamura, Kozo and Streeck, Wolfgang (eds.), *The end of diversity? Prospects for German and Japanese capitalism*, pp. 261–305. Ithaca, NY: Cornell University Press.

Jackson, Gregory, and Miyajima, Hideaki. 2004. Corporate governance in Japan: Institutional change and organizational diversity. Paper read at RIETI Symposium "Corporate Governance in Japan: Converging to Any Particular New Model?" at United Nations University, Tokyo.

Janis, Irving Lester 1982. *Groupthink: Psychological studies of policy decisions and fiascoes*. Boston: Houghton Mifflin.

Japan Fair Trade Commission. 2001. [Concerning the actual state of business groups: Report on the seventh survey]: Japan Fair Trade Commission.

Johnson, Chalmers 1982. *MITI and the Japanese miracle: The growth of industrial policy 1925–1975*. Stanford, CA: Stanford University Press.

Johnson, Gerry 1988. "Rethinking incrementalism," *Strategic Management Journal* 9: 75–91.

Kato, Takao 2001. "The end of lifetime employment in Japan?: Evidence from national surveys and field research," *Journal of the Japanese and International Economies* 15: 489–514.

Katz, Michael L. 1986. "An analysis of cooperative research and development," *RAND Journal of Economics* 17: 527–43.

Katz, Richard 2002. *Japanese phoenix: The long road to economic revival*. Armonk, NY: M.E. Sharpe.

Katznelson, Ira 2003. "Periodization and preferences: Reflections on purposive action in comparative historical social science," in Mahoney, James and Rueschemeyer, Dietrich (eds.), *Comparative historical analysis in the social sciences*, pp. Cambridge, UK: Cambridge University Press.

Kauffman, S. 1995. *At home in the universe*. Oxford, UK: Oxford University Press.

Kawanishi, Hirosuke 1992. *Enterprise unions in Japan*. Translated by Mouer, Ross E. London: Kegan Paul International.

Keddie, Nikki 1995. *Debating revolutions*. New York: New York University Press.

Keohane, Robert O. 1984. *After hegemony: Cooperation and discord in the world political economy.* Princeton, NJ: Princeton University Press.

Kingdon, John W. 1984. *Agendas, alternatives, and public policies.* Boston: Little, Brown and Company.

Kitschelt, Herbert 2003. "Competitive party democracy and political-economic reform in Germany and Japan: Do party systems make a difference?," in Yamamura, Kozo and Streeck, Wolfgang (eds.), *The end of diversity? Prospects for German and Japanese capitalism,* pp. 334–63. Ithaca, NY: Cornell University Press.

Klepper, Steven 1997. "Industry life cycles," *Industrial and Corporate Change* 6: 145–81.

Knight, Jack 1992. *Institutions and social conflict.* Cambridge, UK: Cambridge University Press.

Kobrin, Stephen J. 1982. *Managing political risk assessment: Strategic response to environmental change.* Berkeley, CA: University of California Press.

Kogut, Bruce 1988. "Joint ventures: Theoretical and empirical perspectives," *Strategic Management Journal* 9: 319–32.

Komiya, Ryutaro 1988. "Introduction," in Komiya, Ryutaro, Okuno, Masahiro and Suzumura, Kotaru (eds.), *Industrial policy in Japan,* pp. New York: Academic Press.

Krasner, Stephen 1976. "State power and the structure of foreign trade," *World Politics* 28: 317–43.

Kreps, David M. 1990. *Game theory and economic modelling.* Oxford, UK: Oxford University Press.

Kume, Ikuo 1998. *Disparaged success.* Ithaca, NY: Cornell University Press.

Kumon, Shumpei 1992. "Japan as a network society," in Kumon, Shumpei and Rosovsky, Henry (eds.), *The political economy of Japan, volume 3: Cultural and social dynamics,* pp. 109–41. Stanford, CA: Stanford University Press.

Kunkel, S. W. 1991. The impact of strategy and industry structure on new venture performance. doctoral dissertation, University of Georgia.

Kuroki, Fumio. 2003. *The relationship of companies and banks as cross-shareholdings unwind: Fiscal 2002 cross-shareholding survey.* Tokyo: NLI Research Institute.

Kurosu, Masahi (ed.) 2003. *Japan Almanac 2004.* Tokyo: Asahi Shimbun.

Lebra, Takie Sugiyama 1976. *Japanese patterns of behavior.* Honolulu: University of Hawaii Press.

Lewin, Arie Y., and Kim, Jisung 2004. "The nation state and culture as influences on organizational change and innovation," in Poole, Marshal Scott (ed.) *Handbook of organizational change and development,* pp. Oxford, UK: Oxford University Press.

Lewin, Arie Y., Long, Chris P., and Carroll, Timothy N. 1999. "The coevolution of new organizational forms," *Organization Science* 10: 535–50.

Lewin, Arie Y., and Stephens, Carroll U. 1993. "Designing post-industrial organizations: Combining theory and practice," in Huber, George P. and Glick, William H. (eds.), *Organizational change and redesign*, pp. 393–410. Oxford, UK: Oxford University Press.

Lewin, Arie Y., and Volberda, Henk W. 1999. "Prolegomena on coevolution: A framework for research on strategy and new organizational forms," *Organization Science* 10: 519–34.

Liebeskind, Julia Porter, Oliver, Amalya Lumerman, Zucker, Lynne G., and Brewer, Marilynn B. 1995. *Social networks, learning, and flexibility: Sourcing scientific knowledge in new biotechnology firms*. Cambridge, MA: National Bureau of Economic Research.

Lincoln, Edward J. 1990a. *Japan's unequal trade*. Washington, DC: Brookings Institution Press.

   1999. *Troubled times: U.S.-Japan trade relations in the 1990s*. Washington, DC: Brookings Institution Press.

   2001. *Arthritic Japan: The slow pace of economic reform*. Washington, DC: Brookings Institution Press.

Lincoln, James R. 1990b. "Japanese organization and organization theory," *Research in Organizational Behavior* 12: 255–94.

Lincoln, James R., and Gerlach, Michael L. 2004. *Japan's network economy: Structure, persistence, and change*. Cambridge, UK: Cambridge University Press.

Lincoln, James R., Gerlach, Michael L., and Ahmadjian, Christina L. 1996. "Keiretsu networks and corporate performance in Japan," *American Sociological Review* 61: 67–88.

Lincoln, James R., and McBride, Kerry 1987. "Japanese industrial organization in comparative perspective," *Annual Review of Sociology* 13: 289–312.

Lynn, Leonard H., and McKeown, Timothy J. 1988. *Organizing business: Trade associations in American and Japan*. Washington, DC: American Enterprise Institute for Public Policy Research.

March, James G., and Olsen, Johan P. 1989. *Rediscovering institutions: The organizational basis of politics*. New York: Free Press.

March, James G., and Simon, Herbert A. 1958. *Organizations*. New York: John Wiley & Sons.

Martin, Michael O., Mullis, Ina V. S., Gonzalez, Eugenio J., and Chrostowski, Steven J. 2004. *TIMSS 2003 international science report: Findings from IEA's trends in international mathematics and science study at the fourth and eighth grades*. Boston: TIMSS & PIRLS

International Study Center, Lynch School of Education, Boston College.

Marsh, Robert M. 1992. "A research note: Centralization of decision-making in Japanese factories," *Organization Studies* 13: 261–74.

Martinez, Jon I., and Jarillo, J. Carlos 1989. "The evolution of research on coordination mechanisms in multinational corporations," *Journal of International Business Studies* 20: 489–514.

McGuire, Jean, and Dow, Sandra 2005. "Keiretsu organization in a changing economic context: The evolution of debt and equity ties among keiretsu firms," in Roehl, Thomas and Bird, Allan (eds.), *Japanese firms in transition: Reponding to the globalization challenge*, pp. Oxford, UK: Elsevier.

McKean, Margaret A. 1993. "State strength and the public interest," in Allinson, Gary D. and Sone, Yasunori (eds.), *Political dynamics in contemporary Japan*, pp. Ithaca, NY: Cornell University Press.

Meyer, John W., and Rowan, Brian 1977. "Institutionalized organizations: Formal structure as myth and ceremony," *American Journal of Sociology* 83: 340–63.

Micromachine Center. 2005a. *The national R&D project "Micromachine Technology"*. [cited 3 May 2005]. Available from http://www.mmc.or.jp/e/natio-project/natio-project.html.

2005b. *What is the Micromachine Center (MMC)?* [cited 3 May 2005]. Available from http://www.mmc.or.jp/e/gaiyou-e/gaiyou-e.html.

Miles, Grant, Snow, Charles C., and Sharman, Mark P. 1993. "Industry variety and performance," *Strategic Management Journal* 14: 163–77.

Ministry of Education, Culture, Sports, Science and Technology. 2002a. Japanese government policies in education, culture, sports, science and technology 2002: School in the new era—elementary and secondary education reform in progress. Tokyo: Ministry of Education, Culture, Sports, Science and Technology.

2002b. Japanese government policies in education, culture, sports, science and technology 2002. White Paper. Tokyo: Ministry of Education, Culture, Sports, Science and Technology.

Miwa, Yoshiro 1994. "Subcontracting relationships: The automobile industry," in Imai, Ken'ichi and Komiya, Ryutaro (eds.), *Business enterprise in Japan: Views of leading Japanese economists*, pp. 141–55. Cambridge, MA: MIT Press.

Miwa, Yoshiro, and Ramseyer, J. Mark 2002. "The fable of the keiretsu," *Journal of Economics & Management Strategy* 11: 169–224.

Miyawaki, Ko (ed.) 2005. *Japan Almanac 2006*. Tokyo: Asahi Shimbun.

Mullis, Ina V. S., Martin, Michael O., Gonzalez, Eugenio J., and Chrostowski, Steven J. 2004. *TIMSS 2003 international mathematics report: Findings from IEA's trends in international mathematics and science study at the fourth and eighth grades.* Boston: TIMSS & PIRLS International Study Center, Lynch School of Education, Boston College.

Murakami, Yasusuke, and Rohlen, Thomas P. 1992. "Social exchange aspects of the Japanese political economy: Culture, efficiency, and change," in Kumon, Shumpei and Rosovsky, Henry (eds.), *The political economy of Japan, vol. 3: Cultural and social dynamics*, pp. 63–108. Stanford, CA: Stanford University Press.

Nahapiet, Janine, and Ghoshal, Sumantra 1998. "Social capital, intellectual capital, and the organizational advantage," *Academy of Management Review* 23: 242–66.

Nakamura, Takafusa 1995. *The postwar Japanese economy: Its development and structure, 1937–1994 (2nd ed.).* Tokyo: University of Tokyo Press.

Nakata, Hiroko 2004. METI considers hostile-takeover defenses: Government fears an increase in foreign acquisitions of Japanese firms. *Japan Times*, 7 October 2004.

Nakatani, Iwao 1984. "The economic role of financial corporate grouping," in Aoki, Masahiko (ed.) *The economic analysis of the Japanese firm*, pp. 227–58. Amsterdam: North-Holland.

Nelson, Richard R., and Winter, Sidney G. 1982. *An evolutionary theory of economic change.* Cambridge, MA: Belknap Press.

NHK Broadcasting Culture Research Institute (ed.) 2004. 現代日本人の意識構造[第六版] [*Mental structure of the present-day Japanese, sixth ed.*]. Tokyo: Nihon Housou Shuppan Kyoukai.

Nickell, Stephen, Nunziata, Luca, Ochel, Wolfgang, and Quintini, Glenda 2003. "The Beveridge Curve, unemployment, and wages in the OECD from the 1960s to the 1990s," in Aghion, Philippe, Frydman, Roman, Stiglitz, Joseph and Woodford, Michael (eds.), *Knowledge, information, and expectations in modern macroeconomics: In honor of Edmund S. Phelps*, pp. 394–431. Princeton, NJ: Princeton University Press.

Nihon Keizai Shimbun. 1989. 医療にバイオに超マイクロの機会、蚊は研究者にとって理想的なマイクロマシン [Ultra-micro machines for medicine and biotechnology, the mosquito as the ideal micromachine for researchers]. *Nihon Keizai Shimbun*, 20 February.

1990. 産技審、大型プロジェクト新規テマ決まる [New theme for large project is decided by Industrial Technology Council]. *Nihon Keizai Shimbun*, 24 August 1990.

Niskanen, William A. 1990. "Conditions affecting the survival of constitution rules," *Constitutional Political Economy* 1: 53–62.

Noble, Gregory William. 1988. Between competition and cooperation: Collective action in the industrial policy of Japan and Taiwan. Dissertation, Harvard University, Cambridge, MA.

North, Douglass Cecil 1990. *Institutions, institutional change and economic performance.* Edited by Alt, James E. and North, Douglass Cecil, *Political Economy of Institutions and Decisions.* Cambridge, UK: Cambridge University Press.

1994. "Economic Performance Through Time," *American Economic Review* 84: 359–68.

OECD 2003. *Literacy skills for the world of tomorrow: Further results from PISA 2000.* Paris: OECD.

2004a. *Learning for tomorrow's world: First results from PISA 2003.* Paris: OECD.

2004b. *OECD in figures, 2004 edition: Statistics on the member countries.* Paris: OECD.

2004c. *Statistical Compendium.* OECD 2004 [cited 20 August 2004].

2005. *Economic policy reforms: Going for growth.* Paris: OECD.

Okazaki, Tetsuji 1994. "The Japanese firm under the wartime planned economy," in Aoki, Masahiko and Dore, Ronald Philip (eds.), *The Japanese firm: Sources of competitive strength*, pp. 350–78. Oxford, UK: Oxford University Press.

Okimoto, Daniel I. 1989. *Between MITI and the market: Japanese industrial policy for high technology.* Stanford, CA: Stanford University Press.

Okimoto, Daniel I., and Nishi, Yoshio 1994. "R&D organization in Japanese and American semiconductor firms," in Aoki, Masahiko and Dore, Ronald Philip (eds.), *The Japanese firm: Source of competitive strength*, pp. 178–208. Oxford, UK: Oxford University Press.

Oliver, Christine 1991. "Strategic responses to institutional processes," *Academy of Management Review* 16: 145–79.

1992. "The antecedents of deinstitutionalization," *Organization Studies* 13: 563–88.

Olson, Mancur 1965. *The logic of collective action: Public goods and the theory of goods.* Cambridge, MA: Harvard University Press.

Omori, Takashi, and Yonezawa, Akiyoshi. 2002. Measurement of social capital in Japan. Paper read at Social Capital Measurement Conference (OECD and Office of National Statistics), at London.

Orrù, Marco 1997. "Institutional cooperation in Japanese and German capitalism," in Orrù, Marco, Biggart, Nicole Woolsey and Hamilton,

Gary G. (eds.), *The economic organization of East Asian capitalism*, pp. 297–339. Thousand Oaks, CA: Sage Publications.

Orrù, Marco, Biggart, Nicole Woolsey, and Hamilton, Gary G. 1997. *The economic organization of East Asian capitalism*. London: Sage Publications.

Peck, Merton J., Levin, Richard C., and Goto, Akira 1987. "Picking losers: Public policy toward declining industries in Japan," *Journal of Japanese Studies* 13: 79–123.

Pekkanen, Saadia M. 2003. *Picking winners? From technology catch-up to the space race in Japan*. Stanford, CA: Stanford University Press.

Perez, Carlotta 2002. *Technological revolutions and financial capital: The dynamics of bubbles and golden ages*. London: Edward Elgar.

Pfeffer, Jeffrey, and Salancik, Gerald R. 1978. *The external control of organizations: A resource dependence perspective*. New York: Harper & Row.

Pharr, Susan J. 1990. *Losing face: Status politics in Japan*. Berkeley, CA: University of California Press.

Pierson, Paul 2004. *Politics in time: History, institutions, and social analysis*. Princeton, NJ: Princeton University Press.

Podolny, Joel M., and Page, Karen L. 1998. "Network forms of organization," *Annual Review of Sociology* 24: 57–76.

Porter, Michael E., and Takeuchi, Hirotaka 1999. "Fixing what really ails Japan," *Foreign Affairs* 78: 66–81.

Portes, Alejandro 1998. "Social capital: Its origins and applications in modern sociology," *Annual Review of Sociology* 24: 1–24.

Portes, Alejandro, and Sensenbrenner, Julia 1993. "Embeddedness and immigration: Notes on the social determinants of economic action," *American Journal of Sociology* 96: 626–54.

Powell, Walter W. 1990. "Neither market nor hierarchy: Network forms of organization," *Research in Organizational Behavior* 12: 295–336.

Powell, Walter W., and Brantley, P. 1992. "Competitive cooperation in biotechnology: Learning through networks?," in Nohria, Nitin and Eccles, Robert G. (eds.), *Networks and organizations: Structure, form and action*, pp. Boston: Harvard Business School Press.

Powell, Walter W., Koput, K. W., and Smith-Doerr, Laurel 1996. "Interorganizational collaboration and the locus of innovation: Networks of learning in biotechnology," *Administrative Science Quarterly* 41: 116–45.

Prestowitz, Clyde V. 1988. *Trading places: How we allowed Japan to take the lead*. New York: Basic Books.

Putnam, Robert D. 1993a. *Making democracy work: Civic traditions in modern Italy*. Princeton, NJ: Princeton University Press.

1993b. "The prosperous community: Social capital and public life," *American Prospect* 4: 35–42.

2000. *Bowling alone: The collapse and revival of American community.* New York: Simon & Schuster.

Redding, Gordon 2005. "The thick description and comparison of societal systems of capitalism," *Journal of International Business Studies.*

Redding, S. Gordon 1990. *The spirit of Chinese capitalism.* Berlin: Walter de Gruyter.

Redding, Gordon, and Witt, Michael A. 2004. The role of executive rationale in the comparison of capitalisms: Some preliminary findings. In *INSEAD EAC Working Paper Series.* Fontainebleau, France.

Robinson, Kennth C., and McDougall, Patricia Phillips 1998. "The impact of alternative operationalizations of industry structural elements on measures of performance for entrepreneurial manufacturing ventures," *Strategic Management Journal* 19: 1079–100.

Root, Franklin R. 1988. "Some taxonomies of international cooperative arrangements," in Contractor, Farok J. and Lorange, Peter (eds.), *Cooperative strategies in international business*, pp. 69–80. Lexington, MA: D.C. Heath and Company.

Rosenkopf, Lori, Metiu, Anca, and George, Varghese P. 2001. "From the bottom up? Technical committee activity and alliance formation," *Administrative Science Quarterly* 46: 748–72.

Ruggie, John Gerard 1982. "International regimes, transactions, and change: Embedded liberalism in the postwar economic order," *International Organization* 36: 379–415.

Sakakibara, Eisuke 2003. *Structural reform in Japan: Breaking the Iron Triangle.* Washington, DC: Brookings Institution Press.

Sakakibara, Mariko 1997. "Evaluating government-sponsored R&D cooperatives in Japan: Who benefits and how?," *Research Policy* 26: 447–73.

Sako, Mari 1992. *Price, quality and trust: Inter-firm relations in Britain and Japan.* Cambridge, UK: Cambridge University Press.

Samuels, Richard J. 1987. *The business of the Japanese state: Energy markets in comparative and historical perspective.* Ithaca, NY: Cornell University Press.

Saxonhouse, Gary R. 1986. "Industrial policy and factor markets: Biotechnology in Japan and the United States," in Patrick, Hugh T. (ed.) *Japan's high technology industries: Lessons and limitations of industrial policy*, pp. 97–136. Seattle, WA: University of Washington Press.

2000. "R&D consortia, news, and Japanese high-technology policy: Optoelectronics in Japan," in Aoki, Masahiko and Saxonhouse, Gary

R. (eds.), *Finance, governance, and competitiveness in Japan*, pp. 212–38. Oxford, UK: Oxford University Press.

Schaede, Ulrike 2000. *Cooperative capitalism: Self-regulation, trade associations, and the Anti-Monopoly Law in Japan*. Oxford, UK: Oxford University Press.

Schmidt, Vivien A. 2002. *The futures of European capitalism*. Oxford, UK: Oxford University Press.

Schmitter, Philippe C., and Lehmbruch, Gerhard (eds.) 1979. *Trends toward corporatist intermediation*. London: Sage Publications.

Schneider, Friedrich. 2005. Rückläufige Schattenwirtschaft in Deutschland, Österreich und in anderen OECD-Ländern – Fluch oder Segen? [Receding shadow economy in Germany, Austria, and other OECD countries: Curse or blessing?]. Linz, Austria: Universität Linz.

Schneider, Friedrich, and Enste, Dominik H. 2000a. *Schattenwirtschaft und Schwarzarbeit: Umfang, Ursachen, Wirkungen und wirtschaftspolitische Empfehlungen [Shadow economy and illegal labor: Extent, causes, effects, and recommendations for economy policy]*. Munich: R. Oldenbourg Verlag.

    2000b. "Shadow economies: Size, causes, and consequences," *Journal of Economic Literature* 38: 77–114.

Schoppa, Leonard J. 1997. *Bargaining with Japan: What American pressure can and cannot do*. New York: Columbia University Press.

Schwartz, Frank J. 1998. *Advice and consent: The politics of consultation in Japan*. Cambridge, UK: Cambridge University Press.

    2003. "What is civil society?," in Schwartz, Frank J. and Pharr, Susan J. (eds.), *The state of civil society in Japan*, pp. 23–41. Cambridge, UK: Cambridge University Press.

Seo, Myeong-Gu, and Creed, W. E. Douglas 2002. "Institutional contradictions, praxis, and institutional change: A dialectical perspective," *Academy of Management Review* 27: 222–47.

Sheard, Paul 1989. "The main bank system and corporate monitoring and control in Japan," *Journal of Economic Behavior and Organization* 11: 339–422.

    1994. "Interlocking shareholdings and corporate governance," in Aoki, Masahiko and Dore, Ronald Philip (eds.), *The Japanese firm: Sources of competitive strength*, pp. 310–49. Oxford, UK: Oxford University Press.

Shepherd, W. G. 1975. *The treatment of market power: Antitrust, regulation, and public enterprise*. New York: Columbia University Press.

Sherif, Muzafer 1961. *Intergroup conflict and cooperation: The Robbers Cave experiment*. Norman.

Skocpol, Theda (ed.) 1994. *Social revolutions in the modern world.* Cambridge: Cambridge University Press.

Smith, Clayton G., and Cooper, Arnold C. 1988. "Established companies diversifying into young industries: A comparison of firms with different levels of performance," *Strategic Management Journal* 9: 111–21.

Spence, A. Michael 1984. "Cost reduction, competition, and industry performance," *Econometrica* 52: 101–21.

Stark, David 1996. "Recombinant property in East European capitalism," *American Journal of Sociology* 101: 993–1027.

StataCorp 1999. Stata statistical software: Release 6. College Station, TX: StataCorp LP.

2005. Stata statistical software: Release 9. College Station, TX: StataCorp LP.

Strebel, Paul 1987. "Organizing for innovation over an industry cycle," *Strategic Management Journal* 8: 117–24.

Streeck, Wolfgang, and Thelen, Kathleen 2005. "Introduction: Institutional change in advanced political economies," in Streeck, Wolfgang and Thelen, Kathleen (eds.), *Beyond continuity: Institutional change in advanced political economies*, pp. Oxford, UK: Oxford University Press.

Streeck, Wolfgang, and Yamamura, Kozo 2003. "Introduction: Convergence or diversity? Stability and change in German and Japanese capitalism," in Yamamura, Kozo and Streeck, Wolfgang (eds.), *The end of diversity? Prospects for German and Japanese capitalism*, pp. 1–50. Ithaca, NY: Cornell University Press.

(eds.) 2001. *The origins of nonliberal capitalism: Germany and Japan in comparison.* Ithaca, NY: Cornell University Press.

Stuart, Toby E., Hoang, Ha, and Hybels, Ralph C. 1999. "Internorganizational endorsements and the performance of entrepreneurial ventures," *Administrative Science Quarterly* 44: 315–49.

Surowiecki, James 2004. *The wisdom of crowds: Why the many are smarter than the few and how collective wisdom shapes business, econoimes, societies and nations.* New York: Doubleday.

Szulanski, Gabriel, Cappetta, Rossella, and Jensen, Robert J. 2004. "When and how trustworthiness matters: Knowledge transfer and the moderating effect of causal ambiguity," *Organization Science* 15: 600–13.

Tachibanaki, Toshiaki, and Noda, Tomohiko 2000. *The economic effects of trade unions in Japan.* New York: St. Martin's Press.

Thelen, Kathleen 2004. *How institutions evolve: The political economy of skills in Germany, Britain, the United States, and Japan.* Cambridge, UK: Cambridge University Press.

Tilton, Mark 1996. *Restrained trade: Cartels in Japan's basic materials industries.* Ithaca, NY: Cornell University Press.

Tripsas, Mary 1998. "Accessing external technological knowledge: An evolutionary perspective," in Frank, Nik (ed.) *Innovationsforschung und Technologiemanagement: Gedenkschrift für Stephan Schrader*, pp. Heidelberg: Springer Press.

Trompenaars, Fons, and Hampden-Turner, Charles 1997. *Riding the waves of culture: Understanding cultural diversity in business*. London: Nicholas Brealey Publishing.

Tsebelis, George 1995. "Decision-making in political systems: Veto players in presidentialism, parliamentalism, multicameralism, and multipartyism," *British Journal of Political Science* 25: 289–326.

Tsujinaka, Yutaka 2003. "From developmentalism to maturity: Japan's civil society organizations in comparative perspective," in Schwartz, Frank J. and Pharr, Susan J. (eds.), *The state of civil society in Japan*, pp. Cambridge, UK: Cambridge University Press.

Tullock, Gordon, Seldon, Arthur, and Brady, Gordon L. 2002. *Government failure: A primer in public choice*. Washington, D.C.: Cato Institute.

Tushman, Michael L., and Anderson, Philip 1986. "Technological discontinuities and organizational environments," *Administrative Science Quarterly* 31: 439–65.

Upham, Frank K. 1991. "The man who would import: A cautionary tale about bucking the system in Japan," *Journal of Japanese Studies* 18: 323–43.

Uriu, Robert M. 1996. *Troubled industries: Confronting economic change in Japan*. Ithaca, NY: Cornell University Press.

Utterback, James M. 1994. *Mastering the dynamics of innovation*. Boston: Harvard Business School Press.

Uzzi, Brian 1996. "The sources and consequences of embeddedness for the economic performance of organizations: The network effect," *American Sociological Review* 61: 674–98.

1997a. "Networks and the paradox of embeddedness," *Administrative Science Quarterly* 42: 35–67.

Uzzi, Brian 1997b. "Social structure and competition in interfirm networks: The paradox of embeddedness," *Administrative Science Quarterly* 42: 35–67.

Van de Ven, Andrew H., and Hargrave, Timothy J. 2004. "Social, technical, and institutional change: A literature review and synthesis," in Poole, Marshal Scott and Van de Ven, Andrew H. (eds.), *Handbook of organizational change and innovation*, pp. Oxford, UK: Oxford University Press.

Van de Ven, Andrew H., and Poole, Marchall Scott 1995. "Explaining development and change in organizations," *Academy of Management Review* 20: 510–40.

Vogel, Steven K. 1996. *Freer markets, more rules: Regulatory reform in advanced industrial countries*. Ithaca, NY: Cornell University Press.

2005. "Routine adjustment and bounded innovation: The changing politial economy of Japan," in Streeck, Wolfgang and Thelen, Kathleen (eds.), *Beyond continuity: Institutional change in advanced political economies*, pp. 145–68. Oxford, UK: Oxford University Press.

Volberda, Henk W. 1998. *Building the flexible firm: How to remain competitive*. Oxford, UK: Oxford University Press.

Volberda, Henk W., and Lewin, Arie Y. 2003. "Co-evolutionary dynamics within and between firms: From evolution to co-evolution," *Journal of Management Studies* 40: 2111–36.

Von Hippel, Eric 1987. "Cooperation between rivals: Informal know-how trading," *Research Policy* 16: 291–302.

Wasserman, Stanley, and Faust, Katherine 1994. *Social network analysis: Methods and applications*. Cambridge, UK: Cambridge University Press.

Watanabe, Chihiro, Irawan, Santoso, and Tjahya, Widayanti 1991. *The inducing power of Japanese technological innovation*. London: Pinter Publishers.

Weick, Karl E. 1979. *The social psychology of organizing*. 2nd ed. New York: Random House.

Westney, D. Eleanor 1994. "The evolution of Japan's industrial R&D," in Aoki, Masahiko and Dore, Ronald Philip (eds.), *The Japanese firm: Sources of competitive strength*, pp. 154–77. Oxford, UK: Oxford University Press.

1996. "The Japanese business system: Key features and prospects for changes," *Journal of Asian Business* 12: 21–50.

"Japan," in Rugman, Alan M. and Brewer, Thomas L. (eds.), *The Oxford handbook of international business*, pp. 623–51. Oxford, UK: Oxford University Press.

Westphal, James D., and Zajac, Edward J. 1994. "Substance and symbolism in CEOs' long-term incentive plans," *Administrative Science Quarterly* 39: 367–90.

Whitley, Richard 1999. *Divergent capitalisms: The social structuring and change of business systems*. Oxford, UK: Oxford University Press.

Williamson, Oliver E. 1985. *The economic institutions of capitalism: Firms, markets, relational contracting*. New York: The Free Press.

Witt, Michael A. 2001a. "City banks," in Bird, Allan (ed.) *Encyclopedia of Japanese business and management*, pp. 70–2. London: Routledge.

2001b. "Research cooperatives," in Bird, Allan (ed.) *Encyclopedia of Japanese business and management*, pp. 382–3. London: Routledge.

World Bank 1993. *The East Asian miracle: Economic growth and public policy*. Oxford, UK: Oxford University Press.

Yamagishi, Toshio 2003. "Trust and social intelligence in Japan," in Schwartz, Frank J. and Pharr, Susan J. (eds.), *The state of civil society in Japan*, pp. Cambridge, UK: Cambridge University Press.

Yamamura, Kozo 2003. "Germany and Japan in a new phase of capitalism: Confronting the past and the future," in Yamamura, Kozo and Streeck, Wolfgang (eds.), *The end of diversity? Prospects for German and Japanese capitalism*, pp. 115–46. Ithaca, NY: Cornell University Press.

Yamamura, Kozo, and Streeck, Wolfgang (eds.) 2003. *The end of diversity? Prospects for German and Japanese capitalism*. Ithaca, NY: Cornell University Press.

Zajac, Edward J., and Westphal, James D. 2004. "The social construction of market value: Institutionalization and learning perspectives on stock market reactions," *American Sociological Review* 69: 433–57.

Index

221